Topics i earch

A series of boo
Professor S. V

Mathematical Programming in Practice

Topics in Operational Research

Since the end of the Second World War, studies in the field of Management Sciences and Operational Research have developed at an extraordinary speed, and have gained in width and depth.

The present series of books on "Topics in Operational Research" contains contributions from authors who have special expertise in this field. There exist, of course, excellent texts on the theoretical background, but this series fulfills a need for detailed descriptions of simple numerical or algebraic techniques, and for reports on practical experience with these techniques, useful to managers and executives in many branches of social, commercial, and industrial activity. Knowledge of such techniques will be spread more widely by the publication of these monographs, and further development stimulated thereby.

The texts are written in such a way that little, if any, advanced knowledge from any branch of science will be required of the reader and no mathematical knowledge beyond about A-level G.C.E. or O.N.C.

The various books in the series should thus be of interest not only to management and engineering personnel, but also to teachers in the later forms in schools, and in colleges, as suggestions for possible syllabuses for introductory courses and as sources of interesting problems and examples.

S. VAJDA

Mathematical Programming in Practice

E. M. L. BEALE

Technical Director
Scientific Control Systems Ltd.

Visiting Professor, Department of Mathematics,
Imperial College of Science and Technology,
University of London

Pitman Publishing

First published 1968
Reprinted 1971
Reprinted 1976

Pitman Publishing Ltd
PITMAN HOUSE, 39 PARKER STREET, LONDON WC2B 5PB
PO BOX 46038, BANDA STREET, NAIROBI, KENYA

Pitman Publishing Pty Ltd
PITMAN HOUSE, 158 BOUVERIE STREET, CARLTON, VICTORIA 3053, AUSTRALIA

Pitman Publishing Corporation
6 EAST 43 STREET, NEW YORK, NY 10017, USA

Sir Isaac Pitman (Canada) Ltd
495 WELLINGTON STREET WEST, TORONTO M5V 1G1, CANADA

The Copp Clark Publishing Company
517 WELLINGTON STREET WEST, TORONTO M5V 1G1, CANADA

ISBN: 0 273 40244 7

Reproduced and printed by photolithography and bound in Great Britain at The Pitman Press, Bath
(1157:63)

Preface

Many books on mathematical programming have appeared recently. This reflects the fact that the subject is continuing to grow rapidly, particularly in the range and scale of applications, and that it has many aspects. These can be categorized as follows—

1. Mathematical theory.
2. Development of algorithms. (The word algorithms is widely used to mean procedures for deriving numerical solutions, without specific reference to the precision to which the relevant numbers are to be computed or to the organization of the computations within the store of a computer.)
3. Development of efficient codes to solve practical problems on a computer.
4. Methods of organizing real problems so that they can be solved numerically using standard computer codes.
5. The assessment of actual and potential fields of application of mathematical programming, the economics of these applications, and the problems of co-operating with management to make these applications as profitable as possible.

This book is concerned primarily with the fourth of these aspects, but this cannot be discussed intelligently without reference to the others. In particular, although I have tried to avoid introducing any unnecessary mathematics, this is not a book for anyone who takes a pride in his ignorance of mathematics. On the other hand the book is based on lectures given on a nine-week course on operational research run by C-E-I-R Ltd. for people with widely different mathematical backgrounds; and I believe that people with little mathematical knowledge but who are sympathetic towards the use of mathematics can find out what mathematical programming can do from this book, even if they do not follow all the technical details.

The reader is assumed to know some elementary algebra. Occasional use is made of matrix notation, but only Chapter 7 involves any serious use of matrix algebra. The concepts of this chapter are required for a full understanding of much of the rest of the book, but a reader unfamiliar with matrix algebra should be able to understand these concepts without following the detailed argument. The third part of the book assumes some knowledge of differential calculus.

The book is divided into three parts. The first part, entitled Elementary Linear Programming, covers relatively conventional material. By using numerical examples I have tried to explain the processes of the simplex method (including parametric programming on both the objective function and the right-hand side) with the minimum of formal mathematics. I have said little about special methods for solving transportation problems: the one chapter devoted to this topic is primarily concerned with indicating the range of problems that can be formulated as transportation problems. On the other hand I have gone into more detail than usual about some aspects of linear programming that might otherwise puzzle readers when they come to use a production LP code for a large computer—specifically in the treatment of finding a first feasible solution in Chapter 3, and in Chapter 7 on the inverse matrix method. The product form of inverse, and the reasons for using it, have been strangely neglected in books on linear programming (with the important exception of Gass (1964)); but it is vital to an understanding of why LP codes work the way they do, and why the practical extensions of linear programming have developed in the way they have.

The second part is entitled Organization of LP Calculations. This is a difficult subject to discuss in general terms, but it seems worth while to try to summarize some of the lessons we have learned in C-E-I-R Inc., C-E-I-R Ltd. and C-E-I-R N.V. as a result of having worked on a wide variety of applications of mathematical programming over many years. Institutions that are involved simultaneously in the development and application of mathematical programming systems have special opportunities for advancing these organizational aspects of the subject.

The third part is entitled Special Procedures. It describes various aspects of mathematical programming that lie beyond the simplex method for linear programming and are now being applied to practical problems. Now that one can add a few non-linear constraints or a few integer variables to an otherwise purely linear programming problem and still solve it in essentially the same way on the computer, these applications should continue to grow rapidly.

Reference is made from time to time in this book to C-E-I-R's mathematical programming system for the IBM 7090 and 7094 computers, known as the LP/90/94 system. This system is described briefly from the user's point of view in the Appendix. By the time this book is published, systems with at least some of the facilities of the LP/90/94 system will be available for the next generation of computers, and the best way to use these new systems may well differ in detail from the ways recommended here. This book should remain valid, however, as a basic guide to the use of mathematical programming in practice, to be supplemented by the User's Guide to the particular computing system being used by the reader.

My thanks are due to C-E-I-R Ltd for permission to publish this book. I should also like to thank my colleagues, Peter Windley for permission to use some of his lecture notes in the preparation of Part 2, Tim Glynn for reading the typescript and correcting a number of errors and awkward phrases, and Monica Holland for typing a manuscript that suffered many changes after being first typed.

E. M. L. B.

Contents

Part 1

ELEMENTARY LINEAR PROGRAMMING

1 Introduction to Linear Programming

1.1 A Definition of Mathematical Programming

This book is devoted to one of the most important groups of techniques in operational research, known as *mathematical programming*. This is the name given to the problem of finding a minimum or maximum of some function (known as the *objective function*) of variables, subject to inequality constraints. I admit that this is a slightly unfortunate name, since many people think that mathematical programming means writing computer programs to solve mathematical problems. The confusion is not entirely the fault of mathematical programmers: the term *linear programming* was coined in 1947 for the process of planning a program on the basis of linear constraints on the levels of possible activities. At that time *programming* was not an established term for writing computer instructions—people did not then talk much about writing computer instructions anyway and when they did they usually referred to it as *coding*. The word *linear* has been generalized to *mathematical* now that we are working seriously with non-linear functions. It has been suggested that the term programming should be replaced by *planning* or *optimization*, but it would be foolish to claim that mathematical programming covered all mathematical aspects of planning, and the term optimization is not specific enough to indicate the meaning if used to replace programming in all contexts. For example *quadratic optimization* would give no hint that one was dealing with inequality constraints as well as a quadratic objective function.

The first two parts of the book concentrate on linear programming. This emphasis is justified by the facts that linear programming still covers most of the practical applications of mathematical programming, and that almost all practical methods of solving more general mathematical programming problems are based on the simplex method for linear programming. As in all branches of applied mathematics it is important to avoid allowing irrelevant complications to obscure the main points being studied, and in most mathematical programming work the simplifying assumptions that enable one to use purely linear programming are quite acceptable. Nevertheless, it is quite feasible to apply mathematical programming to problems where these simplifying assumptions cannot be made—it merely involves a little more work both for the analyst and for the computer.

So much for a general introduction. Let us now try to get a clearer picture of what linear programming is about by considering a particular type of situation in which it is used.

1.2 A Distribution Problem

Let us suppose that we are working for a company whose main product, known as Product X, is made at 2 factories, and we are asked to advise on their distribution policy throughout Great Britain. The factories are in Maidstone and Shrewsbury, and it costs 2s. per mile, on the average, to transport 1000 units from the factory to the point of sale.

So far the problem looks delightfully simple: we supply each demand from the nearest factory; but there are further points to be considered. The company operates 3 depots, in Bristol, Leeds and Glasgow, and it may be cheaper to supply some demands via a depot. The economics of depot operation are as follows. The final delivery from the depot costs 2s. per mile for every 1000 units—as with direct delivery from the factory. There is an extra charge associated with handling at the depot which works out at £2 per 1000 units at each depot, but the compensating advantage of depot operation is that goods can be sent in bulk from the factory to the depot, and this *trunking* operation costs only 1s. per mile for every 1000 units. We must also consider the manufacturing costs: these must be divided into fixed costs, essentially independent of the level of activity, and variable costs, assumed to be proportional to the number of units made. The problem of dividing the costs into these 2 categories is both difficult and important: a cost that is fixed for the purposes of a short-term study may be better treated as variable in a long-term study in which greater variations in activity levels are contemplated. However, these problems are outside the scope of the present discussion. Here we are only concerned with the variable manufacturing costs, which we take to be £100 per 1000 units at Maidstone and £105 per 1000 units at Shrewsbury.

These extra complications have not really made the problem any harder. Let us suppose that the sales department have estimates for the annual demand for Product X divided into 12 areas as shown in Table 1.1. The costs can be tabulated as in Table 1.2, where the

TABLE 1.1

Area	*Demand (thousands)*
Northern Scotland	200
Southern Scotland	1200
North-East England	600
North-West England	800
Yorkshire	1000
North Wales	300
South Wales	600
South-West England	300
Southern England	1000
South-East England	2000
Midlands	1500
East Anglia	500
	10000

TABLE 1.2

Manufacturing at	*Cost (£ per thousand)*
Maidstone	100
Shrewsbury	105

Handling at depots	*Cost (£ per thousand)*
Bristol	2
Leeds	2
Glasgow	2

			From		
	Maidstone	Shrewsbury	Bristol	Leeds	Glasgow
Distribution to			*Cost (£ per thousand)*		
Bristol	8	5			
Leeds	11	5			
Glasgow	21	13			
Northern Scotland	52	38	48	31	14
Southern Scotland	40	26	36	19	4
North-East England	31	20	28	9	14
North-West England	25	8	18	6	18
Yorkshire	23	13	21	2	21
North Wales	29	11	21	16	31
South Wales	19	11	4	21	37
South-West England	24	22	12	31	48
Southern England	10	16	8	22	42
South-East England	4	15	12	19	39
Midlands	14	4	9	11	29
East Anglia	13	20	21	17	38

units are £ per thousand. We can now compute the cost of supplying each depot.

It costs 108 units to supply Bristol from Maidstone and 110 units to supply it from Shrewsbury.

It costs 111 units to supply Leeds from Maidstone and 110 units to supply it from Shrewsbury.

It costs 121 units to supply Glasgow from Maidstone and 118 units to supply it from Shrewsbury.

TABLE 1.3

Demands and Total Variable Cost of Supply

Area	*Demand (thousands)*	*Supply from* Maid-stone	Shrews-bury	Bristol	Leeds	Glasgow
Northern Scotland	200	152	143	158	143	*134*
Southern Scotland	1200	140	131	146	131	*124*
North-East England	600	131	125	138	*121*	134
North-West England	800	125	*113*	128	118	138
Yorkshire	1000	123	118	131	*114*	141
North Wales	300	129	*116*	131	128	151
South Wales	600	119	116	*114*	133	157
South-West England	300	124	127	*122*	143	168
Southern England	1000	*110*	121	118	134	162
South-East England	2000	*104*	120	122	131	159
Midlands	1500	114	*109*	119	123	149
East Anglia	500	*113*	125	131	129	158
	10000					

So we should supply Bristol from Maidstone, and Leeds and Glasgow from Shrewsbury.

The total variable cost of supplying any demand is then the sum of the final delivery cost plus an additional cost associated with the depot (or factory if no other depot is used) as follows—

Maidstone	100
Shrewsbury	105
Bristol	$108 + 2 = 110$
Leeds	$110 + 2 = 112$
Glasgow	$118 + 2 = 120$

Adding these numbers onto the final delivery costs we obtain Table 1.3, in which the smallest number in each row is *italic*, indicating the preferred depot for the area.

We see that this solution implies that the number of thousands of units supplied from each depot will be as follows—

Maidstone	3500
Shrewsbury	2600
Bristol	900
Leeds	1600
Glasgow	1400
	10000

And since Bristol is supplied from Maidstone, while the other depots are supplied from Shrewsbury, the numbers of millions of units made at each factory will be

Maidstone	4·4
Shrewsbury	5·6
	10·0

So far this has all been delightfully straightforward, but now the management tell us that our solution is useless. They have 2 objections to it. They say that, while the Maidstone factory could make up to 6 million units per year, the Shrewsbury factory cannot make more than 5 million units per year; also none of the depots can handle more than 1·2 million units per year.

At this point we must firmly resist any temptation to lose our tempers. It was tiresome of the management not to have told us about this beforehand, but we should have asked the right questions. It is very usual in operational research work for an important constraint to come to light only when one proposes a solution that violates it; indeed many problems get solved successfully without the analyst even becoming aware of a lot of complicated constraints because his solutions do not violate them.

Now we have seen that we can supply Leeds almost as cheaply from Maidstone as from Shrewsbury, so the problem would be fairly simple if we did not have any capacity constraints on the depots. The management might well be willing to spend some money on increasing these capacities; but we must find a method of solving the present problem, if only to show how useful this would be.

1.3 A Mathematical Formulation

This problem is a typical linear programming problem that cannot be solved cleanly by commonsense methods. You may be able to find an *ad hoc* solution to this particular problem; but it is much more satisfactory to have a general method for solving problems like this, and that is what linear programming provides. I do not propose to explain such a method in this chapter but I will prepare the ground by formulating the problem algebraically and indicating why the problem cannot be solved by conventional methods.

To formulate the problem algebraically we must introduce some variables. In elementary algebra the first variable is usually called x. The next variable is called y, and if there are as many as 3 variables, the third one is called z. Linear programming models usually involve very many more variables than this. This problem has 71 variables, and practical problems usually have hundreds if not thousands of variables. So we must use a different method of naming them, both because there are not enough letters and because it is very desirable that the name should give some indication of the significance of the variable. We therefore use subscripts, and in this problem it is convenient to use 3 sets of subscripts as follows—

i for factories	$i = 1$ for Maidstone,
	$i = 2$ for Shrewsbury
j for depots	$j = 1$ for Maidstone
	$j = 2$ for Shrewsbury
	$j = 3$ for Bristol
	$j = 4$ for Leeds
	$j = 5$ for Glasgow
k for demand areas	$k = 1$ for Northern Scotland, etc.

All amounts are measured in thousands of units per year.

Let

x_{ij} denote the amount transported from factory i to depot j

y_{jk} denote the amount transported from depot j to demand area k

s_i denote any spare capacity at factory i

t_j denote any spare capacity at depot j

M_i denote the total capacity of factory i

C_j denote the capacity of depot j

D_k denote the demand in area k

Then the constraints of the problem can be written as follows.

The amount received at each depot plus the spare capacity must equal the total capacity, so

$$\sum_{i=1}^{2} x_{ij} + t_j = C_j \qquad (j = 3, 4, 5)$$

The amount received in each demand zone must equal the requirement there, so

$$\sum_{j=1}^{5} y_{jk} = D_k \qquad (k = 1, \ldots, 12)$$

The amount sent out from each factory plus the spare capacity must equal the total capacity, so

$$\sum_{j=3}^{5} x_{ij} + \sum_{k=1}^{12} y_{ik} + s_i = M_i \qquad (i = 1, 2)$$

The amount sent out from each depot plus the spare capacity must equal the total capacity, so

$$\sum_{k=1}^{12} y_{jk} + t_j \qquad = C_j \qquad (j = 3, 4, 5)$$

We now have 20 equations relating our 71 variables, so we may expect that there are a great many possible solutions to the equations. We want to choose the solution that minimizes the total annual cost of the operation. This cost can be written in the form

$$C = \sum_{i=1}^{2} \sum_{j=3}^{5} c_{ij}x_{ij} + \sum_{j=1}^{5} \sum_{k=1}^{12} d_{jk}y_{jk}$$

where

c_{ij} denotes the cost of manufacturing 1000 units at factory i and transporting them to depot j

d_{jk} $(j = 1, 2)$ denotes the cost of manufacturing 1000 units at factory j and transporting them to demand zone k

d_{jk} $(j = 3, 4, 5)$ denotes the cost of handling 1000 units at depot j and transporting them to demand zone k.

The problem has therefore been formulated as one of minimizing a linear *objective function* of variables subject to linear equality constraints. Now we are familiar with the use of differential calculus to solve minimization problems. One writes down a set of equations defining the fact that the partial derivative of the objective function with respect to each of the independent variables is zero. Often this approach is impractical because the resulting equations are too complicated to be solved cleanly, and one resorts to more direct numerical methods. Here the equations are embarrassingly simple—they say that a constant equals zero. Of course we have to consider the constraints, so we can add the variable terms (i.e. the left hand sides) of these times suitable Lagrange multipliers to the objective function. But the modified objective function is still linear, and therefore cannot have a minimum determined by calculus. *The trouble is* *that we have lost sight of a vital feature of the problem. None of our variables can meaningfully take on negative values.* One possible way of dealing with a variable x_j that cannot be negative is to replace it by ξ_j^2, where ξ_j can take any real value. This idea has been proposed at various times: the oldest reference I myself have seen is on pages 149–150 of Hancock (1917).* But all this idea really gives is the fact that at a maximum or minimum either $x_j = 0$ or the derivative with respect to $x_j = 0$, so it is not very helpful computationally. In the next chapter we will turn to a much more effective approach due to George Dantzig, and known as the *simplex method.*

EXAMPLE

Generalize the model to allow units to be sent from one factory to another.

Hint. Consider the depot located on the factory site as logically distinct from the factory, and write equations for these depots similar to those for the other depots.

* See references pp. 189–191.

2 Introduction to the Simplex Method

2.1 A Blending Problem

This chapter describes the simplex method for solving linear programming problems. It was devised by George Dantzig in 1947, though the first published reference is to Dantzig (1951). (For the origins of linear programming see Dantzig (1963).)

It is easiest to introduce the method through a numerical example, but the problem considered in the last chapter is inconveniently large for this purpose. We therefore turn to another typical field of application of linear programming—to blending problems. To avoid confusing the issue with a mass of numbers I have made the example very simple, but more realistic problems of the same type can easily be formulated.

Suppose that we are trying to find an appropriate formula for a canned pet food. Suppose further that we have decided to make this pet food from sago flour, meat meal, and enriched skimmed milk (consisting of skimmed milk enriched with some animal fat); but that we have to decide which of these to use and in what proportions. We want to choose the cheapest formula that will supply a prescribed amount of protein and fat, and satisfy a number of other dietary restrictions on carbohydrates, vitamins, minerals, etc. However for the purpose of this example we assume that the only other constraint is an upper limit on the combined total of fibre plus ash.

The chemical analyses and costs of our three possible ingredients, together with the dietary requirements, are given as a percentage of dry weight in Table 2.1.

The numbers in this table have been adjusted to simplify the numerical work that follows and should not be regarded as factual.

We can now represent our problem mathematically by defining variables x_1, x_2 and x_3 representing the proportions of sago flour, meat meal and enriched skimmed milk respectively in the diet. The problem is then to minimize

$$C = 4x_1 + 5x_2 + 7x_3$$

where

$$\begin{aligned} x_1 + x_2 + x_3 &= 1 \\ 5x_2 + 3x_3 &\geqslant 2 \\ x_2 + 2x_3 &\geqslant 1 \\ 4x_2 + x_3 &\leqslant 2 \end{aligned}$$

TABLE 2.1

	Requirement	*Sago flour*	*Meat meal*	*Enriched skimmed milk*
Protein	$\geqslant 20$	0	50	30
Fat	$\geqslant 10$	0	10	20
Carbohydrate	any	100	0	40
Fibre + Ash	$\leqslant 20$	0	40	10
Cost (£ per ton dry weight)		40	50	70

Our first task is to replace all the inequalities by equations, by introducing an additional variable—known as a *slack variable*—to represent the difference between the two sides of each inequality. We therefore have

$$\begin{aligned} C &= 4x_1 + 5x_2 + 7x_3 \\ x_1 + x_2 + x_3 &= 1 \\ 5x_2 + 3x_3 - x_4 &= 2 \\ x_2 + 2x_3 - x_5 &= 1 \\ 4x_2 + x_3 + x_6 &= 2 \end{aligned}$$

The slacks associated with $\geqslant$ inequalities (x_4 and x_5) are called *negative slacks*, (because they appear in these equations with negative signs). A slack associated with a $\leqslant$ inequality (x_6) is called a *positive slack*. The inequality constraints are now re-written so that all the slack variables are non-negative.

The first step is to solve these equations for the objective function C and some of the variables in terms of the remaining variables.

We shall consider an appropriate systematic way of doing this later. In this example we can immediately write

$$\begin{aligned} C &= 4x_1 + 5x_2 + 7x_3 \\ 0 &= 1 - x_1 - x_2 - x_3 \\ x_4 &= -2 + 5x_2 + 3x_3 \\ x_5 &= -1 + x_2 + 2x_3 \\ x_6 &= 2 - 4x_2 - x_3 \end{aligned}$$

and we can now express the equation with 0 on the left hand side in the form

$$x_3 = 1 - x_1 - x_2$$

and using this to substitute for x_3 in the other equations, we have

$$C = 7 - 3x_1 - 2x_2$$

$$x_3 = 1 - x_1 - x_2$$

$$x_4 = 1 - 3x_1 + 2x_2$$

$$x_5 = 1 - 2x_1 - x_2$$

$$x_6 = 1 + x_1 - 3x_2$$

We call the variables on the left hand sides of these equations the *basic variables*. Those on the right hand side are called *non-basic variables*. Corresponding to this way of writing the problem we associate a trial solution obtained by putting all the non-basic variables equal to zero. The values of the basic variables are then given by the constant terms in the equations.

We can think of the non-basic variables as independent variables, and the basic variables as dependent variables. But we are going to solve the problem by an iterative procedure, in which the set of non-basic variables will be continually changing. So it is reasonable to give them this special name, non-basic, rather than simply calling them independent variables.

At this stage I want to draw your attention to an important fact that is so obvious that you might easily overlook it, and yet is is the key to the simplicity and elegance of the simplex method. The fact is that, although in a sense this solved form of the equations is a deduction from the original equations, it is fully equivalent to the original equations and is a complete statement of the problem. We can therefore forget the original equations, except possibly for a check against round off errors or computing blunders.

Let us therefore concentrate on the solved form of the equations, and the associated trial solution. As it happens, this is feasible, i.e. all the variables that have to be non-negative are non-negative. We shall see later how the simplex method has been extended to solve the problem of finding a first feasible solution, or else show that none exists. For the time being let us just thankfully accept the fact that the trial solution is feasible, and consider whether it is the best possible solution. To find out, we look at the signs of the coefficients of the non-basic variables in the expression for the objective function. A negative sign means that the objective function decreases if we increase this non-basic variable, keeping the others constant (and equal to zero). Since we are minimizing, this represents an improvement. The problem is linear, so it will be profitable to go on increasing this variable as far as we can, provided we do not make any of the basic variables negative. Let us see how this works in our numerical example. The coefficient of x_1 in the expression for C is the most negative, so we choose to increase it. If we do this, keeping $x_2 = 0$, we will have

$$\begin{aligned} x_3 &= 1 - x_1 \\ x_4 &= 1 - 3x_1 \\ x_5 &= 1 - 2x_1 \\ x_6 &= 1 + x_1 \end{aligned}$$

This shows that $x_3 \geqslant 0$ if $x_1 \leqslant 1$, $x_4 \geqslant 0$ if $x_1 \leqslant \frac{1}{3}$, $x_5 \geqslant 0$ if $x_1 \leqslant \frac{1}{2}$, and $x_6 \geqslant 0$ for any positive x_1. So we continue increasing x_1 until x_4 becomes zero.

We should now like to repeat this operation, to see if our new trial solution is the best possible, and if not to improve it. But now $x_4 = 0$ and $x_1 \neq 0$. We should therefore like to have x_4 as a non-basic variable instead of x_1. This is easily done. We perform a *pivoting* operation between x_1 and x_4. That is to say we use the equation for x_4 in terms of the non-basic variables to express x_1 in terms of x_4 and the other non-basic variables. We then substitute for x_1 throughout the expression for the objective function and the other non-basic variables.

Since

$$x_4 = 1 - 3x_1 + 2x_2$$

we have

$$x_1 = \tfrac{1}{3} - \tfrac{1}{3}x_4 + \tfrac{2}{3}x_2$$

and the problem now reads

$$\begin{aligned} C &= 6 + x_4 - 4x_2 \\ x_3 &= \frac{2}{3} + \frac{1}{3}x_4 - \frac{5}{3}x_2 \\ x_1 &= \frac{1}{3} - \frac{1}{3}x_4 + \frac{2}{3}x_2 \\ x_5 &= \frac{1}{3} + \frac{2}{3}x_4 - \frac{7}{3}x_2 \\ x_6 &= \frac{4}{3} - \frac{1}{3}x_4 - \frac{7}{3}x_2 \end{aligned}$$

We now have a new and improved trial solution, with $C = 6$, $x_3 = \frac{2}{3}$, $x_1 = \frac{1}{3}$, $x_5 = \frac{1}{3}$ and $x_6 = \frac{4}{3}$. Since the coefficient of x_2 in the new expression for C is negative we can improve matters further by increasing x_2, keeping $x_4 = 0$. We can continue to do this until $x_2 = 1/7$, when x_5 becomes zero. We therefore now make x_2 basic instead of x_5, and the problem reads

$$C = \frac{38}{7} - \frac{1}{7}x_4 + \frac{12}{7}x_5$$

$$x_3 = \frac{3}{7} - \frac{1}{7}x_4 + \frac{5}{7}x_5$$

$$x_1 = \frac{3}{7} - \frac{1}{7}x_4 - \frac{2}{7}x_5$$

$$x_2 = \frac{1}{7} + \frac{2}{7}x_4 - \frac{3}{7}x_5$$

$$x_6 = 1 - x_4 + x_5$$

This is still not the best possible solution. We can further reduce C by increasing x_4 again. In fact we can increase x_4 until it equals 1, when x_6 becomes zero. So we make x_4 basic instead of x_6, and the problem reads

$$C = \frac{37}{7} + \frac{1}{7}x_6 + \frac{11}{7}x_5$$

$$x_3 = \frac{2}{7} + \frac{1}{7}x_6 + \frac{4}{7}x_5$$

$$x_1 = \frac{2}{7} + \frac{1}{7}x_6 - \frac{3}{7}x_5$$

$$x_2 = \frac{3}{7} - \frac{2}{7}x_6 - \frac{1}{7}x_5$$

$$x_4 = 1 - x_6 + x_5$$

Now the coefficients of all non-basic variables in the expression for C are non-negative. This means that C is not decreased in value if we increase any non-basic variables, either one at a time or together. The only way we could get a smaller value of C would be to make at least one of the non-basic variables negative, which is not allowed. So our trial solution is the final solution to our problem. It says that we should use all our ingredients, 2/7 sago flour, 3/7 meat meal and 2/7 enriched milk. This will provide 10% more than the minimum amount of protein at a total cost of 37/7 tens of pounds, i.e. £52 17s. 2d. per ton dry weight.

One important point about linear programming is that the calculations provide supplementary information as well as the optimum solution and its cost. In particular I should like to draw your attention to the coefficients of the non-basic variables in the final expression for the objective function. They are known as the *reduced costs* of the non-basic variables. What do they tell us here? The reduced cost of x_6 is $\frac{1}{7}$. This means that if we increased x_6 by some small amount θ, i.e. decreased the fibre and ash content by $10\theta\%$ while satisfying the other constraints, the cost would increase by £$(\frac{10}{7})\theta$ per ton dry weight. Equally, if our dietary experts allowed us to increase the fibre and ash content by $10\theta\%$ we could save £$(\frac{10}{7})\theta$ per ton dry weight. Unfortunately the calculation does not tell us for how large a range of values of θ these costs hold. We will return to this point later under the title *parametric programming*. Similarly we see that a reduction in the fat content of $10\theta\%$ would save £$(\frac{110}{7})\theta$ per ton dry weight.

If any of our ingredients had finished as non-basic variables, it would mean that the ingredient was not used in the optimum mix, and the reduced cost would indicate how much the cost of the ingredient had to come down before it would be used.

2.2 Some Properties of the Simplex Method

Before discussion of some of the general issues raised by this method of solving linear programming problems, let us consider the geometrical interpretation of what we have just done.

Any problem with n non-basic variables can be represented in an n-dimensional diagram. This is of course why I chose an illustrative example with $n = 2$. Figure 2.1 represents our problem, with x_1 and x_2 chosen as the independent variables. The lines corresponding to points where each variable equals zero are drawn, and shaded on the side corresponding to negative, i.e. inadmissible, values of this variable. The set of admissible points, known as the *feasible region*, consists of the boundary and interior of the pentagon ABCDE. The arrow in the top right hand corner of the diagram defines the direction of decreasing C, in which we are trying to move. Once we have drawn the diagram, it is obvious that the solution is given by the point D. But this geometrical method of solving the problem is only available when there are just 2 non-basic variables—and even then it is less accurate, and more importantly does not provide information about the reduced costs, which may be just as interesting as the solution itself. The numerical method started from the trial solution A with $x_1 = x_2 = 0$, and moved through the vertices B ($x_1 = x_4 = 0$) and C ($x_4 = x_5 = 0$) before moving to D with $x_5 = x_6 = 0$, which proved to be the final solution.

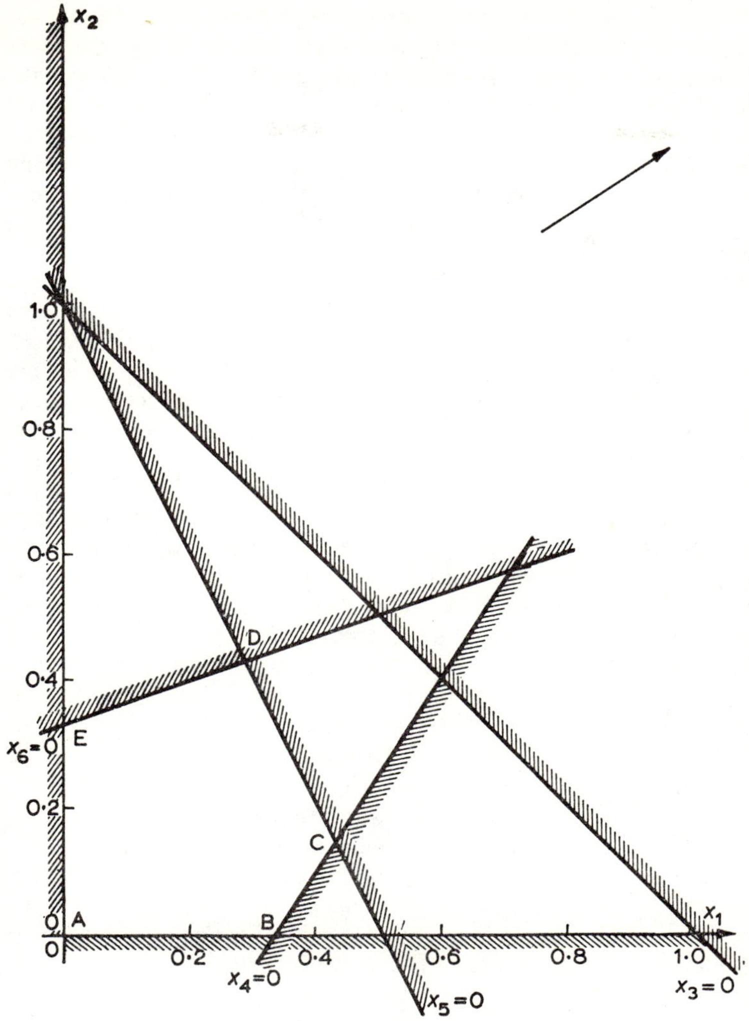

Figure 2.1

It will be seen more generally that the feasible region of a linear programming problem is represented by a polygon, or rather by a polyhedron in as many dimensions as there are non-basic variables. The simplex method starts from some vertex of the polyhedron, and at each stage looks for a neighbouring vertex with a better value of the objective function. When no such vertex can be found one has the final solution.

When presented with this geometrical picture, some people are tempted to criticize the simplex method for creeping round the edges of the feasible region, instead of striding boldly through the middle. But this argument overlooks two things: one is that the final solution is bound to be at a vertex, which may even prove to be very near the starting point; the other is that the geometrical picture, though important, does not tell the whole story. With the simplex method it is very easy to keep track numerically of whether the current trial solution is optimal, and if not what to do to improve it.

If one uses the simplex method, at each stage there is either at least one negative reduced cost, in which case the method produces a better neighbouring vertex, or else there are no negative reduced costs, in which case one has an optimum solution. Since there is only a finite number of vertices, the first case can only arise a finite number of times, so the method must reach an optimum solution in a finite number of steps.

There is just one loophole in this argument. It is not of much practical importance, but it is discussed here as a matter of theoretical interest. One may reach a trial solution where one or more of the basic variables equals zero. (This phenomenon is known as *degeneracy*.) The next iteration may then cause a zero change in the objective function, and there is a remote possibility that the procedure will cycle round endlessly through a loop of alternative representations of the same vertex of the feasible region. Fairly simple theoretical methods have been devised for overcoming this difficulty. They are not used in practice—partly because they would slow the computer program down, unnecessarily in the vast majority of cases, and partly because of the difficulty of recognizing a true zero numerically. A legend has grown up that such cycling never occurs in practice. In fact it does occur sometimes on large problems that have a great many equations with a zero constant term. It is overcome by making small changes in the constant terms of the equations causing the difficulty, and restoring these constant terms to their original values when the difficulty has been overcome.

Before proceeding to the next chapter, the reader is advised to solve a small numerical problem for himself. So this is perhaps a good moment to mention a numerical check that one can apply if things seem to be going wrong. Having obtained a first trial solution one can assign arbitrary numerical values to the non-basic variables, for example putting them all equal to unity, and can compute the corresponding values of the basic variables. These values of the variables should satisfy the equations at all times (although of course some of them may be negative and therefore not represent feasible values). So one can assign the indicated values to the current non-basic variables at any stage, and can check that the basic variables then take the correct values.

EXAMPLE

Suppose that an additional ingredient becomes available in the diet problem—namely soya flour. What is the best formula, given the following expanded table of analyses and costs?

	Requirement	*Sago flour*	*Meat meal*	*Enriched skimmed milk*	*Soya flour*
Protein	⩾20	0	50	30	50
Fat	⩾10	0	10	20	20
Carbohydrate	any	100	0	40	20
Fibre + Ash	⩽20	0	40	10	10
Cost (£/ton dry weight)		40	50	70	60

3 The Simplex Method—Further Details

3.1 Algebraic Summary

This chapter consolidates and formalizes the ideas discussed previously, and also takes up the problem of finding a feasible trial solution when none is readily available.

Let us start with an algebraic summary of the rules of the simplex method. This obviously requires some symbols for the coefficients of the non-basic variables in the expressions for the objective function and the basic variables. And it is conventional to give these coefficients the signs that they would have if all the variables were written on the left hand sides of the equations. The value of this convention will be clearer when we come to the chapter on the inverse matrix method. Meanwhile we can preserve the sign convention and put the non-basic variables in their natural place, on the right hand side, by using minus signs. Another point whose significance will become clearer in terms of the inverse matrix method, but which seems worth taking up now, is that the symbol C, representing the objective function, behaves like any basic variable except that it is not necessarily restricted to non-negative values.

It is therefore convenient to replace it by a symbol x_0 that looks more like a basic variable. But it is conventional to maximize x_0, so we write $x_0 = -C$.

We therefore write

$$x_0 = \bar{a}_{00} + \sum_{j=1}^{n-m} \bar{a}_{0j}(-X_{m+j})$$

$$X_i = \bar{a}_{i0} + \sum_{j=1}^{n-m} \bar{a}_{ij}(-X_{m+j}) \qquad (i = 1, \ldots, m)$$

Variables $X_1, \ldots, X_n$ are a permutation of variables $x_1, \ldots, x_n$: $X_1, \ldots, X_m$ represent the current basic variables and $X_{m+1}, \ldots, X_n$ the non-basic variables. The matrix of coefficients in these equations is known as a *tableau* (It is sometimes called a *contracted tableau* to distinguish it from the *extended tableau*, which includes a unit column for each basic variable. In the extended tableau the columns retain their original order throughout.)

The symbol $\bar{a}_{ij}$ is used because a_{ij} will later be used to denote a coefficient in the original representation of the problem.

The significance of the X_j can perhaps be best explained with reference to the example solved in Chapter [illegible]. In this problem $m =$ [illegible] and $n = 6$, and in the initial tableau

$$X_1 = x_3,\ X_2 = x_4,\ X_3 = x_5,\ X_4 = x_6,\ X_5 = x_1 \text{ and } X_6 = x_2$$

In the first change of basis we exchange the variables x_1 and x_4, and now have

$$X_1 = x_3,\ X_2 = x_1,\ X_3 = x_5,\ X_4 = x_6,\ X_5 = x_4 \text{ and } X_6 = x_2$$

After the next change of basis,

$$X_1 = x_3,\ X_2 = x_1,\ X_3 = x_2,\ X_4 = x_6,\ X_5 = x_4 \text{ and } X_6 = x_5$$

and finally

$$X_1 = x_3,\ X_2 = x_1,\ X_3 = x_2,\ X_4 = x_4,\ X_5 = x_6 \text{ and } X_6 = x_5$$

We assume that all $\bar{a}_{i0} \geqslant 0$. Otherwise we do not have a feasible trial solution. Procedures for finding a first feasible trial solution will be discussed later.

The first step is to study the reduced costs—the coefficients $\bar{a}_{0j}$. (Incidentally some writers use the symbol d_j for $\bar{a}_{0j}$, so the name DJ is also used for reduced cost.) If the $\bar{a}_{0j}$ are all non-negative, then the present trial solution is optimal. Otherwise we take a negative one, $\bar{a}_{0q}$. Theoretically it does not matter which is taken: in practice one usually takes the most negative.

We have now determined the variable X_{m+q} to *enter the basis*, i.e. to be taken to the left hand side of the equations. To determine the variable to leave the basis, we compute $\bar{a}_{i0}/\bar{a}_{iq}$ for all i such that $\bar{a}_{iq} > 0$, and let $\bar{a}_{p0}/\bar{a}_{pq}$ be the smallest such ratio. Then X_p is the variable to leave the basis.

For the sake of completeness, we should consider the possibility that this procedure defines either no variable X_p or alternatively that it defines more than one such variable. It defines no variable if all $\bar{a}_{iq} \leqslant 0$. In these circumstances x_0 can be given an arbitrarily large value by giving X_{m+q} an arbitrarily large value. The problem then has an unbounded solution, which almost certainly means in practice that it has been wrongly formulated. More than one variable may be defined [illegible] of [illegible]. It is then conventional to break [illegible] in favour of the variable that maximizes $\bar{a}_{pq}$, on the grounds that [illegible] values [illegible] tend to produce round-off errors. [illegible] lead to the phenomenon of cycling discussed in [illegible]

Having determined the variables to enter and leave the basis, we must now transform the tableau. The change of variables is easy. We replace X_p and X_{m+q} by each other, the remaining variables are unaltered, and the new coefficients $\bar{a}'_{ij}$ can be computed as follows—

$$\left.\begin{aligned} \bar{a}'_{pq} &= 1/\bar{a}_{pq} \\ \bar{a}'_{pj} &= \bar{a}_{pj}\bar{a}'_{pq} \\ \bar{a}'_{iq} &= -\bar{a}_{iq}\bar{a}'_{pq} \\ \bar{a}'_{ij} &= \bar{a}_{ij} - \bar{a}_{iq}\bar{a}'_{pj} \end{aligned}\right\} \quad i \neq p, j \neq q$$

These are the practical formulae. But it is of some theoretical interest to see what they become if only untransformed coefficients are used on the right hand side. We then have

$$\left.\begin{aligned} \bar{a}'_{pq} &= 1/\bar{a}_{pq} \\ \bar{a}'_{pj} &= \bar{a}_{pj}/\bar{a}_{pq} \\ \bar{a}'_{iq} &= -\bar{a}_{iq}/\bar{a}_{pq} \\ \bar{a}'_{ij} &= \bar{a}_{ij} - \bar{a}_{iq}\bar{a}_{pj}/\bar{a}_{pq} \end{aligned}\right\} \quad i \neq p, j \neq q$$

These formulae emphasize the key role played by the element $\bar{a}_{pq}$ in the transformation. It is given a special name, the *pivot*. The corresponding row and column are called the *pivotal row* and *pivotal column*. The theoretical formulae also illustrate the symmetry between rows and columns of the tableau. We shall explore this later when we discuss duality. But these formulae are not recommended for numerical work, since they require an extra multiplication in the computation of each element that is not in either the pivotal row or in the pivotal column.

Most textbooks on linear programming recommend that the calculations be carried out by operating on the tableau in a mechanical way following these rules. Possibly this is a good idea. But I have never adopted it because no one nowadays is likely to try to earn a living by solving linear programming problems by hand—they will be done on a computer. So one will solve problems by hand only on an occasional basis, and in these circumstances it seems best to keep the equations in explicit form throughout, so that one can always be clear about why one is doing any particular piece of arithmetic.

3.2 Basic Method of Finding a First Feasible Solution

Let us now turn to the problem of finding a first feasible solution to a linear programming problem (sometimes known as *phase* 1 of the simplex method). This is covered in rather more detail than is customary in an elementary course, because otherwise this part of the operation of a practical computer code for linear programming may seem slightly baffling. Let us start with the basic method in the traditional form.

The basic method starts with a first trial solution in which all the genuine variables of the problem equal zero. If some of the constraints are inequalities that are satisfied at this trial solution, then we can solve these constraints for their slack variables in terms of the genuine variables, making the slack variables basic. But if some constraints are equations, or inequalities that are not satisfied at the selected trial solution, this will not do. We then introduce an *artificial variable* representing the discrepancy between the left and right hand side of the equation, with a sign such that the artificial variable is non-negative at our trial solution. We can now solve these constraints for the artificial variables, making them basic. We are then all set to proceed. The only trouble is that we have changed the problem, and any solution to our new problem is not a solution to the original problem unless all the artificial variables equal zero. Since, like all linear programming variables, the artificials are not allowed to take negative values, it is sufficient to make their sum equal to zero. Therefore we start the calculations by minimizing an auxiliary objective function representing the sum of the artificial variables. This sum is usually called the *sum of the infeasibilities*, since each artificial represents the extent to which the present trial solution is infeasible as regards that constraint. If we reduce the sum of infeasibilities to zero, then we have a genuine feasible solution to the original problem, and we can start to improve the genuine objective function in the usual way. If we find that the minimum value of the sum of infeasibilities is positive, then we know that the original problem is infeasible.

Incidentally, note that we may have equations with a constant term of zero. These equations are satisfied at our original trial solution, but we must still introduce an artificial variable to fill out the basis. The artificial will take the value zero in our first trial solution.

While we are minimizing the sum of infeasibilities, artificial variables will become non-basic from time to time. When this happens we need not consider reintroducing them at a later stage, and could in fact drop them from the problem. On the other hand the coefficients of the artificial variables in the tableau do contain some information about the problem, as we shall see later. When we have a genuine feasible solution we will normally find that all artificial variables have become non-basic, and we could carry on as if they had never existed. But we may possibly still have some basic artificial variables, with a value of zero in the trial solution. We must then pivot in one of these rows whenever we want to bring a variable into the basis that has a non-zero coefficient in such a row.

One situation in which one will have basic artificial variables in the final tableau is when the constraints are linearly dependent. You may feel that no-one in his right mind would formulate a problem with linearly dependent equations, since this adds unnecessarily to the arithmetic involved in manipulating the equations; but with a computer to do the arithmetic this may not be serious, and it may be convenient to keep all the equations. For example, the equations considered in Chapter 1 are linearly dependent; but the problem becomes rather unsymmetrical if one equation is suppressed.

Let us now see how these artificial variables work in practice. We again consider the diet problem solved in the last chapter, with the extra ingredient considered in the exercise, but now we require that the carbohydrate content be exactly 50%. The problem now reads as Table 3.1.

TABLE 3.1

Maximize x_0 where

$$
\begin{aligned}
x_0 + 4x_1 + 5x_2 + 7x_3 + 6x_4 &= 0\\
x_1 + x_2 + x_3 + x_4 &= 1\\
5x_2 + 3x_3 + 5x_4 - x_5 &= 2\\
x_2 + 2x_3 + 2x_4 - x_6 &= 1\\
10x_1 + 4x_3 + 2x_4 &= 5\\
4x_2 + x_3 + x_4 + x_7 &= 2
\end{aligned}
$$

The initial tableau is shown in Table 3.2.

TABLE 3.2

$$
\begin{aligned}
x_0 &= 0 - 4x_1 - 5x_2 - 7x_3 - 6x_4\\
A_1 &= 1 - x_1 - x_2 - x_3 - x_4\\
A_2 &= 2 - 5x_2 - 3x_3 - 5x_4 + x_5\\
A_3 &= 1 - x_2 - 2x_3 - 2x_4 + x_6\\
A_4 &= 5 - 10x_1 - 4x_3 - 2x_4\\
x_7 &= 2 - 4x_2 - x_3 - x_4
\end{aligned}
$$

and the [illegible]

$$S = [illegible]$$

We can re[illegible]

TA[illegible]

$S =$	[illegible]	
$x_0 =$	[illegible]	
A	[illegible]	
A	[illegible]	
A	[illegible]	
x_1	[illegible]	
$x_7 =$	[illegible]	

We can now red[illegible]
Table 3.4.

TABLE 3.4

$S =$	$\frac{19}{50}$	[illegible]
$x_0 =$	$-\frac{204}{50}$	[illegible]
$A_1 =$	$\frac{9}{50}$	[illegible]
$x_4 =$	$\frac{20}{[illegible]}$	[illegible]
$A_3 =$	[illegible]	[illegible]
$x_1 =$	[illegible]	[illegible]
[illegible]	[illegible]	[illegible]

We can now reduce S by increasing x_3 until $A_3 = 0$; and obtain Table 3.5.

TABLE 3.5

$$
\begin{aligned}
S &= \frac{6}{40} + \frac{44}{40}A_4 - \frac{14}{40}x_2 + \frac{46}{40}A_3 + \frac{44}{40}A_2 - \frac{4}{40}x_5 - \frac{6}{40}x_6 \\
x_0 &= -\frac{186}{40} + \frac{16}{40}A_4 - \frac{106}{40}x_2 + \frac{114}{40}A_3 - \frac{4}{40}A_2 + \frac{4}{40}x_5 - \frac{114}{40}x_6 \\
A_1 &= \frac{6}{40} + \frac{4}{40}A_4 - \frac{14}{40}x_2 + \frac{6}{40}A_3 + \frac{4}{40}A_2 - \frac{4}{40}x_5 - \frac{6}{40}x_6 \\
x_4 &= \frac{10}{40} - \frac{70}{40}x_2 + \frac{30}{40}A_3 - \frac{20}{40}A_2 + \frac{20}{40}x_5 - \frac{30}{40}x_6 \\
x_3 &= \frac{10}{40} + \frac{50}{40}x_2 - \frac{50}{40}A_3 + \frac{20}{40}A_2 - \frac{20}{40}x_5 + \frac{50}{40}x_6 \\
x_1 &= \frac{14}{40} - \frac{4}{40}A_4 - \frac{6}{40}x_2 + \frac{14}{40}A_3 - \frac{4}{40}A_2 + \frac{4}{40}x_5 - \frac{14}{40}x_6 \\
x_7 &= \frac{60}{40} - \frac{140}{40}x_2 + \frac{20}{40}A_3 - \frac{20}{40}x_6
\end{aligned}
$$

We can now reduce S by increasing x_2 until $x_4 = 0$; and obtain Table 3.6.

TABLE 3.6

$$
\begin{aligned}
S &= \frac{7}{70} + \frac{77}{70}A_4 + \frac{14}{70}x_4 + A_3 + \frac{84}{70}A_2 - \frac{14}{70}x_5 \\
x_0 &= -\frac{352}{70} + \frac{28}{70}A_4 + \frac{106}{70}x_4 + \frac{120}{70}A_3 + \frac{46}{70}A_2 - \frac{46}{70}x_5 - \frac{120}{70}x_6 \\
A_1 &= \frac{7}{70} + \frac{7}{70}A_4 + \frac{14}{70}x_4 + \frac{14}{70}A_2 - \frac{14}{70}x_5 \\
x_2 &= \frac{10}{70} - \frac{40}{70}x_4 + \frac{30}{70}A_3 - \frac{20}{70}A_2 + \frac{20}{70}x_5 - \frac{30}{70}x_6 \\
x_3 &= \frac{30}{70} - \frac{50}{70}x_4 - \frac{50}{70}A_3 + \frac{10}{70}A_2 - \frac{10}{70}x_5 + \frac{50}{70}x_6 \\
x_1 &= \frac{23}{70} - \frac{7}{70}A_4 + \frac{6}{70}x_4 + \frac{20}{70}A_3 - \frac{4}{70}A_2 + \frac{4}{70}x_5 - \frac{20}{70}x_6 \\
x_7 &= 1 + 2x_4 - A_3 + A_2 - x_5 + x_6
\end{aligned}
$$

We can now reduce S by increasing x_5 until $A_1 = 0$; and obtain Table 3.7.

TABLE 3.7

$$
\begin{array}{lllllll}
S = & & A_4 & & + A_3 + A_2 + & A_1 & \\
x_0 = & -\frac{75}{14} & +\frac{1}{14}A_4 & +\frac{12}{14}x_4 & +\frac{24}{14}A_3 & +\frac{46}{14}A_1 & -\frac{24}{14}x_6 \\
x_5 = & \frac{7}{14} & +\frac{7}{14}A_4 & + x_4 & + A_2 & - 5A_1 & \\
x_2 = & \frac{4}{14} & +\frac{2}{14}A_4 & -\frac{4}{14}x_4 & +\frac{6}{14}A_3 & -\frac{20}{14}A_1 & -\frac{6}{14}x_6 \\
x_3 = & \frac{5}{14} & -\frac{1}{14}A_4 & -\frac{12}{14}x_4 & -\frac{10}{14}A_3 & +\frac{10}{14}A_1 & +\frac{10}{14}x_6 \\
x_1 = & \frac{5}{14} & -\frac{1}{14}A_4 & +\frac{2}{14}x_4 & +\frac{4}{14}A_3 & -\frac{4}{14}A_1 & -\frac{4}{14}x_6 \\
x_7 = & \frac{7}{14} & -\frac{7}{14}A_4 & + x_4 & - A_3 & + 5A_1 & + x_6
\end{array}
$$

We now have a feasible solution, but x_0 can be increased by increasing x_4 until $x_3 = 0$; and obtain Table 3.8.

TABLE 3.8

$$
\begin{array}{lllllll}
S = & & A_4 & & + A_3 + A_2 + & A_1 & \\
x_0 = & -5 & & - x_3 & + A_3 & + 4A_1 & - x_6 \\
x_5 = & \frac{11}{12} & +\frac{5}{12}A_4 & -\frac{14}{12}x_3 & -\frac{10}{12}A_3 + A_2 & -\frac{50}{12}A_1 & +\frac{10}{12}x_6 \\
x_2 = & \frac{2}{12} & +\frac{2}{12}A_4 & +\frac{4}{12}x_3 & +\frac{8}{12}A_3 & -\frac{20}{12}A_1 & -\frac{8}{12}x_6 \\
x_4 = & \frac{5}{12} & -\frac{1}{12}A_4 & -\frac{14}{12}x_3 & -\frac{10}{12}A_3 & +\frac{10}{12}A_1 & +\frac{10}{12}x_6 \\
x_1 = & \frac{5}{12} & -\frac{1}{12}A_4 & -\frac{2}{12}x_3 & +\frac{2}{12}A_3 & -\frac{2}{12}A_1 & -\frac{2}{12}x_6 \\
x_7 = & \frac{11}{12} & -\frac{7}{12}A_4 & -\frac{14}{12}x_3 & -\frac{22}{12}A_3 & +\frac{70}{12}A_1 & +\frac{22}{12}x_6
\end{array}
$$

This is the final solution, since x_0 can only be increased by increasing an artificial variable, which is not permitted. What does it tell us? Since $x_0 = -5$, the cost is £50/ton. The values of x_1, x_2, x_3 and [illegible] of the four ingredients in our diet, are [illegible] respectively. Further x_7 = [illegible], meaning that we are [illegible] about 9[illegible]% over the minimum protein requirement, and [illegible] meaning that we are [illegible] of 10% [illegible] maximum [illegible] limit. But what about the reduced costs? The reduced cost of [illegible] is [illegible] indicating [illegible] of increase of cost with $x_{[illegible]}$. The reduced costs of the [illegible] and artificial variables have a special significance. They are known as the *shadow prices* on the rows of the problem, and indicate the rate of change of the objective function with respect to the right hand sides of the restraint equations. In our problem these shadow prices are the reduced costs of the variables A_1, A_2, A_3, A_4 and x_7 and take the values −4, 0, −1, 0 and [illegible] respectively. The reduced cost of A_1 is not of much interest, since it would be physically meaningless to change the right hand side of the first equation, but the other reduced costs represent the effects of small changes in the other limits. It appears that the only crucial requirement is that for fat. The cost increases at a rate of one unit per unit increase in this right hand side, i.e. by £10/ton for every 10% increase in the fat requirement.

3.3 Practical Method of Finding a [illegible]

We now discuss a procedure described by [illegible] (196[illegible]), which can be used to obtain [illegible]. [illegible] that the coefficients of the artificial variables introduced in equations containing slack variables are always just the negatives of the corresponding coefficients of the slack variables (except that an extra 1 is added in the expression for S). So the calculations can be made without writing these artificials explicitly, but allowing the slacks to take negative values. On this basis the initial tableau reads as shown in Table 3.9.

TABLE 3.9

$$
\begin{aligned}
x_0 &= 0 [illegible] \\
A_1 &= 1 - x_1 - x_2 - x_3 - x_4 \\
x_5 &= -2 \quad [illegible] \\
x_6 &= - [illegible] \quad + x_2 + 2x_3 + [illegible] \\
A_4 &= 5 - 10x_1 \quad - 4x_3 - [illegible] \\
x_7 &= 2 \quad [illegible]
\end{aligned}
$$

(The second artificial is called A_4 to make it easier to compare the calculations with the previous ones.)

Using this approach it is probably easiest not to compute S the sum of infeasibilities explicitly. The reduced cost d_j of any non-basic variable $X_{[illegible]}$ is given by the formula

$$d_k = \sum c_i a_{ik}$$

where

$c_i = -1$ if X_i [illegible]

$c_i = +1$ if $a_{ik} < 0$ (and $i > 0$)

$c_i = 0$ otherwise

As before, we see that we can reduce S by increasing [illegible] until A_4 becomes zero as shown in Table 3.10

TABLE 3.10

$$x_0 = -2 + \frac{1}{10}A_4 - 3x_2 - \frac{[illegible]}{10}x_5 - \frac{[illegible]}{10}x_6$$

$$A_1 = \frac{3}{10} - \frac{1}{10}A_4 - x_2 - \frac{6}{10}x_5 - \frac{3}{10}x_6$$

$$[illegible] = -2 \quad + 5x_2 + 2x_5 + 5x_6$$

[illegible]

[illegible]

[illegible] ≥ 0 x_2 x_5 x_6

As before, we can reduce S by increasing x_4, but this is where the important difference between this approach and the original one arises. Previously we stopped increasing x_4 when it reached $\frac{2}{5}$, since an artificial variable became zero, but now all that happens when x_4 reaches $\frac{2}{5}$ is that a variable that was negative becomes positive. There is therefore no reason to stop increasing x_4 if we can find some other variable to be made non-basic. The rule is to continue increasing the selected non-basic variable until either

(*a*) an explicit artificial variable becomes zero
(*b*) a variable that is now positive becomes zero
(*c*) the selected variable could be increased indefinitely without driving any other variables to zero

Note that it is just possible for the sum of infeasibilities to be increased by such a step; but, if so, the number of infeasibilities will be decreased and this is of overriding importance.

In our example we can increase x_4 until $A_1 = 0$, and obtain Table 3.11.

TABLE 3.11

$$
\begin{aligned}
x_0 &= -\frac{42}{8} - \frac{2}{8}A_4 + \frac{12}{8}x_2 - \frac{12}{8}x_3 + \frac{52}{8}A_1 \\
x_4 &= \frac{5}{8} + \frac{1}{8}A_4 - \frac{10}{8}x_2 - \frac{6}{8}x_3 - \frac{10}{8}A_1 \\
x_5 &= \frac{9}{8} + \frac{5}{8}A_4 - \frac{10}{8}x_2 - \frac{6}{8}x_3 - \frac{50}{8}A_1 \\
x_6 &= \frac{2}{8} + \frac{2}{8}A_4 - \frac{12}{8}x_2 + \frac{4}{8}x_3 - \frac{20}{8}A_1 \\
x_1 &= \frac{3}{8} - \frac{1}{8}A_4 + \frac{2}{8}x_2 - \frac{2}{8}x_3 + \frac{2}{8}A_1 \\
x_7 &= \frac{11}{8} - \frac{1}{8}A_4 - \frac{22}{8}x_2 - \frac{2}{8}x_3 + \frac{10}{8}A_1
\end{aligned}
$$

We can now increase x_0 by increasing x_2, until $x_6 = 0$. We therefore get Table 3.12.

TABLE 3.12

$$
\begin{aligned}
x_0 &= -5 - x_6 - x_3 + 4A_1 \\
x_4 &= \frac{5}{12} - \frac{1}{12}A_4 + \frac{10}{12}x_6 - \frac{14}{12}x_3 + \frac{10}{12}A_1 \\
x_5 &= \frac{11}{12} + \frac{5}{12}A_4 + \frac{10}{12}x_6 - \frac{14}{12}x_3 - \frac{50}{12}A_1 \\
x_2 &= \frac{2}{12} + \frac{2}{12}A_4 - \frac{8}{12}x_6 + \frac{4}{12}x_3 - \frac{20}{12}A_1 \\
x_1 &= \frac{5}{12} - \frac{1}{12}A_4 - \frac{2}{12}x_6 - \frac{2}{12}x_3 - \frac{2}{12}A_1 \\
x_7 &= \frac{11}{12} - \frac{7}{12}A_4 + \frac{22}{12}x_6 - \frac{14}{12}x_3 + \frac{70}{12}A_1
\end{aligned}
$$

This is the same result as before, but achieved in half as many iterations. All the shadow prices are still available. The shadow prices on rows containing negative slacks are the negatives of the reduced costs of these slacks.

Finally, we note that if we *guess* at the final solution by solving the equations for some variables in terms of the others and find that some $\bar{a}_{i0} < 0$, indicating that some basic variables take negative values in our trial solution, we can treat these variables in the same way as we treated negative slacks in the example just solved. This is frequently done in practice, particularly with a computer code using the inverse matrix method.

EXAMPLE

Resolve this problem with the ingredient x_3 replaced by 2 ingredients —dried skimmed milk and animal fat—so that the table reads

	Requirement	*Sago flour*	*Meat meal*	*Skimmed milk*	*Soya flour*	*Animal fat*
Protein	$\geqslant 20$	0	50	40	50	0
Fat	$\geqslant 10$	0	10	0	20	100
Carbohydrate	$= 50$	100	0	50	20	0
Fibre + Ash	$\leqslant 20$	0	40	10	10	0
Cost		40	50	60	60	100

4 Transportation Problems

4.1 A Definition of a Transportation Problem

An important special class of linear programming problems, known as *transportation problems* was studied before the general subject of linear programming was explicitly recognized. The original formulation and solution of the transportation problem as we now understand it is due to Hitchcock (1941); and similar ideas were developed earlier by Kantorovich (1939). A transportation problem is one that is mathematically equivalent to the following—

> Given a certain amount of some (homogeneous) commodity available at each of a number of sources, and a certain amount required at each of a number of destinations, where the total amount available altogether equals the total amount required altogether, and given the cost of supplying each destination from each source (as so much per unit), find the cheapest way of meeting the requirements.

The problem can be formulated as a linear programming problem if we define x_{ij} as the number of units sent from source i to destination j. The problem is then to maximize

$$x_0 = -\sum_i \sum_j c_{ij} x_{ij}$$

subject to

$$\sum_j x_{ij} = a_i \quad \text{and} \quad \sum_i x_{ij} = b_j$$

where c_{ij} is the cost of sending one unit from source i to destination j, a_i is the amount available at source i, and b_j is the amount required at destination j.

We assume that $\sum_i a_i = \sum_j b_j$, otherwise the problem is infeasible.

Such problems can be treated as ordinary linear programming problems and solved by the simplex method in the usual way, but more efficient methods have been devised that take advantage of the special structure of these problems. One of many such methods, known as the *stepping stone* [illegible] simplex method but keeps track of the situation [illegible] way, and [illegible] existence of [illegible] computer can [illegible] LP/90/94 [illegible] with up to [illegible] objective [illegible] problems if [illegible] not exceed [illegible] can solve [illegible] of sources [illegible]

3.2 The Formulation of Transportation Problems

Let us therefore consider the range of problems that can be formulated this way. It is clear that transportation problems in this technical sense do not cover all problems involving distribution—not even all [illegible] programming terms, but the range covered is rather wider than might appear at first sight. The following [illegible]

(1) It may be physically impossible to supply some destinations from some sources. If so an effectively infinite cost can be associated with such routes. We call these routes *unspecified routes*.

(2) If the total amount available exceeds the total amount required we can define a fictitious additional destination, a *dummy* destination, to receive the excess material at zero cost. Material sent to the dummy represents unused material.

Similarly if the total amount available falls short of the total amount required, we can define a fictitious source. The costs of shipping from this source to any destination must then represent the penalties or losses associated with not supplying this destination.

(3) There is often a manufacturing (or handling) cost associated with a source. If the total amount to be supplied from the source is fixed, then this is a fixed cost and therefore does not affect the optimum solution. But if this amount is not fixed, then the manufacturing cost (per unit) must be added to the transportation costs to all destinations other than the dummy.

If additional material can be obtained at a higher cost, then this additional material can be thought of as coming from another source. Similarly, one sometimes defines different destinations representing the same geographical area, since one may for example divide the demand into large and small loads, having different delivery costs per unit-mile.

(4) Problems involving intermediate destinations, such as the one involving depots used to introduce linear programming, can be handled by treating the depot as both a source and a destination. The amount available at the source and the amount required at the destination must equal the capacity of the depot. The cost of supplying the depot from itself must be put equal to zero: the amount sent on this route represents the unused capacity at the depot. If the depot capacity is effectively infinite, then some large number should be used for this capacity. This device is due to Orden (1956).

(5) Some multi-time-period problems can be formulated as transportation problems. Each physical source must be treated as a separate mathematical source for each time period, and similarly for the destinations. If storage capacity can be taken as effectively infinite, then the storage costs associated with producing in one time period to meet a demand in a later time period can simply be added to any other costs to produce a corresponding total cost. If the capacity for storage from one time period to the next is limited, this can be put in as an extra source and an extra destination. Let us illustrate these ideas by a specific problem.

Suppose we have to meet a demand for a single product over 4 successive time periods as follows—

12 units in the first period
6 units in the second period
11 units in the third period
18 units in the fourth period.

Production costs vary from period to period, perhaps because of variations in raw material costs. They are (in say thousands of pounds per unit) 5, 3, 7, 8. One must make at least 10 units per period, but up to an additional 5 units can be made by overtime working at an additional cost of 2 (thousand pounds per unit). Up to 5 units can be held in store from one period to the next, at a cost of 1 (thousand pounds per unit) per period plus an additional cost of 2 (thousand pounds per unit) associated with getting the material into and out of the store.

This problem can be formulated as a transportation problem with 11 sources and 8 destinations. The sources can be labelled P_i $(i = 1, \ldots, 4)$ for regular production in period i, O_i $(i = 1, \ldots, 4)$ for overtime production in period i, and S_i $(i = 1, \ldots, 3)$ for storage from period i to period $i + 1$. The destinations can be labelled R_i $(i = 1, \ldots, 4)$ for requirements in period i, S_i $(i = 1, \ldots, 3)$ for storage from period i to period $i + 1$, and dummy representing unused overtime capacity. The matrix of availabilities, demands and costs is shown in Table 4.1.

TABLE 4.1

		Destination	R_1	S_1	R_2	S_2	R_3	S_3	R_4	*Dummy*
		Amount required	12	5	6	5	11	5	18	13
Source	*Amount available*	*Costs:*								
P_1	10		5	7						
O_1	5		7	9						0
S_1	5			0	1	1				
P_2	10				3	5				
O_2	5				5	7				0
S_2	5					0	1	1		
P_3	10						7	9		
O_3	5						9	11		0
S_3	5							0	1	
P_4	10								8	
O_4	5								10	0

Blank spaces in this table represent unspecified routes, i.e. infinite costs.

This type of problem can of course be applied to several different production and demand points, so that it includes an element of ordinary transportation as well as scheduling over time.

(6) There is a formal test, for whether a linear programming matrix represents a transportation problem, that may be of some interest: if the problem can be formulated so that every coefficient outside the objective function and the right hand side is either ± 1, and each variable has at most one $+1$ and at most one -1 in all the constraints taken together, then the problem is a transportation problem. This may seem a strange test, as it is not satisfied by the original equations used to define a transportation problem; but these equations can easily be put into the right form by multiplying the equations relating to sources by -1. This is a natural thing to do on the grounds that each row represents some physical resource and negative coefficients correspond to activities that use or take

away this resource while positive coefficients correspond to activities that create or bring in the resource. To set up a problem that passes the test as a transportation problem, one starts by turning all inequality constraints into equations by adding slack variables. One then writes down a balancing equation, by summing all the other equations and reversing the signs. Each variable will now have precisely one +1 and precisely one −1 coefficient. Equations with only negative coefficients represent sources, and the negative of the right hand side represents the amount available. Equations with only positive coefficients represent destinations, and the right hand side represents the amount required. Equations with both positive and negative coefficients represent both sources and destinations. The amount available at the source must be arbitrarily large. The amount required at the destination must exceed this by the right hand side. The cost of supplying the destination from the corresponding source must be zero. The variables then represent permitted routes, from the source containing the negative coefficient to the destination containing the positive coefficient at the cost given by the coefficient in the objective function.

By such means, a number of simple models of situations not concerned with transport in the normal sense can be formulated as transportation problems. Unfortunately a practical problem often has some additional features that prevents it from being a transportation problem, so transportation problems are not solved as extensively as one might imagine. Nevertheless they are important enough to deserve some special attention. Incidentally, one useful property of transportation problems is that if the amounts available and required are all integers, then all basic solutions are integral. Since any normal algorithm will find an optimum basic solution, one cannot run into the difficulty of interpreting fractional values of the variables that sometimes arises with general linear programming problems.

4.3 The Solution of Transportation Problems

I have mentioned that there are a great many methods for solving transportation problems. Most of them are based on the fact that if we set out the cost coefficients as a matrix, with each row corresponding to a source and each column to a destination, then the problem is unaltered if we subtract a constant from all coefficients in a single row or a single column—since this simply subtracts the constant times the given total (supply or demand) associated with the row or column concerned. The problem is solved if we have a feasible trial solution such that the modified costs associated with all used routes are zero and the modified costs associated with all unused routes are non-negative.

A particular implementation of this strategy, the stepping-stone method, follows the logic of the regular simplex method, and we consider this in rather more detail.

The first task is to find a feasible trial solution—or more specifically a basic feasible trial solution. If there are no unspecified routes, i.e. routes with infinite costs, this is straightforward, and it is still straightforward if we introduce artificial variables, representing the use of these unspecified routes, in the first instance. One way to do this is known as the *north-west corner rule* and works as follows. Consider the first source and first destination. Supply as much as possible along this route until either the source has used all its supply or until the destination had received its full requirement. Then consider a new problem with either one fewer sources or one fewer destinations, in which the amounts available and required are reduced by the amounts already allocated. Continue in this way until the demands are all met. Since the total amount available must equal the total amount required, the supply will simultaneously be all used up.

Let us apply this rule to getting a first feasible solution to the production scheduling problem considered earlier. The first source has 10 units and the first destination requires 12 units. So we send 10 units along this route. This disposes of the first source, but the first destination still requires 2 units. The second source has 5 units, so we send 2 to the first destination to dispose of it. We still have 3 units at the second source and we can send these to the second destination. This can be continued in the straightforward way. In this example it involves sending [illegible] from P_1 to R_1, 5 from Q_1 to R_2, 6 from P_2 to R_2, 2 from Q_2 to R_3 and 6 from $P_{[illegible]}$ to the Dummy.

This rule is apt to produce a very poor initial solution, since it pays no attention to cost. In practice one usually uses a [illegible] *north-west corner* rule in which the next destination considered is chosen as the one with the smallest cost from the source being considered. Applying this to the same problem we assign [illegible] from P_1 to R_1, since R_1 is the cheapest destination from P_1, and 2 units from Q_1 to R_1, since Q_1 is the next source. The remaining 3 units from Q_1 are sent to the Dummy, since this is the cheapest destination from Q_1. The next source (P_2) [illegible] units to the dummy, and the next source (Q_2) supplies the remaining [illegible] units required by the dummy. The other [illegible] not yet considered [illegible] assign [illegible] interchanging sources and destinations. This does not affect the problem, and it is generally better to have more destinations than sources. The same strategy then assigns only 3 units to unspecified routes.

The modified north-west corner rule can be further extended so that the next row is chosen by the same logic as the next column. This also assigns only 3 units to unspecified routes on this problem, but this procedure is often inconvenient in practice for a large problem on a computer.

Normally the solution obtained will use $n + m - 1$ routes (where m is the number of sources and n the number of destinations), and these will be the basic variables. But if any assignment simultaneously exhausts the supply at some source and meets the full demand at some destination—other than at the very end—then we must add a further basic variable with a value of zero. This can be done by pretending that the demand is increased by an arbitrarily small amount, which is then satisfied from the next source.

Having selected $m + n - 1$ basic variables in this way, it is a straightforward matter to select numbers to be subtracted from each row and each column so as to make the modified costs of each basic variable equal to zero. (In fact one of these numbers can be selected arbitrarily.) If the modified costs on all non-basic routes are non-negative the problem is solved, but if any is negative we take one, say the most negative, and make it basic, i.e. increase the amount sent on this route. We must then find another destination to receive less from this source, and then another source to supply more to this destination, and so on until we have completed a circuit using only basic routes other than the one selected non-basic route. This can be done in just one way. We then change the trial solution in the indicated way until some route receives a zero assignment and drops out of the basis. We now recompute the amounts to be subtracted from each row and column, and repeat the process as often as necessary to solve the problem.

Before showing how this works on our example problem, let us note two things:

(1) The costs subtracted from each row and column do not have to be physically subtracted. We can work with the original cost coefficients and numbers associated with each row and column representing the amounts we would subtract. In terms of the simplex method these numbers are in fact the shadow prices on these rows of the matrix.

(2) The modified costs after these (nominal or actual) subtractions are simply the reduced costs of the non-basic variables.

Let us now solve our example problem, starting with a solution obtained by the modified north-west corner rule treating the destinations as rows. This solution is shown in Table 4.2.

TABLE 4.2

	R_1	S_1	R_2	S_2	R_3	S_3	R_4	*Dummy*
P_1	10							
O_1	2	3						
S_1		2	3					
P_2			3	5	2			
O_2								5
S_2					5			
P_3					4	5	1	
O_3								5
S_3							5	
P_4							10	
O_4							2	3

This includes 2 unspecified routes P_2 to R_3 and P_3 to R_4, so we start with an objective function representing the sum of infeasibilities, and form the corresponding shadow prices. Arbitrarily taking 0 for the source P_1, we find we must take 0 for destination R_1, and hence 0 for source O_1 and 0 for destination S_1. Hence we have 0 for source P_2; 0 for destination S_2 and 1 for destination R_3. Hence we have -1 for sources S_2 and P_3; 1 for destination S_3 and 2 for destination R_4. Hence we have -2 for sources S_3, P_4 and O_4; $+2$ for destination dummy, and -2 for sources O_2 and O_3.

The infeasibility costs are shown in Table 4.3.

TABLE 4.3

		R_1	S_1	R_2	S_2	R_3	S_3	R_4	*Dummy*
Shadow prices		0	0	0	0	1	1	2	2
P_1	0	0	0	1	1	1	1	1	1
O_1	0	0	0	1	1	1	1	1	0
S_1	0	1	0	0	0	1	1	1	1
P_2	0	1	1	0	0	1	1	1	1
O_2	−2	1	1	0	0	1	1	1	0
S_2	−1	1	1	1	0	0	0	1	1
P_3	−1	1	1	1	1	0	0	1	1
O_3	−2	1	1	1	1	0	0	1	0
S_3	−2	1	1	1	1	1	0	0	1
P_4	−2	1	1	1	1	1	1	0	1
O_4	−2	1	1	1	1	1	1	0	0

[illegible]

TABLE 4.4

[illegible]

The next iteration can be set out in the same way (Table 4.5) where the trial solution is obtained first, then the shadow prices, then the route to be introduced (O_3 to R_3), and then the cycle.

TABLE 4.5

		R_1	S_1	R_2	S_2	R_3	S_3	R_4	*Dummy*
Shadow prices		0	0	0	0	1	1	0	0
P_1	0	10							
O_1	0	2	2^-						1^+
S_1	0		3^+	2^-					
P_2	0			4^+	5	1^-			
O_2	0								5
S_2	−1					5			
P_3	−1					5	5		
O_3	0					+			5^-
S_3	0							5	
P_4	0							10	
O_4	0							3	2

We can send one unit round this new cycle, and this produces a feasible solution. At the next iteration the shadow prices refer to the genuine cost function. The iteration is summarized in Table 4.6.

TABLE 4.6

		R_1	S_1	R_2	S_2	R_3	S_3	R_4	*Dummy*
Shadow prices		5	7	8	10	7	9	8	−2
P_1	0	10							
O_1	2	2	1^-						2^+
S_1	−7		4^+	1^-					
P_2	−5			5^+	5^-				
O_2	2				+				5^-
S_2	−6					5			
P_3	0					5	5		
O_3	2					1			4
S_3	−7							5	
P_4	0							10	
O_4	2							3	2

We now have a trial solution with a zero basic element, since we cannot drop both O_1 to S_1 and S_1 to R_2 from the basis. Arbitrarily selecting O_1 to S_1 to be dropped, we obtain the iteration shown in Table 4.7.

TABLE 4.7

		R_1	S_1	R_2	S_2	R_3	S_3	R_4	*Dummy*
Shadow prices		10	7	8	10	12	14	13	3
P_1	−5	10							
O_1	−3	2							3
S_1	−7		5	0^-	+				
P_2	−5			6^+	4^-				
O_2	−3				1				4
S_2	−11					5			
P_3	−5					5	5		
O_3	−3					1			4
S_3	−12							5	
P_4	−5							10	
O_4	−3							3	2

This time we make a zero move, but the change of basis allows us to proceed next time, as in Table 4.8.

TABLE 4.8

		R_1	S_1	R_2	S_2	R_3	S_3	R_4	*Dummy*
Shadow prices		10	9	8	10	12	14	13	3
P_1	−5	10							
O_1	−3	2							3
S_1	−9		5		0				
P_2	−5			6	4				
O_2	−3				1				4
S_2	−11					5^-	+		
P_3	−5					5^+	5^-		
O_3	−3					1			4
S_3	−12							5	
P_4	−5							10	
O_4	−3							3	2

The next trial solution and set of shadow prices is shown in Table 4.9.

TABLE 4.9

		R_1	S_1	R_2	S_2	R_3	S_3	R_4	*Dummy*
Shadow prices		10	9	8	10	12	12	13	3
P_1	−5	10							
O_1	−3	2							3
S_1	−9		5		0				
P_2	−5			6	4				
O_2	−3				1				4
S_2	−11					0	5		
P_3	−5					10			
O_3	−3					1			4
S_3	−12							5	
P_4	−5							10	
O_4	−3							3	2

The reduced costs on all feasible routes are now non-negative, so we have the final solution. A fair amount of writing has been needed to find it, but the work is quite quick, essentially because it involves only addition and subtraction, and no multiplication or division.

EXAMPLE

Formulate and solve the problem discussed in Chapter 1 as a transportation problem.

5 Duality and the Dual Simplex Method

5.1 Duality

Let us look again at the rules for manipulating the coefficients in the tableau in their theoretical form. They read as follows—

$$\left.\begin{aligned} \bar{a}'_{pq} &= 1/\bar{a}_{pq} \\ \bar{a}'_{pj} &= \bar{a}_{pj}/\bar{a}_{pq} \\ \bar{a}'_{iq} &= -\bar{a}_{iq}/\bar{a}_{pq} \\ \bar{a}'_{ij} &= \bar{a}_{ij} - \bar{a}_{iq}\bar{a}_{pj}/\bar{a}_{pq} \end{aligned}\right\} i \neq p, j \neq q$$

We have said that these rules relate to the coefficients in the equations

$$x_0 = \bar{a}_{00} + \sum_{j=1}^{n-m} \bar{a}_{0j}(-X_{m+j})$$

$$X_i = \bar{a}_{i0} + \sum_{j=1}^{n-m} \bar{a}_{ij}(-X_{m+j}) \qquad (i = 1, \ldots, m)$$

when the variables X_p and X_{m+q} are interchanged.

We have already commented on the symmetry of the rule with respect to rows and columns of the matrix $(\bar{a}_{ij})$, and as a result of this symmetry we can equally well think of the matrix as the coefficients in the following set of equations

$$y_0 = \bar{a}_{00} + \sum_{i=1}^{m} \bar{a}_{i0} Y_i$$

$$Y_{m+j} = \bar{a}_{0j} + \sum_{i=1}^{m} \bar{a}_{ij} Y_i \qquad (j = 1, \ldots, n-m)$$

and the transformation describes the changes in the coefficients when the variables Y_{m+q} and Y_p are interchanged.

The simplex method terminates when the $\bar{a}_{i0}$ and $\bar{a}_{0j}$ are all non-negative, in which case x_0 has its largest possible value subject to the constraints that all the variables $X_1, \ldots, X_n$ are non-negative.

In these circumstances [illegible] has the smallest [illegible] value subject to the constraints that all [illegible] are non-negative. The two problems are therefore said to be [illegible] *problems.* They are stated [illegible] in terms of [illegible] as follows.

Problem 1 (Primal)

Maximize $B =$ [illegible]

where all variables have to be non-negative and

$$a_{1,1}x_{m+1} + \dots + a_{1,n-m}x_n \leq c_1$$

$$a_{m,1}x_{m+1} + \dots + a_{m,n-m}x_n \leq c_m$$

(so that the variables [illegible] are the slacks on the inequalities).

Problem 2 (Dual)

Minimize $C =$ [illegible]

where all variables have to be non-negative and

$$a_{1,1}y_1 + \dots + a_{m,1}y_m \geq b_1$$

[illegible]

(so that the variables [illegible] are the slacks on the inequalities).

These two problems have the formal relationships implied by the name duality [illegible] that [illegible] problem is the primal problem, and because of the symmetry of the rules for manipulating tableaux discussed above, the solutions to the two problems are related as follows.

If either has a finite optimal solution then so does the other, and the maximum of B equals the [illegible] of C. Furthermore if x_j is basic in the optimal solution to the primal and has a numerical value [illegible], then y_j is non-basic in the corresponding optimal solution to the dual and has a reduced cost of [illegible]; while if x_j is non-basic in the optimal solution to the primal and has a reduced cost of [illegible], then y_j is basic in the corresponding optimal solution to the dual and has a numerical value of [illegible]. Note in particular that the values of the original variables (as opposed to the slack variables) in the dual problem are the shadow prices on the constraints of the primal problem.

Before discussing the significance of duality let us clear up 2 loose ends. Any [illegible] inequalities in the primal problem can be left alone and the corresponding dual variable restricted to non-positive values instead of the customary non-negative values. If there are any equality constraints in the primal problem, the corresponding dual variables are not sign restricted. This can perhaps be seen most easily by treating [illegible] as [illegible] ≥ [illegible] and a ≤ inequality [illegible] would provide [illegible] with identical coefficients [illegible] in all constraints, such that [illegible] to be non-negative while the other had to be non-positive [illegible].

The other loose end concerns the possibility that the problems [illegible] cannot be [illegible]. [illegible] then here is that if either [illegible] the other must be inconsistent. [illegible] it is possible for both primal and dual [illegible] how this comes about.

The primal [illegible] for any i in any tableau,

$$[illegible] \leqslant 0 \quad \text{and} \quad [illegible] \text{ for all } [illegible]$$

[illegible] we have [illegible] of the form

$$X_i = a_{i0} + \sum [illegible]$$

This implies that X_i is negative [illegible] X_j [illegible], and yet it cannot be [illegible] of the [illegible] cannot be negative.

Similarly the primal problem is unbounded if all $a_{i0} \geqslant 0$ and, for any j,

$$a_{0j} < 0 \quad \text{and} \quad a_{ij} \leqslant 0 \text{ for all } i$$

Bearing [illegible] and the changes of sign in the dual tableau, we see that [illegible] if, for any [illegible]

$$a_{i0} < 0 \quad \text{and} \quad a_{ij} \geqslant 0 \text{ for all } j$$

[illegible] the dual problem is unbounded if all $a_{0j} \geqslant 0$ and for any i

$$a_{i0} < 0 \quad [illegible] \geqslant 0 \text{ for all } j$$

[illegible] that [illegible] problem is unbounded [illegible] the other [illegible] can both be inconsistent? This requires that, for some i [illegible]

$$a_{i0} \leqslant 0 \quad \text{and} \quad a_{ij} \geqslant 0 [illegible]$$

[illegible] for some j [illegible]

$$a_{0j} \leqslant 0 \quad \text{and} \quad a_{ij} \leqslant 0 \text{ for all } i$$

[illegible] these [illegible] compatible since [illegible] cannot be [illegible] if [illegible] $[illegible] 0$

So much for the algebra of duality, but is it important? Some people find it very interesting, and argue that it is the only aspect of linear programming of any pure mathematical interest. For myself, I accept this argument without being moved by it, since I am interested in linear programming as a branch of numerical mathematics but not really as a branch of pure mathematics. What else can we say for the duality theorem? It is a generalization of the minimax theorem in the theory of two-person zero-sum games when both players have only a finite number of pure strategies; indeed it provides a very simple proof of this minimax theorem. But I do not want to go into that here.

The dual to a linear programming problem can be given an economic interpretation as follows.

We have pointed out that the values of the dual variables are the shadow prices on the constraints of the primal problem, and we saw earlier that these shadow prices represent the derivatives of the objective function with respect to the right hand sides of these constraints. So a dual variable represents the implied economic cost of a unit of the scarce resource defined by the corresponding primal constraint. On this basis one can price out each primal variable, or activity, taking account not only of the direct cost or profit involved but also of these implied costs of using scarce resources (or implied profits from adding to the supply of scarce resources). If this is done one obtains the reduced costs with which we are already familiar. This assertion can be proved in various ways. One is to note that it amounts to carrying out the numerical check mentioned at the end of Chapter 2 on the dual problem. The trial values assigned to the dual variables are their direct costs.

Now consider the dual objective function. This represents the total value imputed to all the resources available. The dual problem is then to find a set of implied costs on all scarce resources so as to minimize this total value, subject to the constraints that the corresponding reduced costs of all primal activities must be non-negative. The equivalence of the optimum values of the objective functions of the primal and dual problems means that the total value of the resources in this sense is equal to the total profit realizable from using these resources in the best possible way.

5.2 The Dual Simplex Method

So much for theoretical economics. What is the computational importance of duality? The fact that we can obtain the solution to a problem by solving its dual may occasionally be useful, for example if the problem contains more basic than non-basic variables, i.e.

more inequality constraints than original variables. A much more significant fact is that we can solve a linear programming problem by going through the motions of solving the dual problem by the simplex method, but interpreting each step in terms of the original problem. This is the method, due to Lemke (1954), known as the *dual method* or more commonly as the *dual simplex method.* Let us consider this in detail. Consider the tableau

$$x_0 = \bar{a}_{00} + \sum_{j=1}^{n-m} \bar{a}_{0j}(-X_{m+j})$$

$$X_i = \bar{a}_{i0} + \sum_{j=1}^{n-m} \bar{a}_{ij}(-X_{m+j}) \qquad (i = 1, \ldots, m)$$

We suppose that the corresponding trial solution to the dual problem is feasible. This means that the $\bar{a}_{0j}$ are all non-negative, and that the present trial solution would be optimal if the only inequality constraints were that the present non-basic variables must be non-negative. Such a trial solution is called *dual feasible.*

We must now examine the signs of the basic variables to see if we have really solved the problem, or whether some $\bar{a}_{i0}$ is negative, indicating that our trial solution is infeasible. If so, there is an inequality constraint on the current non-basic variables, to the effect that this basic variable must be non-negative, that is not satisfied at our current trial solution. We now find the best trial solution subject to the conditions that this particular constraint must be satisfied, as well as the constraints that all the current non-basic variables must remain non-negative. The new constraint will then be satisfied as an equality, and one of the non-basic variables will become positive; so we make the indicated change of basis and this completes one iteration.

This argument interprets the dual simplex method without any explicit reference to duality, as a cutting plane method. That is to say one has the optimal solution to a problem, but the feasible region is wider than the feasible region of the problem we really want to solve. We find a constraint, or "cutting plane" that excludes part of this wider region, including the present trial solution, but does not exclude any genuinely feasible point, and re-solve the problem taking account of this new constraint. We shall see later how this idea has been applied in other contexts, particularly to the problem of finding integer solutions to linear programming problems.

There remains the problem of getting a first dual feasible solution in the dual simplex method. This can perhaps most easily be resolved as follows. Start by solving the problem for some selected set of basic variables. If the $\bar{a}_{0j}$ are then all non-negative we are all set to proceed, but if not let $\bar{a}_{0q}$ be the most negative of them. Now introduce a new constraint into the problem as follows

$$x_{n+1} = \Omega + \sum_{j=1}^{n-m} (-X_{m+j})$$

where Ω is some arbitrarily large number; so the constraint, which states that the sum of the non-basic variables must be less than or equal to Ω, does not cut out any finite solution to the problem. Finally make x_{n+1} non-basic instead of X_{m+q}. The problem will then be dual feasible, though the tableau will have an extra column, in that some basic variables will have a term in Ω as well as a genuine constant term. If the problem has an unbounded solution, then these Ωs will remain in the problem. If not, x_{n+1} will eventually become basic, and it can be dropped from the problem, together with all Ωs.

Let us illustrate this with an artificial small example. Maximize x_0 where

$$x_0 = 3x_1 - x_2 + 2x_3$$

subject to

$$\begin{aligned} x_4 &= 6 - 2x_1 - x_2 - x_3 \\ x_5 &= -8 + 2x_2 + x_3 \end{aligned}$$

To make the problem formally dual feasible we write

$$x_6 = \Omega - x_1 - x_2 - x_3$$

and pivot between x_1 and x_6. We then have

$$\begin{aligned} x_0 &= 3\Omega - 3x_6 - 4x_2 - x_3 \\ x_4 &= -2\Omega + 6 + 2x_6 + x_2 + x_3 \\ x_5 &= -8 + 2x_2 + x_3 \\ x_1 &= \Omega - x_6 - x_2 - x_3 \end{aligned}$$

Now x_4 is negative, so we make it non-basic. The variable to be made basic must be x_3 if the solution is to remain dual feasible, so we write

$$\begin{aligned} x_0 &= \Omega + 6 - x_6 - 3x_2 - x_4 \\ x_3 &= 2\Omega - 6 - 2x_6 - x_2 + x_4 \\ x_5 &= 2\Omega - 14 - 2x_6 + x_2 + x_4 \\ x_1 &= -\Omega + 6 + x_6 - x_4 \end{aligned}$$

Now [illegible] is negative, so we make it non-basic. The variable to be made basic [illegible] the solution [illegible] that is [illegible] we write

$$x_6 = \quad 12 - x_1 - 3x_? - 2x_?$$

$$x_3 = \quad [illegible]$$

$$x_? = \quad 2 - 2x_? [illegible]$$

$$x_4 = M - 6 + x_? [illegible]$$

We now have [illegible] 6 [illegible] and [illegible] the variable $x_?$ and [illegible]. Since [illegible] we must make it non-basic instead of [illegible]. We then [illegible]

$$x_? = 6 - x_? - [illegible]$$

$$[illegible]\; 4x_? [illegible]$$

$$[illegible] + 2x_? + x_? + x_4$$

Th[illegible] solution [illegible]

EXAMPLE [illegible]

Solve the worked example in Chapter [illegible] by the dual simplex method. [illegible]

6 Parametric Programming

6.1 Parametric Objective Function

Parametric programming is the name given to the problem of tracing out the way the solution to a linear programming problem varies as one or more of the coefficients varies. There are two basic forms of parametric programming—on the objective function and on the right hand side.

Mathematically, parametric programming on the objective function means solving the following problem—

> Maximize $x_0 + \theta x_0^*$ for $0 \leqslant \theta \leqslant \theta_{max}$ where x_0 and x_0^* are linear functions of non-negative variables subject to equality constraints (which may be written as a matrix equation $\mathbf{Ax} = \mathbf{b}$). In practice the expression x_0^* is often a single variable, with either a positive or a negative sign, to explore the effect of changing a single cost or profit coefficient. But the theory is unaffected if one has a more general expression.

This problem is solved by first maximizing x_0 using the simplex (or possibly the dual simplex) method, but keeping track of the expression for x_0^* in terms of the non-basic variables. Then suppose that the final tableau reads

$$x_0 = \bar{a}_{00} + \sum \bar{a}_{0j}(-X_{m+j})$$

$$x_0^* = \bar{a}_{00}^* + \sum \bar{a}_{0j}^*(-X_{m+j})$$

$$X_i = \bar{a}_{i0} + \sum \bar{a}_{ij}(-X_{m+j}) \qquad (i = 1, \ldots, m)$$

Since this is the final tableau, $\bar{a}_{i0} \geqslant 0$ for $i = 1, \ldots, m$, and $\bar{a}_{0j} \geqslant 0$ for $j = 1, \ldots, n - m$. As we increase θ from zero, our composite objective function $x_0 + \theta x_0^*$ becomes equal to

$$(\bar{a}_{00} + \theta\bar{a}_{00}^*) + \sum (\bar{a}_{0j} + \theta\bar{a}_{0j}^*)(-X_{m+j})$$

This is optimized by our present solution as long as $\bar{a}_{0j} + \theta\bar{a}^*_{0j} \geqslant 0$ for all $j = 1, \ldots, n - m$. But we must compute

$$\theta_c = \min_{j, \bar{a}_{0j}^* < 0} \left(\frac{\bar{a}_{0j}}{|\bar{a}^*_{0j}|} \right)$$

and note the corresponding value of j, say $j = q$. When $\theta = \theta_c$ we must make a pivot step, making X_{m+q} basic, and choosing the variable to be removed from the basis in the usual way, i.e. X_p where

$$\bar{a}_{p0}/\bar{a}_{pq} = \min_{i, \bar{a}_{iq} > 0} \left(\frac{\bar{a}_{i0}}{\bar{a}_{iq}} \right)$$

When this has been done we have a new tableau. Some of the $\bar{a}_{0j}$ will no longer be positive, but this does not matter because the current basis is optimal for $\theta = \theta_c$. But we must consider how far it remains optimal as θ is further increased. We therefore compute a new θ_c, and a new change of basis, using the same rules as before. The process continues until one of three things happens

(*a*) $\theta_c \geqslant \theta_{max}$, in which case the current trial solution remains optimal until the end of the prescribed range of values of θ.
(*b*) $\bar{a}^*_{0j} \geqslant 0$ for all j. This is in a sense a special case of (*a*) when $\theta_c = \infty$. It means that the current trial solution remains optimal for all larger θ.
(*c*) $\bar{a}_{iq} \leqslant 0$ for all i. This means that for $\theta > \theta_c$ the objective function is unbounded, i.e. it can be given an arbitrarily large positive value by giving X_{m+q} an arbitrarily large positive value.

At the end we will have mapped out the (finite) set of alternative optimal solutions as θ increases as far as possible from 0 to θ_{max}. The amount of information to be presented from this work obviously depends on circumstances. With small problems it may be worth while to look at each solution in detail. With larger problems one usually does this only for a few specified values of θ, but at each basis change one can summarize the situation by printing

(*a*) the value of θ_c
(*b*) the value of the objective function $(\bar{a}_{00} + \theta_c\bar{a}^*_{00})$
(*c*) the name of the variable entering the basis
(*d*) the name of the variable leaving the basis.

Let us now see how this works in a numerical example. For this purpose we may consider a very simple example of an important field of application of linear programming—the scheduling of production over time. This is typically done for a range of products for which the demand may be seasonal so as to meet the forecast demand without exceeding any machine capacity or other restrictions and finding the best balance between storage costs (incurred when products are made before they are required because there is then spare production capacity) and high production costs (incurred when using overtime labour or when hiring additional labour, or when using a less suitable production route on the grounds that the normal route is fully committed doing something else). In such a model one may also have to consider the seasonal availabilities of some raw materials.

In our numerical example the problem has been kept very simple so that the computations can be done manually.*

Suppose that we have to meet the following sales requirement for 4 successive months

3, 11, 5, 11 units (perhaps millions of items).

Suppose further that a team capable of making 1 unit per month involves an expense of £2000/month. We can recruit additional teams, but we are uncertain of the true cost of this, so we want to explore how the solution varies as the assumed cost of a new team varies from zero up to £10,000. It is contrary to company policy to dismiss staff. It is possible to transfer them to other duties but this does not save money. We neglect the wastage of staff in the model to simplify the arithmetic, although an allowance for this does not complicate the model for a computer.

It is permitted to make units ahead of requirements, but it costs £1000 to store one unit for a month.

We have an initial stock of 2 units, and an initial labour force of 6 teams.

The problem can be formulated in a variety of ways. The smallest number of non-zero coefficients is achieved as follows.

Let

x_i denote the number of units made in month i
y_i denote the spare capacity in month i
z_i denote the number of teams hired in month i
s_i denote the number of units stored at the end of month i.

Then the capacity constraints are of two types.

The labour force in one month equals the labour force in the previous month, plus the number of teams hired [illegible]

[illegible]

[illegible]

[illegible]

Further, the amount stored at the end of a month equals the amount carried forward from the previous month plus the amount produced during the month minus the sales during the month, so

$$s_1 = 2 + x_1 - 3$$
$$s_2 = s_1 + x_2 - 11$$
$$s_3 = s_2 + x_3 - 5$$
$$s_4 = s_3 + x_4 - 11$$

The original objective function is given by

$$x_0 = -2x_1 - 2z_1 - 2x_2 - 2z_2 - 2x_3 - 2z_3 - 2x_4 - 2z_4 - s_1 - s_2 - s_3 - s_4$$

but our additional objective function is given by

$$x_0^* = -t_1 - t_2 - t_3 - t_4$$

The original linear programming problem can be solved by introducing an artificial variable for each equation, but this is a laborious procedure. Let us therefore start by solving for each x_i and each s_i. We then have the tableau shown in Table 6.1.

The sum of infeasibilities is reduced most rapidly by increasing t_1 and we can make the problem feasible by pivoting between t_1 and s_4. We then have Table 6.2.

Now make t_3 basic instead of s_2. We then have Table 6.3.

Now make t_2 basic instead of t_1. We then have Table 6.4.

Now make t_4 basic instead of t_3. We then have Table 6.5.

This gives the final solution when new teams cost nothing to hire.

This solution remains optimal until $\theta = 1$, i.e. until teams cost £1000 to hire. We must then make t_3 basic instead of t_4 and we return to Table 6.4. This remains optimal until $\theta = 3$, i.e. until teams cost £3000 to hire. We must then make s_2 basic instead of t_3 and have Table 6.6.

This solution remains optimal until $\theta = 6$, i.e. until teams cost £6000 to hire. We must then make t_1 basic instead of t_2. We then return to Table 6.2. This remains optimal for all larger θ.

6.2 Parametric Right Hand Side

So much for parametric programming on the objective function. Let us now turn to parametric programming on the right hand side. This is in a sense the dual problem. Mathematically it means solving the following problem—

Maximize x_0, a linear function of non-negative variables subject to

TABLE 6.1

$$
\begin{aligned}
x_0 &= -32 - 18t_1 - 12t_2 - 7t_3 - 3t_4 + 4z_1 + 3z_2 + 2z_3 + z_4 \\
x_0^* &= - t_1 - t_2 - t_3 - t_4 \\
x_1 &= 5 + t_1 - z_1 \\
x_2 &= 5 + t_1 + t_2 - z_2 \\
x_3 &= 5 + t_1 + t_2 + t_3 - z_3 \\
x_4 &= 5 + t_1 + t_2 + t_3 + t_4 - z_4 \\
s_1 &= 4 + t_1 - z_1 \\
s_2 &= -2 + 2t_1 + t_2 - z_1 - z_2 \\
s_3 &= -2 + 3t_1 + 2t_2 + t_3 - z_1 - z_2 - z_3 \\
s_4 &= -8 + 4t_1 + 3t_2 + 2t_3 + t_4 - z_1 - z_2 - z_3 - z_4
\end{aligned}
$$

TABLE 6.2

$$
\begin{aligned}
x_0 &= -68 - \frac{18}{4}s_4 + \frac{6}{4}t_2 + 2t_3 + \frac{6}{4}t_4 - \frac{2}{4}z_1 - \frac{6}{4}z_2 - \frac{10}{4}z_3 - \frac{14}{4}z_4 \\
x_0^* &= -2 - \frac{1}{4}s_4 - \frac{1}{4}t_2 - \frac{2}{4}t_3 - \frac{3}{4}t_4 - \frac{1}{4}z_1 - \frac{1}{4}z_2 - \frac{1}{4}z_3 - \frac{1}{4}z_4 \\
x_1 &= 7 + \frac{1}{4}s_4 - \frac{3}{4}t_2 - \frac{2}{4}t_3 - \frac{1}{4}t_4 - \frac{3}{4}z_1 + \frac{1}{4}z_2 + \frac{1}{4}z_3 + \frac{1}{4}z_4 \\
x_2 &= 7 + \frac{1}{4}s_4 + \frac{1}{4}t_2 - \frac{2}{4}t_3 - \frac{1}{4}t_4 + \frac{1}{4}z_1 - \frac{3}{4}z_2 + \frac{1}{4}z_3 + \frac{1}{4}z_4 \\
x_3 &= 7 + \frac{1}{4}s_4 + \frac{1}{4}t_2 + \frac{2}{4}t_3 - \frac{1}{4}t_4 + \frac{1}{4}z_1 + \frac{1}{4}z_2 - \frac{3}{4}z_3 + \frac{1}{4}z_4 \\
x_4 &= 7 + \frac{1}{4}s_4 + \frac{1}{4}t_2 + \frac{2}{4}t_3 + \frac{3}{4}t_4 + \frac{1}{4}z_1 + \frac{1}{4}z_2 + \frac{1}{4}z_3 - \frac{3}{4}z_4 \\
s_1 &= 6 + \frac{1}{4}s_4 - \frac{3}{4}t_2 - \frac{2}{4}t_3 - \frac{1}{4}t_4 - \frac{3}{4}z_1 + \frac{1}{4}z_2 + \frac{1}{4}z_3 + \frac{1}{4}z_4 \\
s_2 &= 2 + \frac{2}{4}s_4 - \frac{2}{4}t_2 - t_3 - \frac{2}{4}t_4 - \frac{2}{4}z_1 - \frac{2}{4}z_2 + \frac{2}{4}z_3 + \frac{2}{4}z_4 \\
s_3 &= 4 + \frac{3}{4}s_4 - \frac{1}{4}t_2 - \frac{2}{4}t_3 - \frac{3}{4}t_4 - \frac{1}{4}z_1 - \frac{1}{4}z_2 - \frac{1}{4}z_3 + \frac{3}{4}z_4 \\
t_1 &= 2 + \frac{1}{4}s_4 - \frac{3}{4}t_2 - \frac{2}{4}t_3 - \frac{1}{4}t_4 + \frac{1}{4}z_1 + \frac{1}{4}z_2 + \frac{1}{4}z_3 + \frac{1}{4}z_4
\end{aligned}
$$

TABLE 6.3

$$
\begin{aligned}
x_0 &= -64 - \tfrac{14}{4}s_4 + \tfrac{2}{4}t_2 - 2s_2 + \tfrac{2}{4}t_4 - \tfrac{6}{4}z_1 - \tfrac{10}{4}z_2 - \tfrac{6}{4}z_3 - \tfrac{10}{4}z_4 \\
x_0^* &= -3 - \tfrac{2}{4}s_4 + \tfrac{2}{4}s_2 - \tfrac{2}{4}t_4 - \tfrac{2}{4}z_3 - \tfrac{2}{4}z_4 \\
x_1 &= 6 - \tfrac{2}{4}t_2 + \tfrac{2}{4}s_2 - \tfrac{2}{4}z_1 + \tfrac{2}{4}z_2 \\
x_2 &= 6 + \tfrac{2}{4}t_2 + \tfrac{2}{4}s_2 + \tfrac{2}{4}z_1 - \tfrac{2}{4}z_2 \\
x_3 &= 8 + \tfrac{2}{4}s_4 - \tfrac{2}{4}s_2 - \tfrac{2}{4}t_4 - \tfrac{2}{4}z_3 + \tfrac{2}{4}z_4 \\
x_4 &= 8 + \tfrac{2}{4}s_4 - \tfrac{2}{4}s_2 + \tfrac{2}{4}t_4 + \tfrac{2}{4}z_3 - \tfrac{2}{4}z_4 \\
s_1 &= 5 - \tfrac{2}{4}t_2 + \tfrac{2}{4}s_2 - \tfrac{2}{4}z_1 + \tfrac{2}{4}z_2 \\
t_3 &= 2 + \tfrac{2}{4}s_4 - \tfrac{2}{4}t_2 - s_2 - \tfrac{2}{4}t_4 - \tfrac{2}{4}z_1 - \tfrac{2}{4}z_2 + \tfrac{2}{4}z_3 + \tfrac{2}{4}z_4 \\
s_3 &= 3 + \tfrac{2}{4}s_4 + \tfrac{2}{4}s_2 - \tfrac{2}{4}t_4 - \tfrac{2}{4}z_3 + \tfrac{2}{4}z_4 \\
t_1 &= 1 - \tfrac{2}{4}t_2 + \tfrac{2}{4}s_2 + \tfrac{2}{4}z_1 + \tfrac{2}{4}z_2
\end{aligned}
$$

TABLE 6.4

$$
\begin{aligned}
x_0 &= -63 - \tfrac{7}{2}s_4 - t_1 - \tfrac{3}{2}s_2 + \tfrac{1}{2}t_4 - z_1 - 2z_2 - \tfrac{3}{2}z_3 - \tfrac{5}{2}z_4 \\
x_0^* &= -3 - \tfrac{1}{2}s_4 + \tfrac{1}{2}s_2 - \tfrac{1}{2}t_4 - \tfrac{1}{2}z_3 - \tfrac{1}{2}z_4 \\
x_1 &= 5 + t_1 - z_1 \\
x_2 &= 7 - t_1 + s_2 + z_1 \\
x_3 &= 8 + \tfrac{1}{2}s_4 - \tfrac{1}{2}s_2 - \tfrac{1}{2}t_4 - \tfrac{1}{2}z_3 + \tfrac{1}{2}z_4 \\
x_4 &= 8 + \tfrac{1}{2}s_4 - \tfrac{1}{2}s_2 + \tfrac{1}{2}t_4 + \tfrac{1}{2}z_3 - \tfrac{1}{2}z_4 \\
s_1 &= 4 + t_1 - z_1 \\
t_3 &= 1 + \tfrac{1}{2}s_4 + t_1 - \tfrac{3}{2}s_2 - \tfrac{1}{2}t_4 - z_1 - z_2 + \tfrac{1}{2}z_3 + \tfrac{1}{2}z_4 \\
s_3 &= 3 + \tfrac{1}{2}s_4 + \tfrac{1}{2}s_2 - \tfrac{1}{2}t_4 - \tfrac{1}{2}z_3 + \tfrac{1}{2}z_4 \\
t_2 &= 2 - 2t_1 + s_2 + z_1 + z_2
\end{aligned}
$$

equality constraints which may be written as a matrix equation $\mathbf{Ax} = \mathbf{b} + \theta\mathbf{b}^*$, or as a set of ordinary algebraic equations

$$\sum a_{ij}x_j = b_i + \theta b_i^* \qquad (i = 1, \ldots, m)$$

for $0 \leqslant \theta \leqslant \theta_{max}$.

TABLE 6.5

$$\begin{aligned}
x_0 &= -62 - 3s_4 - 3s_2 - t_3 - 2z_1 - 3z_2 - z_3 - 2z_4\\
x_0^* &= -4 - s_4 - t_1 + 2s_2 + t_3 + z_1 + z_2 - z_3 - z_4\\
x_1 &= 5 + t_1 - z_1\\
x_2 &= 7 - t_1 + s_2 + z_1\\
x_3 &= 7 - t_1 + s_2 + t_3 + z_1 + z_2 - z_3\\
x_4 &= 9 + s_4 + t_1 - 2s_2 - t_3 - z_1 - z_2 + z_3\\
s_1 &= 4 + t_1 - z_1\\
t_4 &= 2 + s_4 + 2t_1 - 3s_2 - 2t_3 - 2z_1 - 2z_2 + z_3 + z_4\\
s_3 &= 2 - t_1 + 2s_2 + t_3 + z_1 + z_2 - z_3\\
t_2 &= 2 - 2t_1 + s_2 + z_1 + z_2
\end{aligned}$$

TABLE 6.6

$$\begin{aligned}
x_0 &= -64 - 4s_4 - 2t_1 + t_3 + t_4 - z_2 - 2z_3 - 3z_4\\
x_0^* &= -\frac{8}{3} - \frac{1}{3}s_4 + \frac{1}{3}t_1 - \frac{1}{3}t_3 - \frac{2}{3}t_4 - \frac{1}{3}z_1 - \frac{1}{3}z_2 - \frac{1}{3}z_3 - \frac{1}{3}z_4\\
x_1 &= 5 + t_1 - z_1\\
x_2 &= \frac{23}{3} + \frac{1}{3}s_4 - \frac{1}{3}t_1 - \frac{2}{3}t_3 - \frac{1}{3}t_4 + \frac{1}{3}z_1 - \frac{2}{3}z_2 + \frac{1}{3}z_3 + \frac{1}{3}z_4\\
x_3 &= \frac{23}{3} + \frac{1}{3}s_4 - \frac{1}{3}t_1 + \frac{1}{3}t_3 - \frac{1}{3}t_4 + \frac{1}{3}z_1 + \frac{1}{3}z_2 - \frac{2}{3}z_3 + \frac{1}{3}z_4\\
x_4 &= \frac{23}{3} + \frac{1}{3}s_4 - \frac{1}{3}t_1 + \frac{1}{3}t_3 + \frac{2}{3}t_4 + \frac{1}{3}z_1 + \frac{1}{3}z_2 + \frac{1}{3}z_3 - \frac{2}{3}z_4\\
s_1 &= 4 + t_1 - z_1\\
s_2 &= \frac{2}{3} + \frac{1}{3}s_4 + \frac{2}{3}t_1 - \frac{2}{3}t_3 - \frac{1}{3}t_4 - \frac{2}{3}z_1 - \frac{2}{3}z_2 + \frac{1}{3}z_3 + \frac{1}{3}z_4\\
s_3 &= \frac{10}{3} + \frac{2}{3}s_4 + \frac{1}{3}t_1 - \frac{1}{3}t_3 - \frac{2}{3}t_4 - \frac{1}{3}z_1 - \frac{1}{3}z_2 - \frac{1}{3}z_3 + \frac{2}{3}z_4\\
t_2 &= \frac{8}{3} + \frac{1}{3}s_4 - \frac{4}{3}t_1 - \frac{2}{3}t_3 - \frac{1}{3}t_4 + \frac{1}{3}z_1 + \frac{1}{3}z_2 + \frac{1}{3}z_3 + \frac{1}{3}z_4
\end{aligned}$$

This problem is solved in the usual way with $\theta = 0$, but keeping track of the coefficients of θ in the tableaux. In effect this amounts to treating θ as an additional variable that is never allowed to enter the basis (or more strictly it amounts to treating $-\theta$ in this way, since the coefficients are given the same signs as they would be if the b_i^* were the original right hand sides).

Now suppose that the final tableau reads

$$x_0 = \bar{a}_{00} + \bar{a}_{00}^*\theta + \sum \bar{a}_{0j}(-X_{m+j})$$

$$X_i = \bar{a}_{i0} + \bar{a}_{i0}^*\theta + \sum \bar{a}_{ij}(-X_{m+j}) \qquad (i = 1, \ldots, m)$$

Since this is the final tableau, $\bar{a}_{i0} \geqslant 0$ for $i = 1, \ldots, m$ and $\bar{a}_{0j} \geqslant 0$ for $j = 1, \ldots, n - m$. As we increase θ from zero, the objective function $x_0 = \bar{a}_{00} + \bar{a}_{00}^*\theta$, and the values of the basic variables change: $X_i = \bar{a}_{i0} + \bar{a}_{i0}^*\theta$. Since the $\bar{a}_{0j} \geqslant 0$ this basis remains optimal as long as it remains feasible, but if $\bar{a}_{i0} + \bar{a}_{i0}^*\theta$ becomes negative for any i the variable X_i must be made non-basic.

The formal rule is that we must compute

$$\theta_c = \min_{i, \bar{a}_{i0}^* < 0} \left(\frac{\bar{a}_{i0}}{|a_{i0}^*|} \right)$$

and note the corresponding value of i, say $i = p$. When $\theta = \theta_c$ we must make a pivot step making X_p non-basic, and choosing the variable to enter the basis in the usual way, i.e.

$$X_{m+q} \quad \text{where} \quad \bar{a}_{0q}/|\bar{a}_{pq}| = \min_{j, \bar{a}_{pj} < 0} (\bar{a}_{0j}/|\bar{a}_{pj}|)$$

When this has been done, we have a new tableau. Some of the $\bar{a}_{i0}$ will no longer be positive, but this does not matter because the current basis is feasible for $\theta = \theta_c$. We must next consider how far it remains feasible as θ is further increased. We therefore compute a new θ_c and a new change of basis, using the same rules as before. The process continues until one of three things happens—

(*a*) $\theta_c \geqslant \theta_{max}$, in which case the current basis remains optimal until the end of the prescribed range of values of θ.

(*b*) $\bar{a}_{i0}^* \geqslant 0$ for all i. This is in a sense a special case of (*a*) when $\theta_c = \infty$. It means that the current trial solution remains optimal for all larger θ.

(*c*) $\bar{a}_{pj} \geqslant 0$ for all j. This means that for $\theta > \theta_c$ the problem is infeasible since X_p cannot be made non-negative.

At the end we will have mapped out the (finite) set of alternative optimal solutions as θ increases as far as possible from 0 to θ_{max}.

The amount of information to be presented again depends on circumstances, and the remarks made in this connexion about parametric objective functions are applicable.

Let us now see how this works in a numerical example. We revert to our production scheduling problem, but assume that the cost of hiring a new team has been fixed at £2000/team. Now we wish to explore the possibility that our forecast demand in the last month is in error, and we want to see how the optimal solution varies as this demand decreases from the originally estimated value of 11 units.

The solution to the previous problem with $\theta = 2$ can be written as shown in Table 6.7.

TABLE 6.7

$$
\begin{aligned}
x_0 &= -69 - \frac{9}{2}s_4 - t_1 - \frac{1}{2}s_2 - \frac{1}{2}t_4 - z_1 - 2z_2 - \frac{5}{2}z_3 - \frac{7}{2}z_4 \\
x_1 &= 5 + t_1 - z_1 \\
x_2 &= 7 - t_1 + s_2 + z_1 \\
x_3 &= 8 + \tfrac{1}{2}s_4 - \tfrac{1}{2}s_2 - \tfrac{1}{2}t_4 - \tfrac{1}{2}z_3 + \tfrac{1}{2}z_4 \\
x_4 &= 8 + \tfrac{1}{2}s_4 - \tfrac{1}{2}s_2 + \tfrac{1}{2}t_4 + \tfrac{1}{2}z_3 - \tfrac{1}{2}z_4 \\
s_1 &= 4 + t_1 - z_1 \\
t_3 &= 1 + \tfrac{1}{2}s_4 + t_1 - \tfrac{3}{2}s_2 - \tfrac{1}{2}t_4 - z_1 - z_2 + \tfrac{1}{2}z_3 + \tfrac{1}{2}z_4 \\
s_3 &= 3 + \tfrac{1}{2}s_4 + \tfrac{1}{2}s_2 - \tfrac{1}{2}t_4 - \tfrac{1}{2}z_3 + \tfrac{1}{2}z_4 \\
t_2 &= 2 - 2t_1 + s_2 + z_1 + z_2
\end{aligned}
$$

To vary the assumed demand in the last month we must derive the coefficients of θ in this tableau. In practice on a computer one forms the column of coefficients of θ in the original equations and premultiplies by the inverse of the current basis. This is the forward transformation, or step 3 of a normal iteration, as described in Chapter 7. But for this numerical example we can use more elementary means as follows. Going back to our original equations we see that the only one that is changed is the last, which now reads

$$s_4 = s_3 + x_4 - 11 + \theta$$

Since s_4 and θ occur in no other equation except the objective function, it follows that we can replace s_4 by $s_4 - \theta$ throughout the system and we have Table 6.8.

We note in passing that the coefficients of θ in all rows except the objective function are negative. This means that if we were to decrease θ (i.e. increase the sales forecast for the last month) by any amount the current basis would remain optimal, but we have to consider the effect of increasing θ. We see that the basis ceases to be feasible when $\theta = 2$ (corresponding to a demand of 9 units in the

TABLE 6.8

$$\begin{aligned}
x_0 &= -69 + \frac{7}{2}\theta - \frac{9}{2}s_4 - t_1 - \frac{1}{2}s_2 - \frac{1}{2}t_4 - z_1 - 2z_2 - \frac{5}{2}z_3 - \frac{7}{2}z_4 \\
x_1 &= 5 + t_1 - z_1 \\
x_2 &= 7 - t_1 + s_2 + z_1 \\
x_3 &= 8 - \tfrac{1}{2}\theta + \tfrac{1}{2}s_4 - \tfrac{1}{2}s_2 - \tfrac{1}{2}t_4 - \tfrac{1}{2}z_3 + \tfrac{1}{2}z_4 \\
x_4 &= 8 - \tfrac{1}{2}\theta + \tfrac{1}{2}s_4 - \tfrac{1}{2}s_2 + \tfrac{1}{2}t_4 + \tfrac{1}{2}z_3 - \tfrac{1}{2}z_4 \\
s_1 &= 4 + t_1 - z_1 \\
t_3 &= 1 - \tfrac{1}{2}\theta + \tfrac{1}{2}s_4 + t_1 - \tfrac{3}{2}s_2 - \tfrac{1}{2}t_4 - z_1 - z_2 + \tfrac{1}{2}z_3 + \tfrac{1}{2}z_4 \\
s_3 &= 3 - \tfrac{1}{2}\theta + \tfrac{1}{2}s_4 + \tfrac{1}{2}s_2 - \tfrac{1}{2}t_4 - \tfrac{1}{2}z_3 + \tfrac{1}{2}z_4 \\
t_2 &= 2 - 2t_1 + s_2 + z_1 + z_2
\end{aligned}$$

(The coefficient of θ in the expression for x_0 is derived by noting that s_4 has a direct cost of 1 unit, which does not apply to θ.)

last period). We must then make t_3 non-basic, and t_1 enters the basis. We then have Table 6.9.

TABLE 6.9

$$\begin{aligned}
x_0 &= -68 + 3\theta - 4s_4 - t_3 - 2s_2 - t_4 - 2z_1 - 3z_2 - 2z_3 - 3z_4 \\
x_1 &= 4 + \tfrac{1}{2}\theta - \tfrac{1}{2}s_4 + t_3 + \tfrac{3}{2}s_2 + \tfrac{1}{2}t_4 + z_2 - \tfrac{1}{2}z_3 - \tfrac{1}{2}z_4 \\
x_2 &= 8 - \tfrac{1}{2}\theta + \tfrac{1}{2}s_4 - t_3 - \tfrac{1}{2}s_2 - \tfrac{1}{2}t_4 - z_2 + \tfrac{1}{2}z_3 + \tfrac{1}{2}z_4 \\
x_3 &= 8 - \tfrac{1}{2}\theta + \tfrac{1}{2}s_4 - \tfrac{1}{2}s_2 - \tfrac{1}{2}t_4 - \tfrac{1}{2}z_3 + \tfrac{1}{2}z_4 \\
x_4 &= 8 - \tfrac{1}{2}\theta + \tfrac{1}{2}s_4 - \tfrac{1}{2}s_2 + \tfrac{1}{2}t_4 + \tfrac{1}{2}z_3 - \tfrac{1}{2}z_4 \\
s_1 &= 3 + \tfrac{1}{2}\theta - \tfrac{1}{2}s_4 + t_3 + \tfrac{3}{2}s_2 + \tfrac{1}{2}t_4 + z_2 - \tfrac{1}{2}z_3 - \tfrac{1}{2}z_4 \\
t_1 &= -1 + \tfrac{1}{2}\theta - \tfrac{1}{2}s_4 + t_3 + \tfrac{3}{2}s_2 + \tfrac{1}{2}t_4 + z_1 + z_2 - \tfrac{1}{2}z_3 - \tfrac{1}{2}z_4 \\
s_3 &= 3 - \tfrac{1}{2}\theta + \tfrac{1}{2}s_4 + \tfrac{1}{2}s_2 - \tfrac{1}{2}t_4 - \tfrac{1}{2}z_3 + \tfrac{1}{2}z_4 \\
t_2 &= 4 - \theta + s_4 - 2t_3 - 2s_2 - t_4 - z_1 - z_2 + z_3 + z_4
\end{aligned}$$

This basis remains optimal until $\theta = 4$ (corresponding to a demand of 7 units in the last period). We must then make t_2 non-basic, and z_3 enters the basis. We then have Table 6.10.

TABLE 6.10

$$\begin{aligned}
x_0 &= -60 + \theta - 2s_4 - 5t_3 - 6s_2 - 3t_4 - 4z_1 - 5z_2 - 2t_2 - z_4 \\
x_1 &= 6 + \tfrac{1}{2}s_2 - \tfrac{1}{2}z_1 + \tfrac{1}{2}z_2 - \tfrac{1}{2}t_2 \\
x_2 &= 6 + \tfrac{1}{2}s_2 + \tfrac{1}{2}z_1 - \tfrac{1}{2}z_2 + \tfrac{1}{2}t_2 \\
x_3 &= 10 - \theta + s_4 - t_3 - \tfrac{3}{2}s_2 - t_4 - \tfrac{1}{2}z_1 - \tfrac{1}{2}z_2 - \tfrac{1}{2}t_2 + z_4 \\
x_4 &= 6 + t_3 + \tfrac{1}{2}s_2 + t_4 + \tfrac{1}{2}z_1 + \tfrac{1}{2}z_2 + \tfrac{1}{2}t_2 - z_4 \\
s_1 &= 5 + \tfrac{1}{2}s_2 - \tfrac{1}{2}z_1 + \tfrac{1}{2}z_2 - \tfrac{1}{2}t_2 \\
t_1 &= 1 + \tfrac{1}{2}s_2 + \tfrac{1}{2}z_1 + \tfrac{1}{2}z_2 - \tfrac{1}{2}t_2 \\
s_3 &= 5 - \theta + s_4 - t_3 - \tfrac{1}{2}s_2 - t_4 - \tfrac{1}{2}z_1 - \tfrac{1}{2}z_2 - \tfrac{1}{2}t_2 + z_4 \\
z_3 &= -4 + \theta - s_4 + 2t_3 + 2s_2 + t_4 + z_1 + z_2 + t_2 - z_4
\end{aligned}$$

TABLE 6.11

$$
\begin{array}{rlllllllll}
x_0 = & -55 & - s_4 - 6t_3 & - \frac{13}{2} s_2 & - 4t_4 & - \frac{9}{2} z_1 & - \frac{11}{2} z_2 & - \frac{5}{2} t_2 & - s_3 \\
x_1 = & 6 & & + \frac{1}{2}s_2 & & - \frac{1}{2}z_1 & + \frac{1}{2}z_2 & - \frac{1}{2}t_2 & \\
x_2 = & 6 & & + \frac{1}{2}s_2 & & + \frac{1}{2}z_1 & - \frac{1}{2}z_2 & + \frac{1}{2}t_2 & \\
x_3 = & 5 & & - s_2 & & & & & + s_3 \\
x_4 = & 11 - \theta + s_4 & & & & & & & - s_3 \\
s_1 = & 5 & & + \frac{1}{2}s_2 & & - \frac{1}{2}z_1 & + \frac{1}{2}z_2 & - \frac{1}{2}t_2 & \\
t_1 = & 1 & & + \frac{1}{2}s_2 & & + \frac{1}{2}z_1 & + \frac{1}{2}z_2 & - \frac{1}{2}t_2 & \\
z_4 = & -5 + \theta - s_4 & + t_3 & + \frac{1}{2}s_2 & + t_4 & + \frac{1}{2}z_1 & + \frac{1}{2}z_2 & + \frac{1}{2}t_2 & + s_3 \\
z_3 = & 1 & + t_3 & + \frac{3}{2}s_2 & & + \frac{1}{2}z_1 & + \frac{1}{2}z_2 & + \frac{1}{2}t_2 & - s_3
\end{array}
$$

This basis remains optimal until $\theta = 5$ (corresponding to a demand of 6 units in the last period). We must then make s_3 non-basic, and z_4 enters the basis. We then have Table 6.11.

The basis remains optimal until $\theta = 11$. This corresponds to a demand of zero in the last period, and there is no sense in pursuing the problem any further.

The pattern of solutions is perhaps of some interest. The point is that as the assumed demand in the last period falls off, the labour force required falls off, so labour is taken on earlier to meet the peak demand in the second month with a smaller force.

In practice parametric programming on the right hand side is used much more than parametric programming on the objective function. The reason is that, apart from its use for the explicit purpose of exploring the way the solution changes as the right hand side changes, it is generally the best way of solving a problem with a specific new right hand side, having already solved it with another right hand side. The natural alternatives—either starting again or starting from the previous optimal basis—normally involve an infeasible first trial solution, and many more iterations are then required to make the problem feasible and then optimal. Since the previous basis is necessarily dual feasible, one might think of using the dual simplex algorithm directly. But in a production linear programming code using the product form of inverse this involves appreciably more work per iteration than the primal simplex algorithm. The consequence is that parametric programming is the natural way to re-optimize with a new right hand side, while the normal simplex method is the natural way to re-optimize with a new objective function.

EXAMPLE

Draw diagrams illustrating the changing pattern of solutions as the parameter changes for both of the examples solved in this chapter.

7 The Inverse Matrix Method

7.1 Outline of the Inverse Matrix Method

It is widely known that most production computer codes for solving large linear programming problems use the *product form* of the *inverse matrix method* but it is rather less widely known what this form really involves.

It may be argued that this is a technical detail with which the user of linear programming need not be concerned. Up to a point this is true, but some knowledge of the point will explain the reasons for a number of things with which he is concerned, namely

(*a*) Why is it important to keep down the number of non-zero coefficients in the equations defining a linear programming model; and why does the time taken to solve a linear programming problem depend primarily on the number of rows (equations) and the number of non-zero coefficients, and not particularly on the number of columns (variables)?

(*b*) Why are the coefficients in the equations sorted by columns; and what is the significance of an initial basis, and of the inversion routine incorporated in the normal solution procedure?

(*c*) Why are the shadow prices on all the rows automatically available at the end of the solution process, and why is it computationally easy to accept extra variables (or activities) added to a linear programming problem that has been solved?

(*d*) Why are some extensions of linear programming much more practical than others?

In the original, or straight, simplex method one works with the tableau of coefficients in the expressions for the basic variables as linear functions of the non-basic variables. If there are m equations and n variables this means that one works with an array of

$$(m + 1)(n - m + 1)$$

coefficients—assuming one objective function and one right hand side or column of constant terms. All these coefficients have to be up-dated from one iteration to the next, although only very few of them are actually used in any single iteration. Specifically one uses

(*a*) all the coefficients in the objective function, in order to select the new pivotal column (normally chosen as the one with the most negative reduced cost)
(*b*) the right hand side and the elements in the pivotal column, in order to select the new pivotal row
(*c*) the other elements in the pivotal row, in order to up-date the expression for the objective function.

The remaining columns are up-dated simply because they may be needed as pivotal columns in a subsequent iteration. It is therefore natural to wonder whether, instead of carrying around all this information in case it is needed, one cannot represent the problem more compactly, calculating particular elements of the tableau only when required. It turns out that this is possible. To explain this clearly it seems necessary to use matrix notation.

The original constraints of the problem can be expressed as equations by adding suitable slack variables in all inequality constraints. These constraints can be written as the matrix equation

$$\mathbf{A}\mathbf{x} = \mathbf{b}$$

where $\mathbf{A}$ is an $(m \times n)$ matrix, $\mathbf{x}$ an n-vector and $\mathbf{b}$ an m-vector. The complete problem is defined by the constraints and the objective function, and it is desirable that our matrix equation should include the expression for the objective function. We therefore define a new variable x_0 and a new equation

$$x_0 + \sum a_{0j}x_j = b_0$$

where $\sum a_{0j}x_j - b_0$ represents the expression to be minimized. This minimization can obviously be achieved by maximizing x_0. (This point is worth noting, otherwise one may be puzzled by the sign convention used for a constant term in the objective function of a linear programming problem being solved on a computer.)

We now think of $\mathbf{A}$ as an $(m + 1) \times (n + 1)$ dimensional matrix.

Next, consider the situation at any particular iteration during the solution of this linear programming problem by the simplex method. There will be a set of basic variables, and we can imagine that the variables are re-numbered so that these are the variables $x_1, \ldots, x_m$. Then our matrix equation can be written in the form

$$(\mathbf{B} \mid \mathbf{A}_1)\mathbf{x} = \mathbf{b}$$

where **B** is an $(m + 1) \times (m + 1)$ square matrix of coefficients of the variables $x_0, x_1, \ldots, x_m$, and $\mathbf{A}_1$ denotes the remaining columns of **A**, i.e. the coefficients of the non-basic variables. If we now pre-multiply our matrix equation by $\mathbf{B}^{-1}$, we have it in the form

$$(\mathbf{I} \mid \mathbf{B}^{-1}\mathbf{A}_1)\mathbf{x} = \boldsymbol{\beta}$$

where $\boldsymbol{\beta} = \mathbf{B}^{-1}\mathbf{b}$.

This is matrix notation for a set of equations that define x_0, $x_1, \ldots, x_m$ as linear functions of the variables $x_{m+1}, \ldots, x_n$. The coefficients in the matrix $\mathbf{B}^{-1}\mathbf{A}_1$ are the coefficients in the current tableau, and the coefficients of the column vector $\boldsymbol{\beta}$ are the current right hand sides, the values of the objective function and the basic variables, i.e. the $\bar{a}_{i0}$.

We can now remove the assumption that the basic variables, are x_0. $x_1, \ldots, x_m$. Corresponding to any set of basic variables x_0, $X_1, \ldots, X_m$ we have a basis **B** formed from the coefficients of these variables in **A**, and the matrix $\mathbf{B}^{-1}\mathbf{A}$ defines the coefficients in the extended tableau, while $\boldsymbol{\beta} = \mathbf{B}^{-1}\mathbf{b}$ defines the current right hand sides.

This would still be of very limited computational interest if one had to invert the basis at each iteration, but this is not necessary. The matrix $\mathbf{B}^{-1}$ can be updated directly from one iteration to the next in the same way that one updates a tableau in the straight simplex method: indeed the columns of $\mathbf{B}^{-1}$ can be regarded as columns of the tableau; they correspond to the slack and artificial variables in the original matrix.

In the inverse matrix method, sometimes known as the *revised simplex method*, one therefore works with the original matrix **A**, the list of basic variables $x_0, X_1, \ldots, X_m$, the right hand side vector $\boldsymbol{\beta}$, and some expression for $\mathbf{B}^{-1}$, the inverse of the current basis. In the *explicit inverse* form of the simplex method this is stored as an explicit matrix. Later we shall consider the alternative, product, form.

7.2 The Steps of the Inverse Matrix Method

If we use the inverse matrix method, the work involved in each iteration of the simplex method can be sub-divided into 5 steps as follows—

STEP 1

Produce a pricing vector, i.e. a row vector $\boldsymbol{\pi}$ that can be multiplied into any column of the matrix **A** to determine the reduced cost of the corresponding variable.

The form of this step depends on whether or not the current trial solution is feasible. If it is, the reduced costs are the top row of the matrix $\mathbf{B}^{-1}\mathbf{A}$. This can be expressed in matrix notation as $\mathbf{cB}^{-1}\mathbf{A}$. where $\mathbf{c}$ is a row vector whose first element is 1 and whose remaining elements are zero. So the vector $\boldsymbol{\pi} = \mathbf{cB}^{-1}$, and if $\mathbf{B}^{-1}$ is stored explicitly, this operation simply involves picking out its top row. Note that since the elements of $\boldsymbol{\pi}$ are the reduced costs of the artificial variables, their final values are the shadow prices as defined in Section 3.2.

If the current trial solution is not feasible, we must form reduced costs that measure the rates of increase in the sum of infeasibilities. So we use the same procedure with the row vector $\mathbf{c}$ defined as in Section 3.3. In other words $c_i = -1$ if X_i is artificial and $\bar{a}_{i0} > 0$; $c_i = +1$ if $\bar{a}_{i0} < 0$ (and $i > 0$); $c_i = 0$ otherwise.

STEP 2

Price out the columns of $\mathbf{A}$ to find a variable to remove from the set of non-basic variables. This can be done by forming every element of $\boldsymbol{\pi}\mathbf{A}$ and choosing the most negative; but other methods have been proposed since this step can be a slow one.

STEP 3

Form the up-dated column $\boldsymbol{\alpha}$ of coefficients of the variable to be removed from the set of non-basic variables, i.e. the $\bar{a}_{iq}$, by pre-multiplying the appropriate column of $\mathbf{A}$ by $\mathbf{B}^{-1}$.

STEP 4

Perform a ratio test between the elements of $\boldsymbol{\alpha}$ and the elements of $\boldsymbol{\beta}$ to determine the pivot, and the variable to be made non-basic.

STEP 5

Up-date the set of basic variables, the vector $\boldsymbol{\beta}$ and the inverse $\mathbf{B}^{-1}$. The first of these operations is simply book-keeping. The remainder is the same as the straight simplex method on a smaller matrix consisting of a pivotal column $\boldsymbol{\alpha}$ (whose up-dated value is not needed), the columns of $\mathbf{B}^{-1}$, and a right hand side $\boldsymbol{\beta}$.

7.3 The Product Form of Inverse

Using the product form, the inverse of basis is not recorded explicitly. Instead, it is represented as a product of elementary matrices. Each of these represents the effect of a single pivotal operation.

The effect of pivoting in the pth row, is to premultiply $\mathbf{B}^{-1}$ by a matrix that is a unit matrix except for the pth column, which is computed from the up-dated pivotal column in the tableau. This pivotal column is computed in Step 4 of the inverse matrix method. If its components are denoted by $\bar{a}_{iq}$, then the pth element of the pth column of the elementary matrix is $1/\bar{a}_{pq}$, and the ith element, for $i \neq p$, is $-\bar{a}_{iq}/\bar{a}_{pq}$. These elementary matrices can be stored in the computer very compactly. One simply records the column number p, and the non-zero elements in it; the remaining, unit, columns being understood. In fact these unit columns are so taken for granted that the elementary matrices are often referred to as vectors, specifically *η-vectors.*

The steps of the inverse matrix method can be carried out when $\mathbf{B}^{-1}$ is represented as a product of η-vectors. Step 1 is then called the *backward transformation*, since the row vector $\mathbf{c}$ is post-multiplied by each η-vector successively, in the opposite order to that in which they were generated. It will be noted that each η-vector affects only the pth element of the row vector being built up. Step 2 is carried out as with the explicit inverse. Step 3 is called the *forward transformation*, since the pivotal column of $\mathbf{A}$ is premultiplied by each η-vector successively in the order in which they were generated. Step 4 is carried out as with the explicit inverse, as is Step 5, except that the process of up-dating $\mathbf{B}^{-1}$ is very simple—one just adds another η-vector to the end of the list.

After a while, the list of η-vectors becomes undesirably long, and to shorten it one goes through a process known as re-inversion. It should perhaps be made clear that this re-inversion does not mean recording some explicit inverse which is then simply up-dated by adding η-vectors. One always starts from a unit inverse representing an all slack-or-artificial basis, and adds η-vectors representing pivotal operations to replace unwanted slacks or artificials by genuine variables. Knowing which variables are to be introduced, and which slacks or artificials are to be removed, one can perform these pivotal operations without thinking at all about the signs of the values of the basic variables or of the reduced costs at intermediate stages of the inversion. In fact one has considerable freedom in the choice of pivotal columns and rows during re-inversion. One must choose a column corresponding to a variable that is due to be in the basis but has not yet been used, and one must choose a row corresponding to a slack or artificial that is due to be removed from the basis but has not yet been used, and which will give a non-zero value to the pivot ($\bar{a}_{pq}$); but that is all. If all the elements of $\mathbf{B}$ were non-zero, then it would probably be best to choose pivotal columns and rows to give the largest possible pivot in absolute value, so as to maximize numerical accuracy. In practice matrices arising in large linear programming problems contain a high proportion of zero elements, and the number of non-zero elements in the set of η-vectors depends very significantly on the order in which the pivotal columns and rows are selected. An important computational aspect of linear programming is the choice of pivots during inversion, since this affects the speed of inversion itself and also the speed of subsequent backward and forward transformations.

If **B** were a lower triangular matrix, and one pivoted on the diagonal elements in order, starting with the first and finishing with the last, then the η-vectors would contain no more off-diagonal elements than the original matrix **B**. It is of course possible to invert the matrix using different pivots, or the same pivots in a different order: but this will in general produce more non-zero elements in the resulting η-vectors. In principle therefore what a modern inversion routine does is to permute the rows and columns of **B** so that they are as nearly in lower triangular form as possible, and then pick the pivots in the original matrix **B** corresponding to pivoting on the diagonal elements of the permuted matrix in order.

In practice one often starts a linear programming calculation by inverting to a prescribed initial basis. This initial inversion is performed in exactly the same way as a re-inversion.

7.4 The Advantage of the Product Form

The advantage of the explicit inverse method over the straight simplex method, and of the product form over the explicit inverse, are often summarized as follows—

> In the straight simplex method one has to up-date the complete tableau, involving $(m + 1) \times (n - m + 1)$ numbers, at each iteration. In the explicit inverse method one only has to up-date the inverse, which involves $(m + 1) \times (m + 1)$ numbers. This is a considerable saving if, as is usual, n is much larger than m. The advantage of the product form comes from the fact that even this up-dating is avoided.

From a practical point of view this explanation describes the situation reasonably accurately, but from a theoretical point of view it is so unsatisfactory that it has led a number of workers in the field to think that the inverse matrix is an elaborate hoax and that the straight simplex method is really the best.

The theoretical weakness of the argument lies in the fact that if the matrix **A** were full (i.e. contained no zero coefficients) then the pricing operation, Step 2 of the inverse matrix method, would already involve as much arithmetic as up-dating the tableau, and the, perhaps small, amount of additional work in Steps 1 and 5 would simply make the inverse matrix method even less competitive.

Obviously, in order to get to the heart of the matter we must use the fact that the matrix **A** is usually sparse, i.e. a large proportion of its elements vanish, but we must still be careful. If a proportion ρ of the elements of **A** are non-zero, then pricing in the inverse matrix method will involve about $\rho \times (m + 1) \times (n - m + 1)$ multiplications, since the π-vector will usually be full. (This assumes that one does not price the basic vectors.) On the other hand if a proportion ρ of the elements of the tableau are non-zero, then the up-dating involves only $\rho^2 \times (m + 1) \times (n - m + 1)$ multiplications. So the argument of sparseness can be used to provide further support for the straight simplex method.

What is the true position? Part of the real advantage of the inverse matrix method, and in particular the product form, lies in its greater flexibility. One does not have to complete the pricing operation for every iteration. For example one can use multiple-column-selection techniques in which one uses the pricing operation to select a number of the most promising columns, up-dates them all in Step 3, and then does a few steps of the straight simplex method on this very small sub-problem.

Even without this flexibility the inverse matrix method would still be advantageous on typical large problems because the two ρs in the above formulae are not the same. The original matrix **A** will be much more sparse than typical tableaux during the calculation—since it is obviously much easier for a zero entry in the tableau to become non-zero than it is for a non-zero entry to vanish.

The idea of exploiting the structure of the original A-matrix can usefully be extended in some computers so that elements of ± 1 are treated in a special way. These unit elements can be stored more compactly than general elements. When working with such unit elements during pricing one needs only add or subtract rather than multiply.

Again, the advantage of the product form over the explicit inverse lies not so much in the fact that it simplifies the task of up-dating the inverse as in the fact that it generally provides a more compact expression for the inverse if one has a fast and efficient inversion routine on the lines described at the end of the last subsection.

There is another practical advantage of the inverse matrix method, which applies even more strongly in the product form. Having up-dated a tableau, or even an explicit inverse, one generally has to write it out on to a magnetic tape or some other backing store if one is solving a large problem. It is true that most computers can transfer information in this way at the same time as getting on with other calculations, but these transfers are apt to impede the process of reading further information into the working store for more processing. This bottleneck may be a passing phase in computer technology, but if so it is taking a long time to pass. Vast improvements have been made in the past ten years in methods of moving information from one part of the machine to another, but these are having a hard time keeping up with the vast improvements in arithmetic speed.

Published references to these problems of computational efficiency are somewhat meagre. Some careful theoretical analyses are given in Chapters 4 and 5 of Zoutendijk (1960). Numerical results are reported by Wolfe and Cutler (1963) and by Smith and Orchard-Hays (1963).

7.5 A Numerical Example

The steps of the product form can be illustrated by using it to solve the problem considered in Chapter 3, although this problem is typical of small examples in that it is not sparse enough to give the product form any computational advantage over the straight simplex method. Nevertheless, the product form calculations are quite simple; their only real disadvantage is that they cannot be displayed in a way that is both compact and self-explanatory. This section covers more space than the corresponding part of Section 3.3, but represents a similar amount of work.

We will follow the second method of solution given in Chapter 3, in which we start with the slack variables x_5 and x_6 in the basis at negative levels. We will record the elementary transformation matrices as full matrices, but leaving blanks for zero elements, to make the logic clearer.

The matrix **A** is

$$\begin{bmatrix} 1 & 4 & 5 & 7 & 6 & & & \\ & 1 & 1 & 1 & 1 & & & \\ & & 5 & 3 & 5 & -1 & & \\ & & 1 & 2 & 2 & & -1 & \\ & 10 & & 4 & 2 & & & \\ & & 4 & 1 & 1 & & & 1 \end{bmatrix}$$

and the vector **b** is

$$\begin{bmatrix} 0 \\ 1 \\ 2 \\ 1 \\ 5 \\ 2 \end{bmatrix}$$

We start by introducing the slack variables x_5 and x_6 into the basis so our first 2 transformation matrices are

$$\mathbf{T}_1 = \begin{bmatrix} 1 & & & & & \\ & 1 & & & & \\ & & -1 & & & \\ & & & 1 & & \\ & & & & 1 & \\ & & & & & 1 \end{bmatrix}$$

$$\mathbf{T}_2 = \begin{bmatrix} 1 & & & & & \\ & 1 & & & & \\ & & 1 & & & \\ & & & -1 & & \\ & & & & 1 & \\ & & & & & 1 \end{bmatrix}$$

The initial ordered list of the basic variables is

$$x_0, A_1, x_5, x_6, A_4, x_7$$

and the initial current right hand side

$$\boldsymbol{\beta} = \mathbf{T}_2\mathbf{T}_1\mathbf{b} = \begin{bmatrix} 0 \\ 1 \\ -2 \\ -1 \\ 5 \\ 2 \end{bmatrix}$$

We now form a row vector **c** to represent the fact that we want to reduce A_1, increase x_5 and x_6 and reduce A_4 in order to reduce the sum of infeasibilities, so

$$\mathbf{c} = [0 \quad -1 \quad 1 \quad 1 \quad -1 \quad 0]$$

and

$$\boldsymbol{\pi} = \mathbf{c}\mathbf{T}_2\mathbf{T}_1 = [0 \quad -1 \quad -1 \quad -1 \quad -1 \quad 0]$$

Multiplying $\boldsymbol{\pi}$ into each column of **A** in turn (other than the first column corresponding to the dummy variable x_0), we obtain the reduced costs as

$$-11, -7, -10, -10, 1, 1, 0$$

(These are the coefficients in the expression for S derived from Table 3.9.)

We select the first of these numbers, and bring x_1 into the basis. We must now form the vector $\boldsymbol{\alpha} = \mathbf{T}_2\mathbf{T}_1\mathbf{a}$, where

$$\mathbf{a} = \begin{bmatrix} 4 \\ 1 \\ 0 \\ 0 \\ 10 \\ 0 \end{bmatrix} \quad \text{so } \boldsymbol{\alpha} = \begin{bmatrix} 4 \\ 1 \\ 0 \\ 0 \\ 10 \\ 0 \end{bmatrix}$$

Taking ratios of the elements of $\boldsymbol{\alpha}$ with the corresponding elements of $\boldsymbol{\beta}$ we find that $p = 4$, and our new elementary transformation matrix

$$\mathbf{T}_3 = \begin{bmatrix} 1 & & & & -4/10 & \\ & 1 & & & -1/10 & \\ & & 1 & & & \\ & & & 1 & & \\ & & & & 1/10 & \\ & & & & & 1 \end{bmatrix}$$

The new ordered list of basic variables is

$$x_0, A_1, x_5, x_6, x_1, x_7$$

and the right hand side

$$\boldsymbol{\beta}' = \mathbf{T}_3\boldsymbol{\beta} = \begin{bmatrix} -2 \\ 5/10 \\ -2 \\ -1 \\ 5/10 \\ 2 \end{bmatrix}$$

For the second iteration

$$\mathbf{c} = [0 \quad -1 \quad 1 \quad 1 \quad 0 \quad 0]$$

and $\mathbf{c}\mathbf{T}_3 = [0 \quad -1 \quad 1 \quad 1 \quad 1/10 \quad 0]$

so $\quad \boldsymbol{\pi} = \mathbf{c}\mathbf{T}_3\mathbf{T}_2\mathbf{T}_1 = [0 \quad -1 \quad -1 \quad -1 \quad 1/10 \quad 0]$

Multiplying $\boldsymbol{\pi}$ into the columns of $\mathbf{A}$ we obtain the reduced costs

$$0, -7, -56/10, -78/10, 1, 1, 0$$

We select the fourth of these numbers, and bring x_4 into the basis.

We must now form the vector $\boldsymbol{\alpha} = \mathbf{T}_3\mathbf{T}_2\mathbf{T}_1\boldsymbol{\alpha}$, where

$$\mathbf{a} = \begin{bmatrix} 6 \\ 1 \\ 5 \\ 2 \\ 2 \\ 1 \end{bmatrix} \quad \text{so } \mathbf{T}_2\mathbf{T}_1\mathbf{a} = \begin{bmatrix} 6 \\ 1 \\ -5 \\ -2 \\ 2 \\ 1 \end{bmatrix} \quad \text{and} \quad \boldsymbol{\alpha} = \begin{bmatrix} 52/10 \\ 8/10 \\ -5 \\ -2 \\ 2/10 \\ 1 \end{bmatrix}$$

Comparing this with the elements of $\boldsymbol{\beta}$, we find that this will make the two negative variables positive; so our new elementary transformation matrix

$$\mathbf{T}_4 = \begin{bmatrix} 1 & -52/8 & & & & \\ & 10/8 & & & & \\ & 50/8 & 1 & & & \\ & 20/8 & & 1 & & \\ & -2/8 & & & 1 & \\ & -10/8 & & & & 1 \end{bmatrix}$$

The new ordered list of basic variables is

$x_0, x_4, x_5, x_6, x_1, x_7$

and the new right hand side

$$\boldsymbol{\beta}' = \mathbf{T}_4\boldsymbol{\beta} = \begin{bmatrix} -42/8 \\ 5/8 \\ 9/8 \\ 2/8 \\ 3/8 \\ 11/8 \end{bmatrix}$$

For the third iteration the trial solution is feasible, so

$$\mathbf{c} = [1, 0, 0, 0, 0, 0]$$
$$\mathbf{cT}_4 = [1, -52/8, 0, 0, 0, 0]$$
$$\mathbf{cT}_4\mathbf{T}_3 = [1, -52/8, 0, 0, 2/8, 0]$$

and $\boldsymbol{\pi} = \mathbf{cT}_4\mathbf{T}_3\mathbf{T}_2\mathbf{T}_1 = [1, -52/8, 0, 0, 2/8, 0]$

Multiplying $\boldsymbol{\pi}$ into the columns of $\mathbf{A}$ we obtain the reduced costs

$0, -12/8, 12/8, 0, 0, 0, 0$

We select the second of these numbers, and bring x_2 into the basis. We must now form the vector $\boldsymbol{\alpha} = \mathbf{T}_4\mathbf{T}_3\mathbf{T}_2\mathbf{T}_1\mathbf{a}$, where

$$\mathbf{a} = \begin{bmatrix} 5 \\ 1 \\ 5 \\ 1 \\ 0 \\ 4 \end{bmatrix} \quad \text{so } \mathbf{T}_2\mathbf{T}_1\mathbf{a} = \begin{bmatrix} 5 \\ 1 \\ -5 \\ -1 \\ 0 \\ 4 \end{bmatrix} \quad \mathbf{T}_3\mathbf{T}_2\mathbf{T}_1\mathbf{a} = \begin{bmatrix} 5 \\ 1 \\ -5 \\ -1 \\ 0 \\ 4 \end{bmatrix}$$

and $\boldsymbol{\alpha} = \begin{bmatrix} -12/8 \\ 10/8 \\ 10/8 \\ 12/8 \\ -2/8 \\ 22/8 \end{bmatrix}$

Comparing this with the elements of $\boldsymbol{\beta}$, we find that we must put $p = 3$, so our new elementary transformation matrix

$$\mathbf{T}_5 = \begin{bmatrix} 1 & & & 1 & & \\ & 1 & & -10/12 & & \\ & & 1 & -10/12 & & \\ & & & 8/12 & & \\ & & & 2/12 & 1 & \\ & & & -22/12 & & 1 \end{bmatrix}$$

The new ordered list of basic variables is

$$x_0, x_4, x_5, x_2, x_1, x_7$$

and the new right hand side

$$\boldsymbol{\beta}' = \mathbf{T}_5\boldsymbol{\beta} = \begin{bmatrix} -5 \\ 5/12 \\ 11/12 \\ 2/12 \\ 5/12 \\ 11/12 \end{bmatrix}$$

The trial solution is of course still feasible, so we again put

$$\mathbf{c} = [1, 0, 0, 0, 0, 0]$$
$$\mathbf{c}\mathbf{T}_5 = [1, 0, 0, 1, 0, 0]$$
$$\mathbf{c}\mathbf{T}_5\mathbf{T}_4 = [1, -4, 0, 1, 0, 0]$$
$$\mathbf{c}\mathbf{T}_5\mathbf{T}_4\mathbf{T}_3 = [1, -4, 0, 1, 0, 0]$$
$$\boldsymbol{\pi} = \mathbf{c}\mathbf{T}_5\mathbf{T}_4\mathbf{T}_3\mathbf{T}_2\mathbf{T}_1 = [1, -4, 0, -1, 0, 0]$$

Multiplying $\boldsymbol{\pi}$ into the columns of $\mathbf{A}$ we obtain the reduced costs

$$0, 0, 1, 0, 0, 1, 0$$

These numbers are all non-negative, so the current trial solution is optimal. It corresponds to the final solution given in Chapter 3.

EXAMPLE

Solve the example for Chapter 3 using the product form. Compare the results at each iteration with the corresponding results with the straight simplex method.

Part 2

ORGANIZATION OF LP CALCULATIONS

8 Formulation of Linear Programming Problems

8.1 Introduction

The first part of this book has attempted to give some idea of how linear programming works, and the examples have illustrated some typical fields of application. Let us now concentrate on the user's point of view, and say something about when and how to use linear programming. A general discussion on such topics often promises to be interesting, but in fact turns out to consist of waffle; I will try to cut down the waffle at the expense of some generality by concentrating on specific issues.

Is there anything useful one can say in general terms about when to use mathematical programming? In most operational research work one has, implicitly or explicitly, to make a mathematical model that represents the essential features of the real problem while simplifying other features. Mathematical programming is appropriate if these essential features are inequality constraints on the levels of activities that have to be chosen to give the best possible results in some precisely defined sense. One is often told that the first thing an operational research worker should do about a problem is to define the objective, and indeed one will not get very far until one has done this. But if one wants to consider the possibility of using mathematical programming it is generally best to start with the constraints. This will help to define the main variables of the problem, which may in turn help one to formulate an appropriate objective function. Conversely if one cannot capture the essence of the problem in this way, then mathematical programming is not going to help.

If mathematical programming is in fact appropriate, one can usually represent the constraints to an adequate approximation as linear constraints, and similarly with the objective function. In Part 3 we shall be discussing situations where this is not so, but meanwhile let us concentrate on linear programming problems. The question then arises how are we to solve them? Most real problems have an appreciable amount of special structure that a general simplex code does not recognize in at all an explicit way. So is it worth while devising and programming a special algorithm to take advantage of this structure? The answer to this question is definitely no, if one has a good general purpose LP code that will do the job. It is no longer true that the object in numerical work is to minimize the number of multiplications. One must take account of the time taken to write and debug any new program—or, if someone else has already written the program, the time taken to become familiar with how it works. This last task may sound trivial to anyone who has not had to do it, but I can assure them that it often is not. Furthermore, even when the special program is working it may not run significantly faster than the general program. The general program will be more efficiently organized as a program, so it may well finish up doing more arithmetic in less time than the special program. In the case of linear programming, many of the advantages available from special structure in one's models will in any case be captured by the standard product form of inverse using an efficient inversion routine.

The only exception I would admit to this rule against special linear programming programs is for the transportation problem. This is in itself a fairly general class of problem, and can be solved appreciably quicker with a specific transportation code than by a general simplex code, and, perhaps more importantly, larger transportation problems can be solved on any given computer explicitly as transportation problems rather than as general linear programming problems.

Let us now turn to the specific problems of building a linear programming model. It is helpful to divide the work into 3 stages—technology, costs and right hand sides.

8.2 Technology

First, the purpose of the model must be defined, and the flexibility that exists to enable it to be achieved. Is the objective to minimize production costs, or should variations in transport and selling costs be taken into account? Can one go further and treat the requirements as flexible, within limits, and maximize profit?

Second, one must decide on the scale of detail to be included and the general area to be encompassed. The idea of a single company model to answer all questions is a mirage. Although the use of a computer removes some of the pressure for oversimplification in numerical operational research work, one can still waste a lot of time—both analyst's time and computer time—by going into irrelevant detail over part of the model, and this can distract attention from more important parts. The sort of questions to be considered are: can the plant be regarded as a black box, or must relations be found for the way in which operating conditions affect throughput or yield? Is the model to be of part of a division of the company, or is it to include all relevant activities within the whole company? Is a static model adequate, or is it necessary to consider different time-periods separately? If so, what is the largest time interval that can meaningfully be used? Can useful simplifications be made by taking larger time intervals in the more distant future? With even a moderately complicated situation one should start by formulating and running a one-time-period model, but it is often necessary to consider different time-periods explicitly in the end.

As mentioned earlier, the heart of the model lies in the constraints. These usually fall into 5 main types:

(1) *Availabilities:* of raw materials, etc.
(2) *Capacities:* of plant, warehouse, transport fleet, manpower, etc. These may be fixed, or one may wish to consider activities that change capacities.
(3) *Qualities:* nutritional content of food mix, chemical or physical properties of product.
(4) *Demands:* i.e. sales estimates. These may represent bounds on single activities, but if one has the possibility of doing things in alternative ways they may represent bounds on sums of activities.
(5) *Continuity or material balance:*
Stock at end of previous period (or initial stock)
+ stock bought, transferred in, or made
− stock sold, transferred out, or used
= stock at end of period.

In general one needs a continuity equation for every product or raw material, in every place and every time period. Intermediates must not be forgotten.

It is very desirable to have a consistent sign convention governing continuity rows. This is especially true of large models, where it is the continuity rows that tie individual sub-models together. As a general rule it is desirable to use positive coefficients for activities that transfer materials into a row, and negative coefficients for activities that take away or use materials. We have already considered this point in connexion with transportation problems, discussing availability and demand rows. Availability and demand rows can be treated as special cases of continuity rows. On the other hand since all the coefficients in an availability row have the same sign, one may prefer to treat this is a special type of row and to use positive coefficients.

Costs are usually entered positively into the objective function, profits being entered negatively. Consequently if one's model covers international operations, and one decides to account for income and expenditure in different countries separately—because of different tax structures in different countries and restrictions on movement of money from one country to another—it may be convenient to use the opposite sign convention in money balance rows from that used in physical product balance rows.

Having decided on the rows, and the units in which they are measured, it should not be too difficult to define the activities. These fall into 3 main categories:

(1) *Buying:* Positive coefficients in availability and raw material continuity rows, and perhaps in warehouse capacity row.
(2) *Making:* Positive coefficients in raw material availability rows, or negative coefficients in raw material continuity rows. Positive coefficients in plant capacity rows, possible positive or negative coefficients on quality rows, and a positive yield coefficient on a product continuity or demand row.
(3) *Moving:* Usually a pair of coefficients -1, $+1$ in two continuity rows, but may also have coefficients in capacity rows. This covers moving from plant to market, from plant to plant, or from time-period to time-period (storage vectors).

It is normally good practice, at least during the initial formulation, to define the activities so that each is associated with a single easily defined cost, rather than to produce composite activities such as "the amount made at *A* by a certain process and then sent to *B*." It is better to have separate production and shipping vectors, to separate the two costs and keep the model more natural. One may eventually want to condense the matrix for computational purposes. This point is discussed later on.

8.3 Costs

The appropriate costs are of course the marginal costs, defined as the extra cost of increasing the level of activity by one unit. It is most unusual for such costs to be readily available. The costs in normal use are often the total costs with fixed costs averaged over production. To assess the effective variable cost it will probably be necessary to analyse these total costs into different components, and to consider to what extent each cost component might vary if the level of activity varied to the extent contemplated in the model. It may well be necessary to re-assess the costs after a preliminary run of the model, when one sees the actual changes in activity levels suggested.

In long-term planning models one may well consider expanding capacities. Furthermore it may be that one will need a higher capacity for a limited period of time, and that the optimal throughput (of a particular product in a particular place) may then decline. If so one must consider carefully the extent to which production costs are associated with maintaining the facilities represented by the capacity, and not simply proportional to current throughput. Such maintenance costs should be associated with the activities that create new capacity, and not with the production activities.

8.4 Right Hand Sides

These are normally the availabilities, demands, qualities, etc. There is usually no particular difficulty, though one must remember that if an availability is represented by a continuity equation the amount available should be entered negatively.

There is one recurring problem about multi-time period models that can be discussed here. What final stock level should be specified? There is no very simple answer to this question. If one is studying a seasonal industry and can assume no trend over the years, then one can regard initial and final inventory as variables that must be equal (i.e. put them in as a single variable). Or if one wishes to discover how to get into a good steady state from arbitrary starting conditions one can set up a model covering more than one full year under the assumption that final inventories must equal those a year earlier. This is not always satisfactory if a steady growth (or even decline for some products) is superimposed on a seasonal pattern. Fortunately the first-period decisions are unlikely to be seriously affected by the end conditions, and one will normally re-run the model to assess new information long before the last period, so an approximate method of fixing final inventories should be good enough. One useful approximate method is to treat final inventories as variables, but with specified marginal values. The program will then suggest appropriate final inventories. Often one has to look at the final answer, adjust the marginal values, and do a short re-run. Such re-runs are not to be thought of as particularly undesirable: indeed if the LP model is of any real use the solution to one problem is likely to suggest others in any case.

8.5 Methods of Condensing a Matrix

In reviewing formulations, I have suggested that one should do things in the most natural way, without taking any special steps to economize in either the number of equations or the number of variables. If the resulting problem is still a reasonably small one for the code to be used—in the case of LP/90/94 problems if it is less than say 300 equations—then it is probably best to leave it at that. But one should be aware of the possibilities of using alternative formulations that may be more economical in one way or another. There are really just four points I should like to make in this connexion.

(1) It may be possible to save equations at the expense of adding variables by defining variables representing complete strategies rather than isolated activities. We shall be discussing automatic ways of doing this in a comprehensive way under the heading Decomposition in Chapter 16. But sometimes one can usefully do this manually in a more limited way. The simplest example of this has already been mentioned: introducing variables representing "the amount made at *A* by a certain process and then sent to *B*" avoids the need for an equation to the effect that the total amount shipped out from *A* (summed over all processes) equals the total amount shipped out from *A* (summed over all destinations).

The point can perhaps be made more clearly algebraically. If we have *m* processes and *n* destinations we may introduce *m* variables y_i $(i = 1, \ldots, m)$ representing the amounts made by the *i*th process, and a further *n* variables z_j $(j = 1, \ldots, n)$ representing the amount sent to the *j*th destination. We then need a material balance equation

$$\sum y_i - \sum z_j = 0$$

If instead we introduce *mn* variables x_{ij} representing the amount made by the *i*th process and sent to the *j*th destination, then this material balance equation is unnecessary. What we do is to replace y_i by $\sum_j x_{ij}$ and to replace z_j by $\sum_i x_{ij}$ and the material balance equation becomes the tautology

$$\sum_i \sum_j x_{ij} - \sum_i \sum_j x_{ij} = 0$$

The increase in the number of non-zero coefficients is likely to be too high a price for saving such an equation—unless it is very important to cut down the number of equations, perhaps because the program will not accept the number of rows implied by the original formulation.

Another example concerns the specification of alternative operating conditions for a plant. This can be done by defining explicit constraints on the levels of activities in the plant. Alternatively one can define different modes of operating the plant—being in effect vertices of the feasible region of plant operation—constrained by a single capacity row to the effect that the sum of the levels of the different modes must be either equal to 1 or (more often) less than or equal to 1. It is often convenient to compromise and define different modes and also quality constraints representing further explicit restrictions on the plant operation.

(2) It is often natural to formulate equations of the form

$$x_T = a_1x_1 + a_2x_2 + \cdots + a_nx_n$$

For example x_T might represent the total amount of material produced, and the x_i might represent the total amount supplied to the ith demand point. In this case the a_i will probably all equal one. Alternatively x_T may represent some property of a mixture, say the manganese level, and the a_i are then proportional to the manganese levels of the ingredients of the mixture. Now if the a_i are all non-negative, there is no need to retain this equation to prevent x_T from becoming negative. One can simply substitute the right hand side of the equation for x_T wherever it occurs in the rest of the problem. Is this a good thing to do? The main argument in its favour is that it saves one equation, and also one variable. The arguments against it are

(*a*) It is a nuisance to do, since the problem is most naturally formulated in terms of x_T.
(*b*) The original formulation makes it easier to re-run the problem with changed values for some of the a_i.
(*c*) One wants to see at a glance what is the value of x_T in the final solution.
(*d*) The number of non-zero elements in the matrix may be significantly increased if x_T occurs in more than one other equation.

What are the merits of these arguments? The first is valid for small problems, but becomes less valid as the problem becomes larger, since the time to solve an LP problem increases roughly as the cube of the number of equations. The nuisance is in any case mitigated if one uses a computer program to generate the input data. Similar remarks apply to the second argument. The third argument also has some merit, but its force is diminished if one has a proper output analysis program. The last argument is a very serious one, as I hope is clear from the discussion of the inverse matrix method presented in Chapter 7. It is normally not worth saving a row if this adds more than about half a dozen non-zero matrix elements.

Similar arguments apply to lower bounds. If one has a constraint of the form $y \geqslant 2$, one should really abandon this constraint, and work with a new variable z equal to $y - 2$. The constraint $z \geqslant 0$ will then be taken care of automatically. In practice one may not bother to do this on small problems. Again one may leave the lower bound as an explicit constraint in order to simplify the task of re-running the program with a different lower bound.

(3) Another common problem concerns the representation of limited markets. One may be able to sell a limited amount, say a_1, of some product at a price of £p_1 per unit, and then a further amount a_2 at a lower price £p_2 per unit, and perhaps finally a further amount a_3 at a still lower price of £p_3 per unit. (Similar situations can occur with buying raw materials from increasingly expensive sources.) A natural way to formulate such a problem is to define variables say x_1, x_2 and x_3 denoting the amounts sold in the different markets. The total amount sold is then $x_1 + x_2 + x_3$, and the total revenue from the operation is £$(p_1x_1 + p_2x_2 + p_3x_3)$. One then has to define the constraints

$$x_1 \leqslant a_1$$
$$x_2 \leqslant a_2$$
$$x_3 \leqslant a_3$$

This formulation is quite convenient if one is using a linear programming code with special facilities for representing upper bound constraints, but with other codes it is more convenient to treat the revenue from the sale of this product as a concave piecewise linear function of the total amount offered for sale. Instead of the 3 variables x_1 x_2 and x_3 one defines 4 variables, say λ_0, λ_1, λ_2 and λ_3 and the one constraint

$$\lambda_0 + \lambda_1 + \lambda_2 + \lambda_3 = 1$$

The total amount sold is then

$$c_1\lambda_1 + c_2\lambda_2 + c_3\lambda_3$$

and the total revenue from the operation is

$$£(d_1\lambda_1 + d_2\lambda_2 + d_3\lambda_3)$$

where

$$c_1 = a_1$$
$$c_2 = a_1 + a_2$$
$$c_3 = a_1 + a_2 + a_3$$
$$d_1 = a_1p_1$$
$$d_2 = a_1p_1 + a_2p_2$$
$$d_3 = a_1p_1 + a_2p_2 + a_3p_3$$

To define the amount sold on the *i*th market from the values of the λ_j one merely has to compute

$$\left(1 - \sum_{j=0}^{i-1} \lambda_j\right) a_i$$

Similarly, to obtain the shadow price on the right hand side of the constraint defining the upper bound on the size of any market when this constraint is not written down explicitly, one works with the shadow price on the material balance row defining the amount of the material available for sale. This shadow price defines the marginal cost of producing a small amount more; so the advantage of an increase in the market size is represented by the difference between the price p_i and this marginal production cost, provided this difference is positive.

In this formulation one cannot do parametric programming explicitly on the right hand side of a market size constraint, but the effects can be deduced from a parametric programming run on the right hand side of the material balance row. If the material balance row has a right hand side of θ, one has the consequences of producing an extra amount θ and not selling it. So if one now sells it at a price of £p_i per unit the objective function is increased by £$p_i\theta$. This increase can be carried out in the computer by putting a coefficient of p_i in the objective function in the right hand side representing the change vector, though it should be noted that this formulation implies that the additional material *must* be sold in the *i*th market. So if the objective function starts to decrease as the parameter θ increases beyond a certain point, one may be able to avoid this decrease in practice by not supplying the full potential of the market.

This method of representing non-linear functions is discussed again in Chapter 14 on separable programming.

(4) My fourth point is more specialized, but it does arise in a number of contexts. It concerns the representation of capacity increases in a multi-time-period model. One can generally save non-zero coefficients, though not equations or variables, by expressing these in the form

Capacity this period = capacity last period + increase in capacity becoming effective this period

rather than in the form

Capacity this period = initial capacity + sum of increases in capacity that have become effective since the initial time period

The preferred form can be derived algebraically from the alternative by writing the constraints as equations (by adding slack variables representing unused capacity) and subtracting last period's constraint from the current period's constraint, but it is preferable to think of the constraint as a directly meaningful condition. The capacity in each period will be represented by the sum of the activities using the capacity plus a variable representing unused capacity.

8.6 Scaling

Having decided on the structure of the matrix, one must decide on the units in which to measure each activity, and each constraint. It is desirable to make all non-zero matrix elements approximately equal to 1 in magnitude. Values of 10 or 0·1 are quite acceptable, but values of 1000 or 0·001 are apt to slow the program down. This is because at each iteration most codes choose the variable with the most negative reduced cost as the one to enter the basis. Imagine for example that some quantities are measured in tons when they should be measured in pounds, or thousandths of a ton, in order to keep the numbers in balance. Then the change in the objective function per unit change in such a quantity is likely to be numerically large. So whenever it happens to be positive one will probably bring it into the basis. One will therefore tend to spend an unreasonable amount of time bringing such variables into the basis and then removing them. And furthermore this may generate enough rounding off errors to be a nuisance.

It is possible to get the mathematical programming code to take care of the scaling. The LP/90/94 system has an agendum called SCALEM, which multiplies each row of the matrix by a constant so that the largest element in absolute value is ± 1. The scaling factors are stored (on magnetic tape), and there is an agendum called UNSCALE to restore the original scaling before printing the final results.

8.7 Degeneracy

Good computer codes will deal correctly with most degenerate problems in practice, but there are two sets of conditions in which this is not always so. First, the all-slack basis can be very degenerate if there are hundreds of zero elements in the right hand side. It may be desirable to run these problems with small non-zero right hand sides, equal to say 0·000001; though one must be careful to choose these in such a way that the problem remains feasible. Second, some production facility may be included in a general-purpose matrix, but not be permitted in particular runs. The normal way to deal with this is to put a zero RHS on the relevant capacity row. The equation is then of the form $\sum a_i x_i \leqslant 0$, where all $a_i \geqslant 0$. Thus all x_i must be zero, but one will be in the basis at zero level. One may make a large number of futile iterations bringing in different x_i at a zero level; and furthermore rounding-off errors may lead to the x_i taking a small nonzero value and creating an apparent infeasibility. Also the shadow prices and reduced costs may be misleading since the basis is degenerate. This problem can be tackled in one of 2 ways: replace the zero right hand side by a small positive number, say 0·001; or temporarily remove all variables that cannot take non-zero values from the problem. This latter approach is only feasible if it can be done by program. The LP/90/94 system has an agendum FLAGS, ZEROVECTORS that does this, and it has been found most useful both for speeding up the solution of LP problems and for detecting errors in the matrix—since a list of vectors suppressed in this way is printed out, and if it includes vectors that can in fact be used some coefficient must be in error.

EXAMPLE

Consider the situation described below. Formulate a linear programming model that represents the problem. If you have access to a computer with a suitable LP code, use it to solve the problem.

A company makes 3 products, *X*, *Y*, and *Z*. These products are made on 2 groups of machines, of type *A* or type *B*. The technological conditions are as follows.

Product *X* can only be made on type *A* machines, at a rate of 2000 units/week on each machine.

Product *Y* can only be made on type *B* machines, at a rate of 1000 units/week on each machine.

Product *Z* can be made on either type of machine, at a rate of 5000 units/week, but of course while the machine is working on *Z* it cannot make either *X* or *Y*. Change-over costs are negligible.

The uses of raw materials in each product is given in the following table—

Each unit of *X* uses 1·5 lb of R_1 and no R_2

Each unit of *Y* uses 0·5 lb of R_1 and 1·0 lb of R_2

Each unit of *Z* uses no R_1 and 2·0 lb of R_2

The demand for each product over the next year has been forecast for each of 13 4-week periods as shown in Table 8.1.

TABLE 8.1

Period	*Demand (thousands)*		
	X	*Y*	*Z*
1	15	10	30
2	12	11	30
3	10	12	30
4	12	12	30
5	14	12	30
6	16	12	30
7	20	12	30
8	22	12	30
9	24	12	30
10	22	12	30
11	20	12	30
12	18	12	30
13	16	12	30

3 type *A* machines and 4 type *B* machines are available, and we have an initial stock of

1000 lb of R_1
2000 lb of R_2
5000 units of *X*
4000 units of *Y*
20000 units of *Z*

The forecast cost of seasonal raw materials is as shown in Table 8.2.

TABLE 8.2

Period	£/1000 lb	
	R_1	R_2
1	80	160
2	80	150
3	80	140
4	90	160
5	100	190
6	120	220
7	120	250
8	120	280
9	120	310
10	120	340
11	120	360
12	110	300
13	100	200

It costs £20 to store 1000 lb of either raw material for a month. It also costs £20 to store 1000 units of any product for a month.

How should the operation be planned to meet the demand as cheaply as possible?

9 Input for Linear Programming Problems

9.1 Initial Input

Having formulated a linear programming problem, one has to get the information into the computer. The most straightforward way to do this is to punch the coefficients explicitly onto cards (or paper tape). If one is following this route, the SHARE standard system, used in LP/90/94 and described in the Appendix, is probably as good as any. On the other hand the problem is at its most expanded form when written out as an LP matrix, so this is really the worst possible point at which to enter the computer for the first time. This perhaps suggests that one needs an LP subroutine rather than an independent LP program. For some purposes this is true and it is likely to become increasingly true in the future, as machines and problems get bigger and more complex. But fortunately the distinction between a subroutine and an independent program is not nearly so marked as it used to be now that we have such things as magnetic tapes. It is quite feasible to have a program that writes a matrix as card images on magnetic tape to be read by the LP program. This may seem to be an inefficient route, since the card-image is a very expanded way of representing the coefficient, which will immediately be put into a more compact form in the LP code. But the actual time taken to read and write a matrix is very small compared with the time taken to solve the LP problem, and the use of card images in this way makes it very easy to check the matrix generator program.

What does a matrix generator program consist of? This varies widely. The most primitive—but still useful—matrix generator is really a format converter. The user may wish to specify his coefficients in one format, and the program converts them into the standard format. For example most people first coming into practical linear programming think in terms of equations rather than activities, so that they would rather put all coefficients of an equation together rather than all coefficients of a variable. After a while one gets used to thinking in terms of activities, and this has advantages, in that one is more likely to be adding or deleting activities than equations. This approach forces one to think of the physical significance of each row of the problem. I regard this as an advantage, though some people might consider it an imposition. But if you don't like this you can certainly have a matrix generator that accepts the data in rows and puts it out in columns. Equally, particularly for small matrices, one may wish to punch several matrix coefficients on the same card, with the understanding that successive numbers refer to successive variables (or equations as the case may be).

Probably the most widely used matrix generators are more sophisticated but more special purpose programs, written for a particular application. It is difficult to generalize about what form these programs will take, but the unit matrix coefficients will normally be generated automatically, and the numerical values of other coefficients will be specified in the data to the matrix generator only once, even though the same number may be used in various places. The generator will usually do a modest amount of arithmetic: some of this will consist of changing units—for example a processing rate may be given in tons/hour, but the coefficient to go in the capacity constraint must be in hours/ton, i.e. the reciprocal. There will often be more arithmetic to be done on cost coefficients: adding up different components of cost, making allowances for tax rebates, and in multi-time-models discounting the costs by a suitable factor to give net present worth. This type of matrix generator is particularly useful on multi-time-period models, when the matrix is largely repeated from one time period to the next, with different variable and constraint names and different right hand sides.

One important feature of a good matrix generator is that the key input data are printed out in an easily readable form. A major part of getting an LP model operating usefully consists of getting the data right. This in turn is made easier by having a tidy print-out that you can show to people and ask them to say whether the numbers are correct: the chances are that they are not correct because you have had to guess at some of the numbers in the first instance (hopefully on the basis of related information supplied by the user) in order to get something moving.

With a matrix generator of this type various alterations can be made to the matrix by simply changing the data, without altering the program. For example one can change the numerical value of some yield factor, or one can change the discount factor to be applied to future incomes or expenditures to determine present worth. In a multi-time-period model one can presumably change the number of time periods. But it is impossible to foresee all possible ways in which one might wish to extend the model, and it is foolish to try to do so.

One should expect to have to change the program itself from time to time. If it is written in a reasonably straightforward way in say FORTRAN, then this is not difficult.

Various groups are working on much more general matrix generator programs. It is clear that a certain amount of equation generation can be done automatically if the constraints are all of the standard types indicated in the previous chapter. I am not convinced that this is really going to save effort in the long run for people who are familiar with FORTRAN or some other suitable language for writing special purpose matrix generators—although these special purpose generators do tend to become more general as new features are added to deal with new types of problem.

9.2 An Example of a Matrix Generator

The significance of the previous discussion may be clearer from a specification of a typical matrix generator. Let us therefore consider one designed and written by Mr. M. Minns, Mrs. A. F. Grundy, Miss W. Hunt and C-E-I-R for the Mond Division of ICI. This description does not include all facilities now available in the generator, but it should be adequate for illustrative purposes.

This matrix generator is for a single time-period model. The model deals with up to 100 plants grouped into not more than 20 regions. It recognizes up to 100 raw materials and up to 200 products that can be made at one or more of the plants, although some may also be bought. The data cards define the system as follows.

First, region cards define the code letter and name (up to 24 characters) of each region, and the number of plants in the region.

The region cards are followed by product cards, which define the code number and name (up to 12 characters) of each raw material and product. For products (as opposed to raw materials) these cards also indicate the way in which the product can be sold, according to the following code—

0 = No sales possible
1 = Market sales
2 = Unlimited sales, in which case the card also defines the selling price. This selling price may be negative if it represents the cost of disposing of a waste product.
3 = Customer sales, in which case the card also defines the number of customers. (This is to enable the program to create the ROWIDS for the customers before reading the cards defining the sales details.)

The significance of market and customer sales will be explained later when the data for these sales are defined.

The product cards are followed by data on each region. First there are cards defining the cost of transporting a product to another region. (This is assumed to be impossible unless specified in this way, although any product can be freely transported within any region.) Then there are cards defining the purchase prices of raw materials and other products in the region. (Again, purchases are assumed to be impossible unless specified in this way.) Then there are cards defining the operation of each plant in the region. These plant cards take the following form—

> The first card gives the name of the plant (up to 24 characters), and says whether or not there are any quality constraints on the operation of the plant. A plant normally has a finite capacity and may be operated at any level up to this capacity, but it is possible to specify here that a particular plant must be operated at full capacity, or that it has no capacity limit.
>
> The non-zero coefficients, right hand sides and slack indicators of any quality constraints follow next. These can be any constraints relating the amounts of different products made at the plant.
>
> Finally there are the modal cards. These define the variable operating costs, the amounts of different materials that must be input, and the corresponding types and amounts of material produced in each mode of operation. The capacity of the plant in each mode is also indicated.

After the data on all plants in all regions, there are data on market and customer sales. With market sales it is assumed that the difference in transport costs to different markets from different regions is unimportant, but that there may be a number of markets for the product with different realizations and different sizes. Two cards are specified for each market. The first gives the name (up to 12 characters) of the market and the realization and the second gives the size of the market (inserted as a negative number if the requirement for this market must be met in full). Customer sales are similar, except that transport costs are not negligible, so these two cards are followed by further cards defining the transport costs from all regions from which the customer can be supplied.

Throughout the data cards, reference to raw materials and products are by code number and to regions by code letter. This is to avoid confusion from variants in the spelling of names.

This matrix generator does not involve any large amount of arithmetic in computing the coefficients. The costs of the raw materials that are not intermediate products are added to the variable operating costs for each mode, and the coefficients for each modal variable are multiplied by the capacity of the plant in this mode. Also the coefficients for market sales variables are cumulated as indicated in the previous chapter, and the distribution cost is subtracted from the realization to define the profit from customer sales, but that is all. Furthermore, although a few numbers (the costs of raw materials for different plants in the same region, and the selling prices for unlimited sales products in different regions) are used in the computation of more than one matrix element, the number of input coefficients for the matrix generator is not dramatically less than the number that would be required to define all matrix coefficients explicitly. So what are the advantages of using this particular generator? They can be summarized under the following headings.

(1) The size of the LP matrix is much smaller than with the previous manual formulation of the same problem. Some of these economies could have been achieved without the matrix generator, but others—the elimination of material balance rows for raw materials and the elimination of rows for each market—would not be very convenient in practice without the generator to do the arithmetic associated with this elimination.

(2) The size of the data deck is smaller (by a factor of about 2) than the corresponding deck for direct input. This is largely because the unit elements associated with transporting product to sales and from one region to another are generated automatically.

(3) The matrix generator automatically provides a reasonable starting basis for the LP calculations. The calculation of the basis is less elaborate in this generator than in some others: it is handicapped by the fact that the data are too voluminous to be held entirely in the core of the IBM 7094 computer, but artificial variables in the natural starting basis are replaced by the following—

Variables defining the total make at any plant, of each product involved in quality rows.
Variables representing selling any product to either unlimited or market sales.
Variables representing operating each plant in its first mode.
Variables representing the first 2 points on the curve defining income from market sales as a function of the amount of product available for sale.

This starting basis can be overwritten by the final basis from the solution to a previous problem if this seems expedient, but so far the generated basis has always been found satisfactory.

(4) Finally, but perhaps most importantly, we must consider the things the matrix generator does in addition to writing the LP matrix. It checks that the data cards are assembled in the correct order, and prints suitable messages about incorrect cards. It produces a clear language print-out of the specification of the problem for data-checking purposes, with names as well as numbers given for each region, each plant, each raw material or product and each market or customer. It also generates compile cards to enable the LP system to provide a suitable clear-language report on the solution to the problem.

In practice ICI Mond Division used linear programming without matrix generators initially but found that even after the first problem was correctly formulated, the task of modifying the matrix to solve other similar problems was extremely slow and expensive. This applied particularly to studies of plans for 4 or 5 years hence, which inevitably change rather rapidly.

9.3 Revising the Matrix

Most LP problems are not correctly specified first time, and some debugging of data is necessary. Furthermore, at some stage it is likely that the model will have to be revised to include up-to-date cost coefficients and right hand sides. If the matrix was generated by the program, this should not cause much difficulty: one just re-runs the matrix generator. It will still be possible to use the optimum basis from the previous run as an initial starting basis if this seems expedient. This requirement may have some influence on the format of the data input to the matrix generator: for example if one element of the cost of some activities is a transport cost, computed as so much per ton mile, then the number of miles should be primary data. Another number can represent the cost per ton mile, which can then be changed if necessary.

In some ways I think that progress has been hindered by the fact that the LP/90/94 system has a number of facilities to help manual matrix revisions. Nevertheless these facilities have been quite widely used, and are convenient. The basic one is the agendum REVISE, which essentially does the same as INPUT except that existing numbers are maintained unless explicitly deleted. Another is the agendum RECOST, which allows one to build up a new cost row as a linear combination of existing rows that may represent the components of total cost.

Occasionally it is expedient to use these methods to revise a matrix that has been generated by program—for example to create a new right hand side for a special purpose parametric programming study; although it is usually tidier and more efficient to make these revisions by changing the matrix generator.

9.4 Row and Column Names

One aspect of input that deserves some special discussion is the naming of variables (columns) and constraints (rows). In some codes the variables are given consecutive numbers, and similarly for the constraints. This is understandable on a small computer, and I believe that there still are people who think that it is satisfactory on any computer, on the grounds that the name inside the LP routine itself is of no concern to the user.

The LP/90/94 system is like many others in that the constraints and variables are given names of 6 characters (any of which can be blank). The first character has to be either blank, 1, 2, 3, 4, 5, 6, 7, 8, or 9; although & is also used for special purposes. What advantages do these names provide? One advantage is that certain features of the names are used as markers in some extensions of linear programming, as we shall see later in the book. Perhaps more importantly, a logical coding system simplifies the writing of a flexible special purpose matrix generator, and makes it easier to debug a matrix from print-outs directly from the LP system. Also it simplifies some matrix revisions, for example one can flag (or temporarily exclude from the problem) any variables with a particular character in a specified position in its name.

The row and column names created by the matrix generator should be reasonably mnemonic, primarily to help the analyst studying the LP output, but also to simplify matrix revisions as discussed in Section 9.3.

9.5 The Importance of Matrix Generators

The use of sophisticated special purpose computer programs to assemble the input data for linear programming calculations, and to prepare reports about the results of the calculations, is almost as important an advance as the use of computers to carry out the calculations themselves. But these programs have only recently started to be widely used, so this chapter concludes with a summary of their advantages.

Linear programming calculations are of 2 types: they may be carried out on a production basis, being run every 6 months, or every 3 months, or even more frequently, to indicate the operating strategy for the next time period. Or they may be undertaken on a research basis, being carried out once in order to throw light on the relative merits of different ways of organizing the business, but without the intention of ever using them for routine decision making. Now one might question whether it was worth while to write a special input program to marshal the data for a one-off exercise. But I am sure that it is worth while, for a number of reasons:

(1) The task of getting the data marshalled correctly without a program is a major one. It is easy to underestimate it because of its low intellectual content.
(2) Although the exercise may only be carried out once, several computer runs will probably be required, in order to eliminate clerical-type errors, mathematical errors, and missing constraints that only become apparent when one sees the consequence of optimizing without these constraints. After that one may well want to run the program under a variety of assumptions. Many of these re-runs will involve changing the matrix generator program, but this is likely to be a far less tedious and unreliable process than changing the matrix manually. Furthermore the number of runs will almost certainly exceed the number originally estimated—particularly if this latter number is only 1 or 2.
(3) An important by-product of a linear programming study is that it provides a framework for assembling the relevant data for any operational research study into the problem being investigated. It is therefore desirable to take the opportunity to print out at least the main features of the data in a tidy format, both to help detect errors and for future reference. This business of printing out the input data is often the major part of writing a matrix generator, but it is nevertheless well worth while.

When one turns to production jobs, the case for special purpose matrix generators appears much stronger, but I must report that a lot of production LP work is done without matrix generators. One has a *get off* tape representing the state of the problem when last solved. One restarts it, revises a few coefficients using cards punched with the changed numbers, and away one goes. I do not really approve of this, but I cannot deny that it works.

10 Output from LP Calculations

10.1 Normal Operating Output

One may be tempted to think that all one needs to do to use mathematical programming in practice is to formulate the problems and assemble the input data in a form acceptable to the LP code of one's computer. However if one wants to use mathematical programming for anything other than occasional research projects, one must give serious attention to methods of presenting the results of the calculations.

The standard unscrambled output from the LP/90/94 system is very convenient for the analyst, once he has learnt how to read it. It consists of 5 columns giving

(1) The names of the basic variables in their original order.
(2) The corresponding values of the basic variables.
(3) The names of the rows (or constraints).
(4) The shadow prices on these rows.
(5) The original right hand side elements on these rows.

The value of printing the basic variables and their numerical values surely needs no comment. I hope that the importance of the shadow prices on the rows (the dual variables) has been illustrated by previous discussions. I find that the easiest way to think about them is as the marginal values of small increments to the right hand sides. Some of these marginal values are liable to be more meaningful than others: for example changes in right hand sides representing availabilities or demands can easily be interpreted. Changes in capacities have a clear interpretation in single-time-period models. In multi-time-period models it may be unnatural to think of increasing a capacity temporarily: but the sum of the shadow prices on capacity rows from one time period to the end of the program indicates the utility of a permanent increase in capacity. Changing zero or unit right hand elements may have less immediate significance, but note that the shadow price on a continuity row represents minus the marginal value of an extra unit of the material being balanced.

It may seem illogical to include the original right hand side, but it is useful, both because there may be several right hand sides on the matrix tape, and it may be helpful to have written confirmation that one is using the right hand side one intended to use; and also because it often helps one to understand a solution, and to reveal errors. For example if one has a capacity constraint, one may be able to see at a glance that one activity uses all the available capacity. If the solution looks suspicious, it may for example be worth checking that the sum of the activities using a capacity, plus the spare capacity, equals the given right hand side.

Although this output is convenient for the analyst, it is not convenient for the general user, and he should certainly be presented with a tidy report containing the relevant information about the solution in plain language. Different systems have different report-writing facilities. With the LP/90/94 system two approaches are possible. One is to use the report-writing facilities of the LP system itself, which requires the preparation of a set of compile cards defining the form of the report. The other is to write the details of the solution on a special tape, which we call an *unravel tape*, and to have a special FORTRAN program to prepare the report. The report-writer has advantages for simple reports, in that the report is generated during the same run on the computer as the linear programming problem is solved. On the other hand, generating the control cards to compile the report is in effect programming in a special language that is rather like FORTRAN but is much more limited.

If a matrix generator is used to prepare the input data, this may well have some bearing on the output analysis. If the report-writer facility is being used, then the matrix generator can be programmed to produce the cards to compile the report. The limitations on the language in which compile cards are written are then less serious. Specifically the fact that one cannot write DO loops in compile statements means that one sometimes needs many more compile statements than one would need FORTRAN statements to achieve the same results in the FORTRAN output analyser. These compile statements can however often be generated fairly painlessly using DO loops in the matrix generator. If a FORTRAN output analyser is being used, then it should normally include the part of the matrix generator that reads the data and prints it out. There may be some additional data required by the output analyser, in addition to the unravel tape, that define quantities that are independent of the activity levels and are therefore irrelevant to the LP matrix. But the operation is greatly simplified from a data-handling point of view if one has an identical input deck for both programs, as well as taking advantage of the tidy print-out prepared for the matrix generator to allow one to check against errors before embarking on an expensive LP run.

The necessity with the LP/90/94 system to run the matrix generator and output analyser under a different monitor system from the LP calculations themselves is a slight nuisance. In these circumstances, if one has many problems to run it is sometimes expedient to run them "in parallel", i.e. to generate all the matrices, then do all the LPs, and then do all the output analyses. There are compensating advantages for this interrupted procedure that apply particularly if the unravel tape is prepared in BCD as card images. The fact that the unravel tape can easily be printed helps in debugging the output analyser. The output analyser can also be used to prepare a report on a strategy that is not optimal in a mathematical sense but has been suggested, perhaps by management, as being convenient for reasons that cannot be adequately quantified in a mathematical model. (Such analyses can be derived by adding constraints to the LP model to force the desired strategy, but it is often easier to prepare a synthetic unravel tape, perhaps by just punching the cards.)

One further piece of information is provided automatically by some codes, namely the reduced costs of all variables in the final solution. This is easily computed, and is often of some interest. In the LP/90/94 system it is optional. One can call the agendum UNSCRAMBLE, which provides the output discussed originally followed—or not according to taste—by the agendum DO.D/J, which provides the reduced costs. Alternatively one can call the agendum SOLUTION, which provides the scrambled and unscrambled output, together with the reduced costs and a punchout of the final basis.

10.2. Other Output

Sometimes more extensive output is desirable for analytical purposes, particularly for debugging a matrix. Some examples of additional output available on the LP/90/94 system, and indications of its value, are as follows.

(*a*) PICTURE

It is difficult to get an overall view of a large matrix, since only a small part of it will fit on a piece of paper, and it can be very troublesome to detect matrix elements that are missing, or inserted in the wrong place, or inserted with the wrong sign, or with the wrong scale factor. This agendum represents all non-zero matrix elements by a 2-character code. The first is the sign. The second indicates the magnitude: 1 is printed explicitly. Other magnitudes are indicated by a letter code described on the first page of the picture. In this way 61 vectors and 60 rows can be represented on a page—and the pages are numbered in matrix notation for easy identification.

It tends to be particularly difficult to sort out errors in the matrix if the problem as formulated has no feasible solution. Sometimes this is genuine. The constraints as formulated may represent what people would like to be able to do. In practice they are interpreted flexibly, and the analyst must find out about this and represent the flexibility mathematically before proceeding further. Whether or not this is the reason, some vector or right hand side must be changed before resolving the problem. At this stage the shadow prices represent the derivatives of the sum of infeasibilities with respect to the right hand sides, so it is natural to concentrate attention on rows with a numerically large shadow price. The agendum PICTURE HELP does the same as PICTURE except that it suppresses some vectors, but it includes all vectors having non-zero coefficients in any row for which the absolute value of the shadow price is greater than or equal to unity. It also includes other vectors having nonzero coefficients in rows where there is an infeasibility (either an artificial or a variable at negative level). If in fact the trouble is an incorrect vector and not simply an impossible set of right hand side elements, then the erroneous vector will usually be among those selected by these criteria. One should of course check the possibility that some vector is missing from the picture precisely because its coefficient in the relevant row is missing.

(*b*) TABLEAU

This gives either the whole of the current tableau, or else selected columns from the tableau. On a large problem this can be a very slow and expensive operation, but it can be useful—particularly for debugging purposes—on smaller problems.

(*c*) EXTSOL

This prints out a basic vector times its value in the solution. This may be useful in debugging—to check material balances or quality rows. It can be done for all basic vectors, or alternatively for a selection of them.

(*d*) SENSIT

This agendum may be used to help assess the accuracy to which a coefficient needs to be determined. It measures the derivative of the objective function with respect to small changes in the *non-zero* coefficients in the current basis—or one can restrict the calculation to selected vectors. The formula for this derivative is $-\beta_j\pi_i$, i.e. the negative of the current value of the basic variable times the shadow price on the row in which one is changing the coefficient. This formula is almost obvious, since if the matrix element a_{ij} is increased by a small amount Δ one would have to change the right hand side of the ith row by $\beta_j\Delta$ in order to restore the original solution. This latter change could increase the objective function by $\pi_i\beta_j\Delta$, so the original change must have decreased the objective function by this amount. The same result can be deduced more formally by considering the current tableau, pivoting between x_j and the slack-or-artificial associated with the ith row, changing the transformed pivot by Δ, and then pivoting back.

The difficulty with these sensitivities is that the derivatives concerned are only relevant for small changes, and are discontinuous when the basis changes. Nevertheless they can be useful in giving an overall first impression of the importance of different factors.

11 Post-optimal Analysis

11.1 Introduction

It is sometimes said that obtaining the first optimal solution to a linear programming problem is of no importance in itself. It is merely a necessary preliminary to the further post-optimal analyses that are the really valuable results of a LP study. This is certainly true if post-optimal analysis is deemed to include thinking about the significance of the results of the calculation—though otherwise I think it is a considerable exaggeration.

Let us therefore start by discussing the process of thinking about the solution to an LP problem. One certainly has not achieved very much if one simply has an optimal solution unless one can understand (after the event) why the general pattern of the solution is as it is. There is some temptation even among sophisticated people to feel that numbers printed in a tidy lay-out by a computer have some mystical significance independent of any assumptions made in deriving them, but this temptation must be resisted—unless one can see in general terms why such a solution is after all plausible, the chances are that it isn't right. It may be a consequence of having omitted some important constraint, or of having formulated some constraint in an unfortunate way, or of having lost some coefficient from the matrix, or of having put it in with the wrong sign. Or perhaps the model is basically right, but the result is a consequence of a badly chosen value of some important input parameter. Theoretically it is reprehensible to cook the input data because you don't like the look of the answer, but in practice this is often the only way to detect bad guesses at the values of some of these data.

When the analyst or formulator has studied a solution carefully enough to have some confidence in it, various supplementary questions are likely to suggest themselves. In addition to the values of the basic variables, one will also have the shadow prices on each constraint—these in effect define the partial differential coefficients of the objective function with respect to the right hand sides of the constraints. One may also decide, as a matter of routine, to print out the reduced costs on each of the non-basic variables. These can be interpreted as the amounts by which the direct cost of each activity must be reduced before it is profitable to engage in it.

11.2 Standard Facilities

Other types of supplementary question can perhaps best be appreciated by considering the main facilities provided in general linear programming systems.

The basic requirement for post-optimal analysis is a facility for revising individual numbers in the formulation of the problem, re-inverting to the basis that had been optimal (although it may now be neither optimal nor feasible), and re-optimizing. The larger the problem the less relevant other post-optimal analysis facilities become, since one comes more and more up against the situation that any small change in the data makes a small change in the solution.

Other facilities are the possibility of defining alternative objective functions or alternative right hand sides (i.e. constant terms) in the equations. This does not of course mean that one can use two objective functions simultaneously; it merely means that one may wish to investigate the way the solution varies if the input data (on either costs or requirements) change, and it may be convenient to define the alternatives in advance rather than revise the problem after one optimization.

Parametric programming, discussed in Chapter 6, is an extension of the concept. One can study the way the optimum solution varies for a one-parameter family of alternative right hand sides or objective functions. In practice it is most usual to explore the effect of changing a single cost coefficient, or a single right hand side element (representing say the size of some market).

Other facilities related to parametric programming that may be of interest, particularly in small problems, are cost ranging and right hand side ranging. Cost ranging means in effect starting to do parametric programming to vary each coefficient in the objective function in turn, either up or down, and noting how big a change can be made without changing the solution—as well as which variables would enter the basis if one slightly exceeded the limits. Similarly right hand side ranging means in effect starting parametric programming to vary each constant term in turn either up or down, and noting how big a change can be made without changing the basis—as well as which variables would leave the basis if one slightly exceeded the limits. (Of course the numerical values of some basic variables will change with any changes in the constant terms.)

Another useful facility that can conveniently be discussed in connexion with post-optimal analysis is flags. One may wish to resolve a problem with a side condition that certain variables are not allowed to be used. This can be achieved by altering their costs to be arbitrarily large, but it is somewhat more efficient to flag them as variables that are ineligible to enter the basis. The costs will then not be computed at all.

11.3 Uses of Post-optimal Analyses

So much for the general types of analyses that are sometimes carried out. It is more difficult to give general guidance as to what analysis to make in any given situation, but some comments may be helpful.

Parametric programming may be used as a more efficient procedure for resolving the problem with a new right hand side than simply re-optimizing—since one does not then ever send the problem infeasible.

Parametric programming, on either the objective function or the right hand side, is a convenient tool if one is uncertain of the relative weights to be given to two different objectives. For example, in a diet problem one might be uncertain how strictly to define the dietary requirements. By mapping out the family of solutions as the permitted limits (or ranges) are decreased one can see the consequences of different assumptions.

There are many other circumstances in which one wants to explore the consequences of changing right hand sides, perhaps after looking at the final solution to the problem as originally formulated and finding large shadow prices on some rows indicating the possibility of a substantial saving from changing the sales target of some product, or increasing the availability of some raw material, or (in a longer-term model) increasing some capacity. Similar considerations may apply to the terminal stocks in a multi-time-period model.

There are many problems for which a continuous mathematical programming model is useful without providing a complete solution. these are typically scheduling-type problems that involve an important discrete element. The primary purpose of the mathematical programming model is then to determine shadow prices on the rows corresponding to the use of scarce resources. The post-optimal analysis will then be some non-mathematical programming calculation using these shadow prices. It may simply amount to taking each task in turn and arranging to do it in the cheapest available way—the use of the shadow prices should prevent any scarce resource from becoming grossly overloaded.

In some circumstances the post-optimal analysis can be done in a more highbrow way—the replacement of the inequality constraints by additional costs may simplify the problem to such an extent that one can use dynamic programming. One may be able to go even further and use dynamic programming to generate variables for a master linear programming problem representing the inequality constraints. This approach has been applied for example by Gilmore and Gomory (1961) to cutting-stock problems, and by Dzielinski and Gomory (1965) to certain production-scheduling problems involving set-up costs.

Part 3

SPECIAL PROCEDURES

12 Lagrange Multipliers and Kuhn-Tucker Conditions

12.1 Theory of Optimization

This part of the book is concerned with extensions of mathematical programming beyond the simplex method for linear programming. Specifically we shall be concerned with non-linear programming; that is with non-linear constraints or a non-linear objective function or both in an otherwise linear programming problem; also with integer programming, that is with problems containing variables that must take integer values; and with decomposition—a method of solving some large linear and other programming problems. Before embarking on the practical aspects of these procedures it seems desirable to review the basic mathematical theory of optimization from a more general point of view than was convenient when introducing linear programming.

Suppose that we wish to minimize some differentiable function $f(x)$, defined for all values of x. Then it is well known that a necessary condition for a minimum is that $df/dx = 0$. A value of x for which $df/dx = 0$ does not necessarily minimize $f(x)$ but under certain conditions it does. One such condition arises if the function $f(x)$ is convex: a function is said to be convex if it is never underestimated by linear interpolation, i.e. if

$$f[x + \theta(y - x)] \leqslant f(x) + \theta[f(y) - f(x)] \tag{12.1}$$

for any x, y and θ such that $0 < \theta < 1$. Convexity is related to the possibly more familiar condition for a minimum based on the second derivative, since it is easy to show that if a convex function has a second derivative it must be non-negative. However this is not the place to explore the mathematical properties of convex functions in any detail.

We shall later wish to refer to a *strictly convex* function. This means one for which (12.1) holds with a $<$ sign instead of the $\leqslant$ sign.

A precisely analogous situation arises if we wish to minimize a differentiable function of several variables, say $f(x_1, \ldots, x_n)$. It is convenient to call this a function of a vector $\mathbf{x}$, i.e. $f(\mathbf{x})$, where $\mathbf{x}$ simply denotes the n-dimensional array $(x_1, \ldots, x_n)$. (The vectors with which one deals in elementary mechanics are of course special cases of these more abstract vectors.) A necessary condition for a minimum is now that

$$\frac{\partial f}{\partial x_1} = 0, \frac{\partial f}{\partial x_2} = 0, \ldots, \frac{\partial f}{\partial x_n} = 0$$

Again, if $f(\mathbf{x})$ is a convex function any point where all these partial derivatives vanish must be a minimum. A convex function of a vector is defined in the same way as a convex function of a scalar quantity; the definition can be written in elementary terms as follows—

$$f[x_1 + \theta(y_1 - x_1), \ldots, x_n + \theta(y_n - x_n)] \leqslant$$
$$f(x_1, \ldots, x_n) + \theta[f(y_1, \ldots, y_n) - f(x_1, \ldots, x_n)]$$

for any values of $x_1, \ldots, x_n, y_1, \ldots, y_n$ and such that $0 < \theta < 1$.

Again, the function is strictly convex if the $\leqslant$ sign can be replaced by a $<$ sign.

The problem becomes a little more difficult if one has to consider *equality constraints*. Suppose we wish to find the values of $x_1, \ldots, x_n$ minimizing $f(x_1, \ldots, x_n)$ subject to the constraints that $g_i(x_1, \ldots, x_n) = b_i$ for $i = 1, \ldots, m$. One may be able to overcome the problem by using the constraints to solve for m of the variables in terms of the others, but sometimes this is not convenient. We can then solve the problem by using *Lagrange multipliers*, as follows.

Since each function $g_i(\mathbf{x})$ must equal b_i, the problem is unaffected if we replace the objective function $f(\mathbf{x})$ to be minimized, by

$$F(\mathbf{x}) = f(\mathbf{x}) + \sum_{i=1}^{m} \pi_i[g_i(\mathbf{x}) - b_i]$$

for any values of the quantities $\pi_1, \ldots, \pi_m$, which are known as Lagrange multipliers. On the other hand if we can find values of $\pi_1, \ldots, \pi_m$ such that the point $\mathbf{x}$ where $F(\mathbf{x})$ is minimized happens to satisfy all the constraints $g_i(\mathbf{x}) = b_i$, then our problem is solved. The method of Lagrange multipliers therefore consists of finding values of $\pi_1, \ldots, \pi_m, x_1, \ldots, x_n$ such that

$$\frac{\partial f}{\partial x_j} + \sum_{i=1}^{m} \pi_i \frac{\partial g_i}{\partial x_j} = 0 \qquad (j = 1, \ldots, n)$$

$$g_i(x_1, \ldots, x_n) = b_i \qquad (i = 1, \ldots, m)$$

Note that if we were to increase some b_i by an arbitrarily small quantity Δb_i we would decrease $F(\mathbf{x})$ by $\pi_i \Delta b_i$. If we regard the minimum value of the objective function as a function of $(b_1, \ldots, b_m)$, the right hand sides of the constraints, then the Lagrange multipliers are the negatives of the partial derivatives of the objective function with respect to each right hand side element.

Lagrange multipliers can be generalized to apply to inequality constraints $g_i(\mathbf{x}) \leqslant b_i$. To see intuitively how this works, it is perhaps easiest to think again of functions of a single variable. We know that the minimum of some function $f(x)$ subject to the constraint $x \leqslant b$ will be attained *either* when $df/dx = 0$, *or* when $df/dx < 0$ and $x = b$. This can be expressed by the conditions $df/dx + \pi = 0$, $\pi \geqslant 0$ and $\pi(x - b) = 0$. The corresponding condition on the Lagrange multiplier π_i when the constraint $g_i(\mathbf{x}) = b_i$ is replaced by $g_i(\mathbf{x}) \leqslant b_i$ is that either $\pi_i = 0$ or $\pi_i > 0$ and $g_i(\mathbf{x}) = b_i$, i.e. that $\pi_i(g_i(\mathbf{x}) - b_i) = 0$.

If all the constraints are of the form $g_i(\mathbf{x}) \leqslant b_i$, and the functions $g_i(\mathbf{x})$ are all convex and differentiable, we obtain the famous *Kuhn-Tucker conditions* (see Kuhn and Tucker (1951)) to the effect that $\mathbf{x} = (x_1, \ldots x_n)$ minimizes $f(\mathbf{x})$ subject to the constraints if and only if there exist values of $\pi_1, \ldots, \pi_m$ such that

$$\frac{\partial f}{\partial x_j} + \sum_{i=1}^{m} \pi_i \frac{\partial g_i}{\partial x_j} = 0 \qquad (j = 1, \ldots, n)$$

$$g_i(\mathbf{x}) \leqslant b_i \qquad (i = 1, \ldots, m)$$

$$\pi_i \geqslant 0 \qquad (i = 1, \ldots, m)$$

$$\sum_{i=1}^{m} \pi_i(g_i(\mathbf{x}) - b_i) = 0$$

Actually this theorem requires a *constraint qualification* to exclude some pathological situations. Perhaps the easiest way to express this constraint qualification is to say that there must exist some point $\mathbf{x}$ where all the constraints are satisfied and $g_i(\mathbf{x})$ is strictly less than b_i for all i such that the function $g_i(\mathbf{x})$ is non-linear. (Note that this does not exclude problems where some linear constraints can only be satisfied as equalities.)

It is clear that the Kuhn-Tucker conditions are necessary conditions for a local minimum even for problems lacking the convexity properties needed to ensure a global minimum.

Note that the Kuhn-Tucker conditions can be interpreted as conditions on the direction of the gradient of the objective function at the minimum. For an unconstrained problem the gradient must vanish. When there are equality constraints the gradient does not necessarily vanish, but it must be representable as a linear combination of the normals to the constraints. The same applies to inequality constraints, except that if there is a component parallel to the normal to such a constraint it must be pointing inward and not outward, and the constraint must be *active*, i.e. satisfied as an equality at the point under consideration.

12.2 Conditions for Quadratic Optimization

A great deal has been written about *quadratic programming*. This is the name given to the problem of minimizing a quadratic function of variables subject to linear constraints. This is the subject of the next chapter, but it is convenient to relate it here to the Kuhn-Tucker conditions. If we wish to minimize

$$f(\mathbf{x}) = \sum_j c_j x_j + \frac{1}{2}\sum_j \sum_k d_{jk} x_j x_k$$

where $d_{kj} = d_{jk}$ and the constraints are written

$$x_j \geqslant 0 \qquad (j = 1, \ldots, n)$$

$$\sum_j a_{ij} x_j = b_i \qquad (i = 1, \ldots, m)$$

then the Kuhn-Tucker conditions become the $m + n$ linear equations

$$\sum_k d_{jk} x_k + \sum_i a_{ij} \pi_i - y_j = -c_j \qquad (j = 1, \ldots, n)$$

$$\sum_j a_{ij} x_j = b_i \qquad (i = 1, \ldots, m)$$

where the variables π_i $(i = 1, \ldots, n)$ are the Lagrange multipliers associated with the equality constraints, which are not sign-restricted; and the y_j $(j = 1, \ldots, n)$ are the Lagrange multipliers associated with the requirements that the x_j must be non-negative. The y_j must also be non-negative and satisfy the complementarity condition $\sum_j x_j y_j = 0$.

As a footnote, these equations can be expressed more compactly in matrix notation. If $f(\mathbf{x}) = \mathbf{c}'\mathbf{x} + \frac{1}{2}\mathbf{x}'\mathbf{D}\mathbf{x}$, $\mathbf{A}\mathbf{x} = \mathbf{b}$, $\mathbf{x} \geqslant 0$, the Kuhn-Tucker conditions are

$$\mathbf{D}\mathbf{x} + \mathbf{A}'\boldsymbol{\pi} - \mathbf{y} = -\mathbf{c}$$

$$\mathbf{A}\mathbf{x} = \mathbf{b}$$

Many algorithms for quadratic programming have been published based on a more or less direct solution of these equations. The best known of these, due to Wolfe (1959), amounts computationally to a simple modification of the artificial variable technique for finding a first feasible solution to a linear programming problem. We add an artificial variable with the appropriate sign to each of the $m + n$ Kuhn-Tucker conditions, and then use the ordinary simplex method to minimize the sum of infeasibilities with one additional rule: if x_j is basic then y_j is not eligible to enter at this iteration, and similarly if y_j is basic then x_j is not eligible. (The first m iterations can be used to bring the π_i into the basis, where they will stay since they are not sign-restricted.) This algorithm is obviously finite, since it is the ordinary simplex method with extra restrictions that could cause it to terminate earlier. But Wolfe showed that if the matrix **D** of coefficients (d_{jk}) is *positive definite*, i.e. if the objective function is strictly convex, the algorithm must lead to a solution with the objective function equal to zero, i.e. to the true solution of the problem.

Dantzig (1963) has developed a slightly more compact version of the algorithms that works rather faster if **D** is either positive definite or semi-definite, but that may not terminate at all if it is indefinite.

13 Quadratic Programming

13.1 Introduction

Quadratic programming is the name given to the problem of finding a minimum, or at least a local minimum, of a quadratic function of variables subject to linear inequality constraints. Mathematically this is a natural first extension beyond the realm of purely linear programming, and one of many methods for solving the problem was outlined in Chapter 12. This chapter is devoted to a single method, known as Beale's method. The method was originally published in Beale (1955). Further work on it is reported in Beale (1959), and a more complete account is given in Beale (1967). The method has two important advantages over other methods—

(1) As implemented in the C-E-I-R mathematical programming system LP/90/94, it imposes no real limit on the total number of variables in the problem, provided that the number of variables entering the quadratic part of the objective function is not more than a few hundred. So in this respect there is no difference between quadratic and linear programming problems.
(2) If the objective function is not convex, the method will give a local optimum, although this may not be a global optimum.

Perhaps the most used application of quadratic programming is with problems that would be linear programming problems except that the coefficients in the objective function have to be treated as random variables. One may then choose to minimize the variance of this function, subject to the constraint that the mean is at least equal to some prescribed value, together with any other constraints that may be imposed on the problem. One can then map out the solution for a range of values of the mean. In principle this mean and variance approach seems appropriate to a variety of problems, but the only one to which I know it has been applied in practice is to the study of portfolios of stock-exchange investments. This work was pioneered by H. M. Markowitz (1959).

Quadratic programming is also applicable to the problem of fitting a linear model to numerical data by the method of least squares when there are inequality constraints on the values of the parameters. In particular some parameters may be required to take non-negative values.

It also arises in some problems in mechanics and in electrical engineering.

More generally, it may be appropriate to make a local quadratic programming approximation to a general non-linear programming problem. If so, it is important to take account of the non-linearities in any active constraints. This can be done using the shadow prices; the details are given for example in Beale (1967).

13.2 The Simplex Method

The simplex method will now be reviewed in a way that covers its application to Beale quadratic programming. Since the constraints are all linear, we can select basic variables and solve for these in terms of the remaining, non-basic, variables in the usual way. Leaving the objective function aside for the moment, the constraints can then be expressed in tableau form as follows—

$$X_i = \bar{a}_{i0} + \sum_j \bar{a}_{ij}(-z_j)$$

where the X_i represent m of the variables x_j. In this equation the symbol z_j is used for a typical non-basic variable, rather than x_j, because we shall later consider the introduction of additional non-basic variables that are not original variables of the problem.

We may assume that the $\bar{a}_{i0}$ are all non-negative—otherwise our trial solution (obtained by putting all the non-basic variables equal to zero) is infeasible. The problem of finding a basic feasible trial solution is the same in linear and quadratic programming, since the ultimate objective function is irrelevant at this stage.

We can now use the equations for the basic variables to express the objective function C, which we are minimizing, in terms of the non-basic variables. We can then consider the partial derivative of C with respect to any one of them, say z_q, assuming that the other non-basic variables remain fixed and equal to zero.

If now $\partial C/\partial z_q > 0$, then a small increase in z_q, with the other non-basic variables held equal to zero, will not reduce C; but if $\partial C/\partial z_q < 0$, then a small increase in z_q will reduce C. If C is any linear or non-linear function with continuous derivatives, then it will be profitable to go on increasing z_q until either

(*a*) one has to stop to avoid making some basic variable, say X_p, negative, or

(*b*) $\partial C/\partial z_q$ vanishes and is about to become positive.

In case (*a*), which is the only possible case when C is linear, we change the basis by making X_p non-basic instead of z_q, using the equation

$$X_p = \bar{a}_{p0} + \sum \bar{a}_{pj}(-z_j)$$

to substitute for z_q in terms of X_p and the remaining non-basic variables throughout the constraints and also the expression for C.

In case (*b*) we are in trouble if C is an arbitrary function; but if C is a quadratic function, then $\partial C/\partial z_p$ is a linear function of the non-basic variables.

The form of the expression for C is the primary difference between the first, or theoretical, and the second, or practical, version of the method. The theoretically simplest way to express C is as a symmetric matrix $(\bar{c}_{jk})$ for $j, k = 0, 1, \ldots$, such that

$$C = \sum \sum \bar{c}_{jk} z_j z_k$$

where $z_0 = 1$ and $z_1, \ldots$ denote the non-basic variables. Then

$$\frac{1}{2}\frac{\partial C}{\partial z_q} = \bar{c}_{q0} + \sum \bar{c}_{qk} z_k$$

and if this quantity becomes positive as z_q is increased (keeping the other non-basic variables equal to zero) before any basic variable goes negative, then we define a new variable

$$u_t = \bar{c}_{q0} + \sum \bar{c}_{qk} z_k$$

(where the subscript t simply indicates that this is the tth such variable introduced into the problem). We then make u_t non-basic, using the above equation to substitute for z_q in terms of u_t and the other non-basic variables throughout the constraints and the expression for C.

Note that if z_q is an x-variable, then there will be one more basic x-variable after this iteration than there was before.

The mechanics for substituting for z_q in the expression for C will be discussed later. Let us first consider the theory of the procedure in a little more detail.

Note that u_t is not restricted to non-negative values. It is therefore called a free variable, to contrast it with the original x-variables which are called restricted variables. But there is no objection to having a free non-basic variable. One simply has to remember that if $\partial C/\partial u_t > 0$, then C can be reduced by making u_t negative (or alternatively by replacing u_t by the variable $v_t = -u_t$ and increasing v_t in the usual way). In fact $\partial C/\partial u_t$ will remain equal to zero until another x-variable becomes non-basic. At this stage all previously defined non-basic free variables are made basic in turn, being either increased or decreased so as not to increase C. When a free variable is removed from the set of non-basic variables we can forget about it. There are only two reasons for keeping track of the expressions for the basic variables: one is to know their values in the final solution, but the more important reason is to prevent such a variable from surreptitiously becoming negative. Neither reason applies to these free variables.

There remains the problem of justifying this particular choice of free variable to be made non-basic. It is obviously convenient to have a set of non-basic variables that all vanish at the trial solution, since the values of the basic variables are then simply given as the constant terms in the tableau, but many other expressions would achieve this.

The mathematically correct way to express this justification is to say that the new variable is chosen so that the direction defined by increasing it and keeping the other non-basic variables constant is conjugate (with respect to the quadratic objective function) to any direction defined by changing some other non-basic variable and keeping the new variable constant. In other words we try to choose the new variable u_t so that it will not be profitable to change its value when we change the values of any other non-basic variables. It is shown in any of the references to this method that we succeed in this objective until some other x-variable becomes non-basic. It is also shown that the method terminates in a finite number of steps.

13.3 Up-dating the Tableau

A few words should be said about up-dating the tableau from one iteration to the next. The expressions for the constraints are handled exactly as in linear programming, but the objective function must also be considered. This is handled very differently in the theoretical and practical versions of the method; but it seems worth saying a little more about the theoretical version, since this is convenient for doing small-scale examples by hand.

The essential problem can be formulated algebraically as follows. Given the expression

$$C = \sum \sum \bar{c}_{jk} z_j z_k$$

and given the transformed pivotal row, in the form

$$z_q = e_0 + e_q N + \sum_{k \neq p} e_k z_k$$

substitute for z_q in terms of N (the new non-basic variable, which is not present in the given expression for C) and the other non-basic variables.

The new expression can be written as

$$C = \sum \sum \bar{c}'_{jk} z_j z_k$$

where $\bar{c}'_{qq}$ denotes the coefficient of N^2, and $\bar{c}'_{qj} = \bar{c}'_{jq}$, the coefficient of $2Nz_j$, so that the variable N has replaced z_q. We then find that the $\bar{c}'_{jk}$ are given in terms of the $\bar{c}_{jk}$ and the e_k by the formulae

$$\bar{c}'_{qq} = \bar{c}_{qq} e_q^2$$

$$\bar{c}'_{jq} = \bar{c}'_{qj} = \bar{c}_{jq} e_q + \bar{c}_{qq} e_q e_j$$

$$\bar{c}'_{jk} = \bar{c}_{jk} + \bar{c}_{jq} e_k + \bar{c}_{qk} e_j + \bar{c}_{qq} e_j e_k$$

where $j, k \neq q$.

These formulae simplify if we write

$$c_q^* = \tfrac{1}{2} \bar{c}_{qq} e_q$$

$$c_j^* = \bar{c}_{jq} + \tfrac{1}{2} \bar{c}_{qq} e_j \qquad (j \neq q)$$

for we then have

$$\bar{c}'_{qq} = 2c_q^* e_q$$

$$\bar{c}'_{jq} = \bar{c}'_{qj} = c_j^* e_q + c_q^* e_j$$

$$\bar{c}'_{jk} = \bar{c}_{jk} + c_j^* e_k + c_k^* e_j$$

13.4 A Numerical Example

The process will now be illustrated using the numerical example given in Beale (1959). The details of the working are slightly different from those given in that paper, since the quantities c_j^* were not used at that time.

Suppose that we want to minimize

$$C = 6 - 6x_1 + 2x_1^2 - 2x_1 x_2 + 2x_2^2$$

subject to the constraints

$$x_1 \geqslant 0, \ x_2 \geqslant 0, \ x_1 + x_2 \leqslant 2$$

Introducing x_3 as a slack variable, and making it basic in our initial tableau we can write the problem in the form

$$\begin{aligned} x_3 &= 2 + 1(-x_1) + 1(-x_2) \\ C &= 6 - 3x_1 \\ &\quad + (-3 + 2x_1 - x_2)x_1 \\ &\quad + (- x_1 + 2x_2)x_2 \end{aligned}$$

This method of displaying the objective function shows the coefficients $\bar{c}_{jk}$, and can also be read as an intelligible equation.

We see that $\frac{1}{2}\,\partial C/\partial x_1 = -3$, so we increase x_1. This remains possible as far as the only basic variable x_3 is concerned until $x_1 = 2$, and at this stage $\frac{1}{2}\,\partial C/\partial x_1 = -3 + 2 \times 2 = +1$, so our first new non-basic variable is a free variable u_1, defined by

$$u_1 = -3 + 2x_1 - x_2$$

i.e. $x_1 = \frac{3}{2} + \frac{1}{2}u_1 + \frac{1}{2}x_2$

Hence

$$q = 1, \quad e_0 = \tfrac{3}{2}, \quad e_1 = \tfrac{1}{2}, \quad e_2 = +\tfrac{1}{2},$$

$$\tfrac{1}{2}\bar{c}_{qq} = 1, \quad c_0^* = -\tfrac{3}{2}, \quad c_1^* = \tfrac{1}{2}, \quad c_2^* = -\tfrac{1}{2}$$

and the new tableau reads

$$\begin{aligned} x_1 &= \tfrac{3}{2} - \tfrac{1}{2}(-u_1) - \tfrac{1}{2}(-x_2) \\ x_3 &= \tfrac{1}{2} + \tfrac{1}{2}(-u_1) + \tfrac{3}{2}(-x_2) \\ C &= (\tfrac{3}{2} - \tfrac{3}{2}x_2) \\ &\quad + (\tfrac{1}{2}u_1)u_1 \\ &\quad + (-\tfrac{3}{2} + \tfrac{3}{2}x_2)x_2 \end{aligned}$$

We now see that $\frac{1}{2}\,\partial C/\partial x_2 = -\frac{3}{2}$, so we increase x_2. This remains possible until $x_2 = \frac{1}{3}$, and at this stage

$$\tfrac{1}{2}\,\partial C/\partial x_2 = -\tfrac{3}{2} + \tfrac{3}{2} \times \tfrac{1}{3} = -1$$

so our next non-basic variable is x_3.

The transformed pivotal row then reads

$$x_2 = \tfrac{1}{3} - \tfrac{1}{3}u_1 - \tfrac{2}{3}x_3$$

Hence

$$q = 2, \quad e_0 = \tfrac{1}{3}, \quad e_1 = -\tfrac{1}{3}, \quad e_2 = -\tfrac{2}{3},$$

$$\tfrac{1}{2}\bar{c}_{qq} = \tfrac{3}{4}, \quad c_0^* = -\tfrac{5}{4}, \quad c_1^* = -\tfrac{1}{4}, \quad c_2^* = -\tfrac{1}{2}$$

and the new tableau reads

$$\begin{aligned}
x_1 &= \tfrac{5}{3} - \tfrac{1}{3}(-u_1) + \tfrac{1}{3}(-x_3) \\
x_2 &= \tfrac{1}{3} + \tfrac{1}{3}(-u_1) + \tfrac{2}{3}(-x_3) \\
C &= (\tfrac{2}{3} + \tfrac{1}{3}u_1 + \tfrac{2}{3}x_3) \\
&\quad + (+\tfrac{1}{3} + \tfrac{2}{3}u_1 + \tfrac{1}{3}x_3)u_1 \\
&\quad + (+\tfrac{2}{3} + \tfrac{1}{3}u_1 + \tfrac{2}{3}x_3)x_3
\end{aligned}$$

Since we have made an x-variable non-basic, we must make u_1 basic. Since $\partial C/\partial u_1 > 0$ we decrease u_1. This is possible until $u_1 = -5$, when $\frac{1}{2}\,\partial C/\partial u_1 = \frac{1}{3} - 10/3 = -3$, so our next non-basic variable is a free variable u_2, defined by

$$u_2 = \tfrac{1}{3} + \tfrac{2}{3}u_1 + \tfrac{1}{3}x_3$$

i.e.

$$u_1 = -\tfrac{1}{2} + \tfrac{3}{2}u_2 - \tfrac{1}{2}x_3$$

Hence

$$q = 1, \qquad e_0 = -\tfrac{1}{2}, \qquad e_1 = \tfrac{3}{2}, \qquad e_2 = -\tfrac{1}{2}$$

$$\tfrac{1}{2}\bar{c}_{qq} = \tfrac{1}{3}, \qquad c_0^* = \tfrac{1}{6}, \qquad c_1^* = \tfrac{1}{2}, \qquad c_2^* = \tfrac{1}{6}$$

and the new tableau reads

$$\begin{aligned}
x_1 &= \tfrac{3}{2} - \tfrac{1}{2}(-u_2) + \tfrac{1}{2}(-x_3) \\
x_2 &= \tfrac{1}{2} + \tfrac{1}{2}(-u_2) + \tfrac{1}{2}(-x_3) \\
C &= (\tfrac{1}{2} \qquad\qquad + \tfrac{1}{2}x_3) \\
&\quad + (\qquad + \tfrac{3}{2}u_2 \qquad\qquad)u_2 \\
&\quad + (+\tfrac{1}{2} \qquad\qquad + \tfrac{1}{2}x_3)x_3
\end{aligned}$$

This is the final tableau. The solution is

$$x_1 = \tfrac{3}{2}, \qquad x_2 = \tfrac{1}{2}, \qquad C = \tfrac{1}{2}$$

The steps towards the solution are illustrated in Fig. 13.1. The feasible region consists of the triangle ABC. The contours of constant value of the objective function are ellipses centred at the point $x_1 = 2$, $x_2 = 1$—two such ellipses are shown as broken lines. The first trial solution was at the point A, with x_1 and x_2 as non-basic variables. We found it profitable to increase x_1, moving towards B, but it was not profitable to proceed all the way to B. We therefore stopped at D which is where C is minimized conditional on x_2 taking some prescribed value—geometrically $u_1 = 0$ is the set of points at

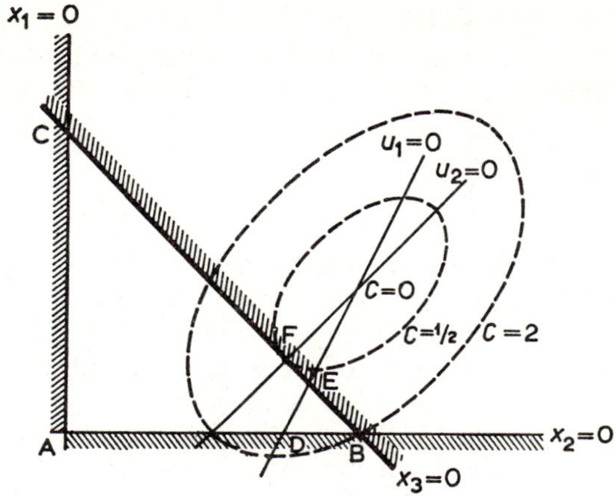

Figure 13.1

which the contours of constant values of C have horizontal tangents. We next found it expedient to increase x_2 keeping $u_1 = 0$, and if it had not been for the constraint that $x_3 \geqslant 0$ we would have reached the final solution at the centre of the system of ellipses at this iteration. In fact we are stopped at the point E by the basic variable x_3 becoming zero. At this stage we must remove the free variable u_1 from the set of basic variables—we are no longer interested in horizontal tangents. We find we can reduce C by decreasing u_1, moving to the point F where C is minimized conditional on x_3 being equal to zero, and we introduce the new non-basic variable u_2 that is equal to zero at all points where C is minimized conditional on x_3 taking some prescribed value. This is the final solution.

13.5 The Practical Version of the Method

The theoretical version of the method outlined above suffers from the disadvantage that the number of coefficients needed to represent the quadratic part of the objective function is of the order of the square of the number of non-basic variables. In practice this means using as many rows as there are non-basic variables. Even if the quadratic part of the objective function consisted of a single term, say x_1^2, this would blow up into a complicated expression if x_1 became basic, and the expression for x_1 in terms of the non-basic variables had many non-zero coefficients.

This disadvantage is overcome by representing C in a more compact form, from which the required coefficients from the theoretical version can be computed as required. This exploits the same philosophy as that represented by the inverse matrix method, and a vital feature of this approach is that it combines very conveniently with the product form of inverse method of carrying out the computations.

The method used to represent C is as a linear term plus or minus sums of squares, i.e.

$$C = -\lambda_0 + \frac{1}{2}\sum_{i=1}^{r} s_i\lambda_i^2$$

where $s_i = \pm 1$ and the λ_i are linear functions of the original variables of the problem, which can be updated in terms of the current non-basic variables from one iteration to the next. The index r need never be more than the rank of the matrix of quadratic coefficients, and in particular this cannot exceed the number of variables involved in the quadratic terms. If the objective function is given as a general quadratic expression, it is a straightforward matter to reduce it to a sum of squares. For if $C = \sum\sum c_{jk}z_jz_k$, where $c_{11} > 0$ it is easy to see that

$$C = \tfrac{1}{2}\lambda_1^2 + C_1$$

where

$$\lambda_1 = (\tfrac{1}{2}c_{11})^{-\frac{1}{2}}\sum c_{1k}z_k$$

and C_1 does not involve z_1, i.e. it contains at least one fewer variables than C. Methods of dealing with problems where c_{11} is not positive are described for example in Beale (1967).

In a computer code there is of course the problem of indicating how many rows represent quadratic components of the objective function, and which sign should be associated with each. In the LP/90/94 system the quadratic rows must come immediately after the linear objective functions (which in turn come at the top of the matrix). The quadratic rows are identified by their names. The first character must be an &. The next 4 characters are arbitrary, but the last character must be a + for a convex quadratic term (i.e. if $s_i = +1$) or a− for a concave quadratic term (i.e. if $s_i = -1$).

So much for the problem of defining the objective function. Let us now consider how the computations can be carried out when the objective function is defined in this way.

We must keep track (implicitly or explicitly) of the expressions for the λ_i in terms of the current non-basic variables. So let us write these in the form

$$\lambda_i = d_{i0} + \sum d_{ij}(-z_j)$$

Then

$$\frac{\partial C}{\partial z_q} = \bar{a}_{0q} = d_{0q} + \sum_{i=1}^{r}(-s_i d_{i0} d_{iq})$$

Using the product form of inverse, this is not really any more difficult to calculate than the reduced cost in linear programming. All that happens is that the backward transformation starts with a row vector containing elements $-s_i d_{i0}$ in the positions corresponding to the quadratic rows of the objective function in addition to the unit element in the position corresponding to the linear part of the objective function. The resulting π-vector is then applied to the columns of the original matrix in the usual way to determine the modified reduced costs.

When we have found a non-basic variable z_q to be increased, we must compute the coefficient of z_q^2 in the objective function, in order to decide whether the new non-basic variable is to be an x-variable or a u-variable. This coefficient is given by the expression

$$\bar{c}_{qq} = \frac{1}{2} \sum_{i=1}^{r} s_i d_{iq}^2$$

so if θ denotes the amount by which z_q can be increased without driving any basic x-variable negative, the new variable should be a free variable if and only if

$$\bar{a}_{0q} + 2\bar{c}_{qq}\theta \geqslant 0$$

If a new free variable has to be made non-basic, we must compute the expression for it in terms of the present non-basic variables. This is

$$u_t = \tfrac{1}{2}\bar{a}_{0q} + \sum \bar{c}_{qj} z_j$$

where

$$\bar{c}_{qj} = \frac{1}{2} \sum_{i=1}^{r} s_i d_{iq} d_{ij}$$

Using the product form of inverse, these coefficients are computed by taking a row vector with components d_{iq} in the positions corresponding to the quadratic rows of the objective function, performing a backward transformation to produce a pricing vector, and then multiplying this into each column of the matrix in turn to deduce the coefficient $\bar{c}_{qj}$.

We should perhaps also note that the current value of the objective function is given by

$$-d_{00} + \frac{1}{2} \sum_{i-1}^{r} s_i d_{i0}^2$$

14 Separable Programming

14.1 Introduction

Separable programming (due to Miller (1963)) is probably the most useful non-linear programming technique. It allows one to use non-linear functions of single arguments in either the constraints or the objective function of an otherwise linear programming problem. It is called separable programming because it assumes that all the non-linear expressions in the problem can be separated out into sums and differences of non-linear functions of single arguments. This assumption may seem to severely restrict the usefulness of the method but we shall see later that the restriction is not as severe as one might imagine.

Suppose we have some variable z, and that we want to deal with some function $f(z)$. Suppose that the graph of $f(z)$ looks something like Fig. 14.1. We now replace this function by a piecewise linear approximation based on a finite number of points on the graph. In the diagram I have taken 7 points $P_1, \ldots, P_7$.

Now let the co-ordinates of these points be (a_i, b_i) and introduce 7 new non-negative variables $\lambda_1, \ldots, \lambda_7$, which can be thought of as weights attached to the points $P_1, \ldots, P_7$ respectively, and the equations

$$\lambda_1 + \cdots + \lambda_7 = 1 \tag{14.1}$$

$$a_1\lambda_1 + \cdots + a_7\lambda_7 = z \tag{14.2}$$

$$b_1\lambda_1 + \cdots + b_7\lambda_7 = f(z) \tag{14.3}$$

We call these new variables a single group of *special variables*. The equations (14.1) and (14.2) are known respectively as the *convexity row* and the *reference row* for this group of special variables.

Note that the quantities z and $f(z)$ are not necessarily non-negative, but this causes no trouble—we will not normally want to introduce them explicitly into the mathematical programming model in any case.

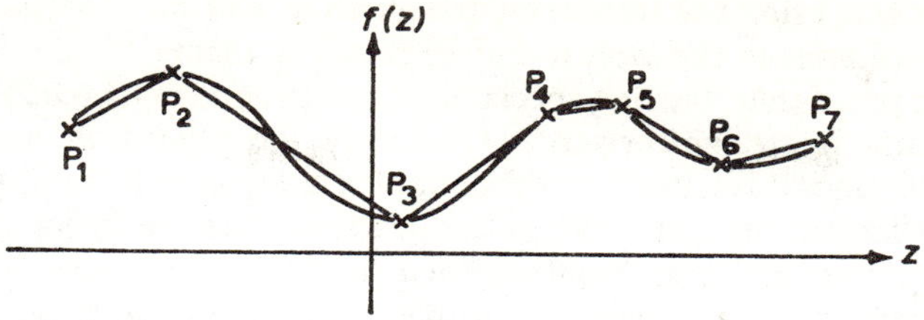

Figure 14.1

It is clear that the vertices of the piecewise linear approximation to $f(z)$ are obtained by putting all but one special variable of the group equal to zero. Any other point on the graph can be obtained by giving 2 neighbouring special variables of the group non-zero values, and putting the others equal to zero. The other sets of values of the special variables may correspond to points off the graph.

Now if $f(z)$ is convex, then non-neighbouring special variables always overestimate it; and this does not matter if $f(z)$ is either part of an objective function to be minimized, or else is on the right hand side of a $\geqslant$ inequality constraint and does not appear elsewhere in the problem. In these circumstances we do not need the special procedures of separable programming, though we may use the interpolation procedures described later in this chapter.

Miller's special contribution was to point out and exploit the fact that the rules of the simplex method can easily be modified to ensure that meaningless sets of values of the special variables cannot occur even if the problem is not convex. In this way one can reach a local optimum, which may possibly not be a global optimum, solution to a non-convex problem. (Actually the point reached may conceivably not even be a local optimum if one is trapped by a phenomenon which Miller called *special degeneracy*. It must be a *virtual local optimum*, i.e. a point that could be turned into a local optimum by arbitrarily small changes in the constant terms of the constraints. This possible difficulty does not need to be taken any more seriously in practice than the risk of cycling in the normal linear programming calculation.)

All we have to do is to restrict the set of variables to be considered as candidates to enter the basis. If two special variables of a group are in the current basis, then we do not consider allowing a third. If one is already in the basis we consider only its neighbours.

Hadley (1964) suggests that one should consider introducing any variable into the basis if it has a suitable reduced cost, and only reject the variable if the resulting basis includes an illegal combination of special variables. This would be an inefficient strategy, particularly if one was using the inverse matrix method and had to up-date all these columns in the tableau before rejecting them.

The proof that, barring special degeneracy, one must reach a local optimum is straightforward. Obviously the algorithm must terminate, since it is a version of the simplex method with the possibility of earlier termination. When it does terminate we know that we have a true optimum solution to a linear programming problem obtained from our original problem by suppressing all special variables other than those in the basis, and their neighbours when they are the only variables of the group in the basis. This is a local optimum if all the basic special variables take positive values—and they can be given positive values by arbitrarily small changes in the right hand sides of the reference rows.

The implementation of separable programming is easy in any mathematical programming code in which the variables are indexed by names—as opposed to serial numbers. For example in the LP/90/94 system, if the program is in the separable mode, then all variables with a 9 as their first character are treated as special ones. The next 3 characters define the group of special variables, and the last 2 are decimal digits defining the sequence of the special variables.

Incidentally, as Miller (1963) points out, one can very easily deal with several different non-linear functions of the same variable in the same problem. One simply writes down an equation of the type (14.3) for each function. And in practice one does not usually have to include these equations explicitly in the model, since the left hand side can be substituted for the right wherever it occurs.

14.2 Product Terms

A number of mathematical programming problems are linear except for the presence of a few product terms.

The price of some commodity may be a linear function of other variables of the problem—such as the quantity bought. The amount spent on this commodity is then the product of the price and the quantity. If this amount enters only into the objective function it may be more convenient to solve the problem by quadratic programming, but if there are other non-linearities it may be more convenient to use separable programming.

In oil production problems, the productivity of a well may be an approximately linear function of variables relating to production from this reservoir in previous years. The production available in the current year is then given by the product of the well productivity and the number of wells drilled. Similar considerations may apply in long-term planning models for other extractive industries.

A typical application of separable programming is described by Beale, Coen and Flowerdew (1965). This relates to the choice of ores for burdening iron-making furnaces. Various raw materials are available at various costs, and they have different physical and chemical properties. So far this looks like a typical application of linear programming, in which the problem is to determine the cheapest combination of raw materials that meet certain specifications on the overall properties of the input material.

But non-linearities arise if some raw material can be fed into a preprocessing unit whose output can then be fed into more than one type of main production unit. In the iron-making application the preprocessor is a sinter plant, which removes some impurities and improves the physical properties of the ore. If the preprocessor has to feed only one type of main unit, then linear methods may still be applicable, but if the preprocessor has to be run in a fixed way to feed several types of main unit, then the problem is apt to be non-linear.

A good way to handle such problems is often to define variables representing the proportion of the output from the preprocessor that is fed to each main unit. The amount of some chemical element in the preprocessed material that is supplied to a main unit is then the product of this new variable and the amount of this element in the output from the preprocessor. This amount is itself linearly related to the inputs to the preprocessor.

So it is important to be able to handle product terms. The expression u_1u_2 is not a non-linear function of a single variable, so it might appear that it was not amenable to separable programming. If that were true, then separable programming would be of very limited value. Fortunately it is not true.

We note that

$$u_1u_2 = \left(\frac{u_1 + u_2}{2}\right)^2 - \left(\frac{u_1 - u_2}{2}\right)^2 \tag{14.4}$$

so we can always express a product of 2 linear variables as a difference between 2 non-linear functions of linear variables. This is a special case of the fact that any quadratic function can be represented as a sum or difference of squares.

Any such function is therefore amenable to separable programming, and we could then handle the product of such a quadratic function with another variable in the same way; so in theory there is no limit to the class of functions that can be represented in this way. In practice of course a very involved representation would be cumbersome computationally.

So we can deal with a simple product term by introducing 2 groups of special variables. This involves 4 extra equations—2 convexity rows to represent the conditions that the sum of the special variables in each group must equal 1, and 2 reference rows to represent the values of the arguments of the non-linear functions in terms of the special variables. These correspond to equations (14.1) and (14.2), in general with some linear combination of the basic variables of the problem substituted for z in (14.2). In practice we will generally not write down an equation corresponding to (14.3) explicitly, since we can substitute the left hand side of this equation for $f(z)$ wherever it occurs.

Another application of separable programming is discussed by Akeroyd (1966). Mylander (1966) has pointed out that this particular problem can be reformulated to avoid all non-linearities; but this does not affect the point of Akeroyd's paper, which is to show that separable programming can deal effectively with many non-linear formulations that might superficially seem beyond the range of linear programming techniques.

14.3 Defining the Ranges of the Variables

The next point to notice is that separable programming only deals with non-linear functions over definite ranges of their arguments. It is clear from equation (14.2) that z cannot be less than a_1 or greater than a_7. Occasionally the fact that the program automatically fixes lower and upper bounds on the argument defining a non-linear function is a useful bonus to the formulator of the problem. More often it is a minor chore to have to fix realistic bounds for these arguments. In this connexion it is often convenient to work with the proportion of something that is obtained or treated in a certain way. This proportion must obviously lie between 0 and 1. And if one has a variable z defined by

$$z = \sum_{i=1}^{n} e_i x_i$$

where the x_i are proportions and are therefore non-negative and sum to 1, then z must lie between the smallest and the largest of the e_i.

When dealing with product terms, it is desirable to define the quantities u_1 and u_2 to which one applies the identity (14.4) so that each lies between 0 and 1. If one has a product term $v_1 v_2$ with arbitrary, but specified, ranges for v_1 and v_2, one can always write

$$v_1 = a_1 + b_1 u_1$$

$$v_2 = a_2 + b_2 u_2$$

where $0 \leqslant u_1 \leqslant 1$ and $0 \leqslant u_2 \leqslant 1$. Then

$$v_1v_2 = a_1a_2 + a_1b_2u_2 + a_2b_1u_1 + b_1b_2u_1u_2$$

i.e.

$$v_1v_2 = -a_1a_2 + a_2v_1 + a_1v_2 + f_1(z_1) + f_2(z_2)$$

where

$$f_1(z_1) = b_1b_2z_1^2, \quad f_2(z_2) = -b_1b_2z_2^2$$

and

$$z_1 = 0{\cdot}5(-a_1b_1^{-1} - a_2b_2^{-1} + b_1^{-1}v_1 + b_2^{-1}v_2)$$

$$z_2 = 0{\cdot}5(-a_1b_1^{-1} + a_2b_2^{-1} + b_1^{-1}v_1 - b_2^{-1}v_2)$$

so that $0 \leqslant z_1 \leqslant 1$, $-\frac{1}{2} \leqslant z_2 \leqslant \frac{1}{2}$.

14.4 Defining the Grid

Just one further decision has to be taken; how fine a grid of points do we need to represent our non-linear function? As a rough rule I recommend taking between 4 and 6 points on each curve, on the grounds that the running time on the computer is apt to increase quite sharply if one seeks more accuracy by reducing the spacing of the points much further. This decision is obviously easier to make if one has a facility for automatically interpolating extra points in relevant parts of the range on each curve. The C-E-I-R interpolation scheme is described below. It is based on the assumption that each non-linear function $f(z)$ can be adequately approximated by a cubic function of z between any 4 neighbouring grid points on the graph, and by a quadratic between the first 3 and the last 3 points. Note that the grid points need not be evenly spaced. Note also that one may have a choice of which row to make the reference row for a group of special variables. For example one might want to define a quantity z as a linear function of other variables and to use $\sqrt{z}$ in some constraint. We can make our interpolations exact by making the constraint involving $\sqrt{z}$ the reference row, i.e. regarding $w = \sqrt{z}$ as the argument and w^2 as the non-linear function. Similarly when working with logarithms it is probably better to regard the logarithm as the argument and take its exponential as the dependent variable.

14.5 Interpolation

It has been pointed out by Miller (1963) that separable programming problems are liable to take as much as 4 times as long to run as ordinary linear programming problems of the same size. This is because of the need to creep round the curves defining the non-linear functions. This difficulty can be mitigated by starting with a coarse grid and interpolating extra points in the relevant parts of the curves. For practical reasons it would be undesirable to have to refer back to the original formation of the problem to carry out this interpolation but this is not necessary.

As an example of what can be done, let us consider the C-E-I-R agendum INTERPOLATE in some detail. The agendum INTERPOLATE, *n* can be called any time; but it is normally called after reaching an optimum solution to the problem with the original grid. The matrix tape is then scanned until a group of variables with a name beginning with a 9 is reached. If any interpolation is required, the reference row will have the same name as the variables of the group, except for the last 2 characters, which will be **. If there is no such row name, or if no variables of the group are in the basis, then no action is taken with this group of variables. But if there is just one variable of the group in the basis, say the ith, then the program inserts n equally spaced new variables between the $(i - 1)$th and the ith point, and a further n equally spaced new variables between the ith and the $(i + 1)$th point (unless the ith point is an end point, in which case the points that would have to be extrapolated are suppressed). If there are 2 adjacent special variables of the group in the basis, the program inserts n equally spaced new variables between them. If for any reason the basis contains non-adjacent special variables in the group, or variables at negative levels, then the program does no interpolation for this group but selects two suitable adjacent variables of the group to enter the basis. Any others are replaced by artificials.

When the interpolations have been carried out, the special variables are renumbered so that the previous basis represents the best estimate of the corresponding basis of the interpolated problem. The program then re-inverts the new problem to this basis, and automatically enters the agendum NORMAL to re-optimize. Because of this re-numbering, and the fact that variables with indices outside the range 00 to 99 are suppressed, it is best to give the original special variables indices between 40 and 60. (They may start anywhere, as long as they are consecutive.)

When interpolating, the entries in the reference row are linearly interpolated with equal spacing. The formulae for the entries in the other rows are as follows. Let the entries in the reference row at points P_{i-1}, P_i, P_{i+1} and P_{i+2} be r_{-1}, r_0, r_1 and r_2, and let the corresponding entries in any other row be s_{-1}, s_0, s_1 and s_2. We define the two ratios

$$\mu_{-1} = (r_{-1} - r_0)/(r_1 - r_0) \quad \text{and} \quad \mu_2 = (r_2 - r_0)/(r_1 - r_0)$$

Then a new element in the row in which we are interpolating at a fraction f of the distance from P_i to P_{i+1} is

$$a_0 + a_1 f + a_2 f^2 + a_3 f^3$$

where

$$a_0 = s_0$$

$$a_1 = \mu_2 t_{-1} + (\mu_{-1} + \mu_2 + \mu_{-1}\mu_2)t_0 + \mu_{-1}\mu_2 t_1 + \mu_{-1} t_2$$

$$a_2 = -(1 + \mu_2)t_{-1} - (1 + \mu_{-1} + \mu_2)t_0 - (\mu_{-1} + \mu_2)t_1 - (1 + \mu_{-1})t_2$$

$$a_3 = t_{-1} + t_0 + t_1 + t_2$$

and

$$t_{-1} = s_{-1}/\mu_{-1}(\mu_{-1} - 1)(\mu_{-1} - \mu_2)$$

$$t_0 = -s_0/\mu_{-1}\mu_2$$

$$t_1 = s_1/(1 - \mu_{-1})(1 - \mu_2)$$

$$t_2 = s_2/(\mu_2 - \mu_{-1})\mu_2(\mu_2 - 1)$$

Similarly if P_{i+2} is undefined, the new element is $a_0 + a_1 f + a_2 f^2$, where

$$a_0 = s_0$$

$$a_1 = -t_{-1} - (1 + \mu_{-1})t_0 - \mu_{-1} t_1$$

$$a_2 = t_{-1} + t_0 + t_1$$

and

$$t_{-1} = s_{-1}/\mu_{-1}(\mu_{-1} - 1)$$

$$t_0 = +s_0/\mu_{-1}$$

$$t_1 = s_1/(1 - \mu_{-1})$$

Note that after an interpolation, the program may decide that the solution lies in a quite different part of the curve. It would be rather undesirable to have a very fine grid of points in an irrelevant part of the curve, so it is usual to restrict the parameter n to a value of 3 or 4, and to perform 3 or more successive interpolations, re-optimizing after each one.

14.6 An Example of Separable Programming Formulation

Some problems are formulated naturally in terms of non-linear functions over finite ranges of single arguments. The separable programming formulation is then straightforward.

Some of the detailed considerations involved in setting up a more complicated separable programming application can be illustrated by considering the problem of planning the development of a number of oil reservoirs over a number of years. We assume that a target total production has been fixed for the group of reservoirs as a whole for each year, and we have to decide how to meet it. The variables of the problem will represent such things as

the amount of oil to be produced at each reservoir
the amount of oil to be sent from each reservoir to each terminal
the number of wells to drill at each reservoir
the amount of additional capacity to install in the surface facilities at each reservoir
the amount of additional pipeline capacity to install from each reservoir to each terminal.

The constraints are all linear and present no difficulty except for the constraints defining well productivities. For each reservoir in each year of the program we will have a constraint of the form

$$q_t \leqslant p_t n_t \tag{14.5}$$

where q_t denotes the production for the year

p_t dneotes the average well productivity
n_t denotes the number of producing wells.

We can write

$$n_t = w_0 + \sum_{s=1}^{t-1} w_s \tag{14.6}$$

where w_0 is the number of wells available at the start of the program and w_s is the number drilled in the *s*th year.

We also need a formula to represent the way the well productivity depends on previous production at the reservoir. We may be able to approximate this by the formula

$$p_t = a\left(1 - b\sum_{s=1}^{t} q_s\right) \tag{14.7}$$

where a represents the initial well productivity, and $1/b$ represents the ultimate potential cumulative production from the reservoir.

So (14.5) represents a product of two terms that are both variable, and we must decide precisely how to express this in our mathematical programming matrix.

Our first task is to fix bounds on these 2 terms. We note that p_t must lie between 0 and a, and n_t must be between w_0 and $w_0 + W_{\text{max}}$, where W_{max} is the maximum number of new wells that we might consider drilling.

So we can now re-write (14.5) as

$$q_t \leqslant aw_0u_t + aW_{\max}u_tv_t \tag{14.8}$$

where

$$u_t = 1 - b\sum_{s=1}^{t} q_s \tag{14.9}$$

$$v_t = \frac{1}{W_{\max}}\sum_{s=1}^{t-1} w_s \tag{14.10}$$

and we know that $0 \leqslant u_t \leqslant 1$, $0 \leqslant v_t \leqslant 1$.

We now apply the identity (14.4), and (14.8) becomes

$$q_t \leqslant aw_0u_t + aW_{\max}z_{1t}^2 - aW_{\max}z_{2t}^2 \tag{14.11}$$

where

$$z_{1t} = \tfrac{1}{2}(u_t + v_t) \tag{14.12}$$

$$z_{2t} = \tfrac{1}{2}(u_t - v_t) \tag{14.13}$$

The quantity z_{1t} lies between 0 and 1, so we may choose 6 special variables $\lambda_{1t}, \ldots, \lambda_{6t}$ representing 6 points on the graph of the function z_{1t}^2 at $z_{1t} = 0{\cdot}0, 0{\cdot}2, 0{\cdot}4, 0{\cdot}6, 0{\cdot}8$ and $1{\cdot}0$. Similarly z_{2t} lies between $-0{\cdot}5$ and $+0{\cdot}5$, so we may choose 6 special variables $\mu_{1t}, \ldots, \mu_{6t}$ representing 6 points on the graph of the function z_{2t}^2 at $z_{2t} = -0{\cdot}5, -0{\cdot}3, -0{\cdot}1, +0{\cdot}1, +0{\cdot}3$, and $+0{\cdot}5$. We then have the approximate equations

$$\begin{aligned} q_t \leqslant aw_0u_t + aW_{\max}\{&0{\cdot}04\lambda_{2t} + 0{\cdot}16\lambda_{3t} + 0{\cdot}36\lambda_{4t} \\ &+ 0{\cdot}64\lambda_{5t} + 1{\cdot}00\lambda_{6t} - 0{\cdot}25\mu_{1t} - 0{\cdot}09\mu_{2t} \\ &- 0{\cdot}01\mu_{3t} - 0{\cdot}01\mu_{4t} - 0{\cdot}09\mu_{5t} - 0{\cdot}25\mu_{6t}\} \end{aligned} \tag{14.14}$$

$$0{\cdot}2\lambda_{2t} + 0{\cdot}4\lambda_{3t} + 0{\cdot}6\lambda_{4t} + 0{\cdot}8\lambda_{5t} + 1{\cdot}0\lambda_{6t} = \tfrac{1}{2}(u_t + v_t) \tag{14.15}$$

$$\lambda_{1t} + \lambda_{2t} + \lambda_{3t} + \lambda_{4t} + \lambda_{5t} + \lambda_{6t} = 1 \tag{14.16}$$

$$\begin{aligned} -0{\cdot}5\mu_{1t} - 0{\cdot}3\mu_{2t} - 0{\cdot}1\mu_{3t} + 0{\cdot}1\mu_{4t} + 0{\cdot}3\mu_{5t} + 0{\cdot}5\mu_{6t} \\ = \tfrac{1}{2}(u_t - v_t) \end{aligned} \tag{14.17}$$

$$\mu_{1t} + \mu_{2t} + \mu_{3t} + \mu_{4t} + \mu_{5t} + \mu_{6t} = 1 \tag{14.18}$$

The constraints that actually appear in the matrix are deduced from (14.14), (14.15), (14.16), (14.17) and (14.18) by substituting for u_t and v_t from (14.9) and (14.10). The one non-linear constraint (14.5) has led to 4 additional rows—2 reference rows (14.15) and (14.17), and 2 convexity rows (14.16) and (14.18).

The arithmetic involved in computing the coefficients of the variables (the q_s, w_s, λ_{it} and μ_{it}) in these constraints would be very tedious without a suitable matrix generator program—but it is not difficult to write such a generator.

14.7 Parametric Separable Programming

Parametric programming—on either the right hand side or the objective function—can be carried out while using separable programming, but it requires one modification to the standard parametric procedures.

When a special variable leaves the basis, the other neighbour of the variable in this group that remains in the basis becomes eligible to enter the basis, and its reduced cost must be examined. If this reduced cost is non-negative then parametric programming can proceed in the usual way. If it is negative it means that one has come to the end of a family of local optima (for changing values of the parameter), and one must re-optimize for the current value of the parameter before continuing with parametric programming.

This feature of parametric programming makes it a useful tool for exploring alternative local optima if one knows enough about the problem to be able to choose appropriate alternative right hand sides.

Note that in parametric programming on the right hand side, the variable to leave the basis in each iteration is chosen first, and may therefore be considered as out of the basis when deciding which special variables are eligible to enter the basis.

14.8 The Limitations of Separable Programming

Separable programming with interpolation is a powerful non-linear programming technique, but it may be appropriate to close this chapter with some remarks about its limitations.

Some problems contain important non-linearities associated with set-up costs. The cost of undertaking an activity at level x may be somewhat as shown in Fig. 14.2. Separable programming can find

Figure 14.2

local optimum solutions to such problems, but these may not be of much interest. Sometimes one can usefully solve these problems not in separable mode, and then call INTERPOLATE (with the parameter $n = 0$) to obtain a good and legal starting point for a separable programming analysis. One may then proceed further and use integer programming to explore other possible combinations of activities. This point is taken up in Chapter 15.

A good quadratic programming code is likely to be more efficient than separable programming when it is applicable, and it avoids the necessity to define the ranges of the variables; but problems with a few quadratic constraints are quite suitable for separable programming.

Separation may not be convenient for some problems. For example, it is unlikely to be feasible to cope with a hundred or more product terms, or with general non-linear functions of several variables that are defined numerically (as opposed to analytically). In these circumstances a technique known as the *method of approximation programming*, due to Griffith and Stewart (1961) is more appropriate. In outline this is a very simple technique: one simply makes linear approximations to all non-linear functions valid in the neighbourhood of one's present trial solution, and fixes bounds on the amounts by which the non-linear variables may move away from their present trial values. In this way one solves a sequence of linear programming problems. It may be better to make local quadratic programming approximations. Such a scheme has been pioneered by Wilson (1963), who has written a FORTRAN program for solving general convex programming problems with not more than 100 variables. This approach is discussed further in Beale (1967).

15 Integer Programming

15.1 Introduction

Integer programming is the name given to the problem of solving linear programming problems when variables have to take integer values. The field is divided into *pure integer programming*, in which all variables have to be integers, and *mixed integer programming*, in which only some variables have to be integers.

The subject may be said to date from 1958, when Ralph Gomory published an outline of his first method for pure integer programming, known as the *method of integer forms*, see Gomory (1958). Since that time many approaches to both pure and mixed integer programming have been proposed. Surveys of this work have been made for example by Beale (1965) and Balinski (1965), and no attempt will be made to review this work as a whole here. After discussing some fields of application of integer programming, we restrict our attention to three methods for which reliable computer codes exist.

15.2 Applications of Integer Programming

There are a great many programming problems in which non-integral values of some or all of the variables are physically meaningless, and it may be worth while to use an integer programming code to make the appropriate adjustments to allow for this. However the most important applications of integer programming would seem to lie elsewhere. Almost any combinatorial problem can be formulated in integer programming terms, though this is probably not useful if it involves more than a few hundred constraints. If one has to choose the most profitable combination of objects satisfying some conditions one may define the variable x_i to denote the probability that the ith object is included. The constraints will often have to be formulated in such a way that they are only meaningful if x_i is either 0 or 1, so the problem must be regarded as one in integer programming. We call an integer variable that must be either 0 or 1 a *zero-one variable*. Such problems are particularly amenable to integer programming if many of the constraints are covering equations representing the fact that a subset of the variables must sum to unity. The most spectacular applications of integer programming have been to aircrew scheduling, where the variables have represented the probability that some crew follows a specified tour of duty, and the constraints represent the fact that each leg of the time-table must be covered—though there are often some additional constraints.

Other problems require more variables: x_{ijt} may represent the probability that event i takes place on machine j in time period t, or that event i immediately precedes event j in time period t. The practicality of such formulations must still be regarded as uncertain, since apparently quite simple problems are apt to involve a fair number of variables and constraints. Some of these constraints are covering equations of the type discussed above, and there is some evidence that these lead to relatively easy integer programming problems.

Another important class of integer programming problems deals with non-convex objective functions, and specifically with fixed charges. Suppose that some activity can be undertaken at any level x between 0 and M, at a cost cx; but suppose that there is an additional fixed charge f associated with any non-zero level of the activity. This situation can be represented by defining a zero-one variable δ representing the probability that the activity is used, so that the cost is represented by $cx + f\delta$, and one has the constraint $x \leqslant M\delta$, so that δ must equal 1 unless $x = 0$.

This can be further generalized to provide a global optimum to problems for which separable programming provides a local optimum, at the expense of a considerable amount of extra computation. Methods of doing this will now be discussed.

15.3 Integer Programming Formulation of Non-linear Functions

There are several ways of representing non-linear functions of a single argument in mixed integer programming terms. Three in particular are worth considering explicitly.

The first method follows the same approach as that used in separable programming, but uses integer variables and some extra constraints to replace the "arbitrary" rules restricting the choice of special variable to enter the basis.

Suppose that the cost $c(z)$ of some activity can be approximated as a function of its level z by a piecewise linear function as indicated in Fig. 15.1.

The curve passes through the points $P_0, P_1, \ldots, P_6$. As in the separable programming formulation we define variables λ_i representing the weights to be attached to the points P_i, and we have the equations

$$\sum \lambda_i = 1 \tag{15.1}$$

$$\sum a_i\lambda_i = z \tag{15.2}$$

$$\sum b_i\lambda_i = c(z) \tag{15.3}$$

where (a_i, b_i) are the co-ordinates of the point P_i. These equations will be treated in the same way as in separable programming, that is

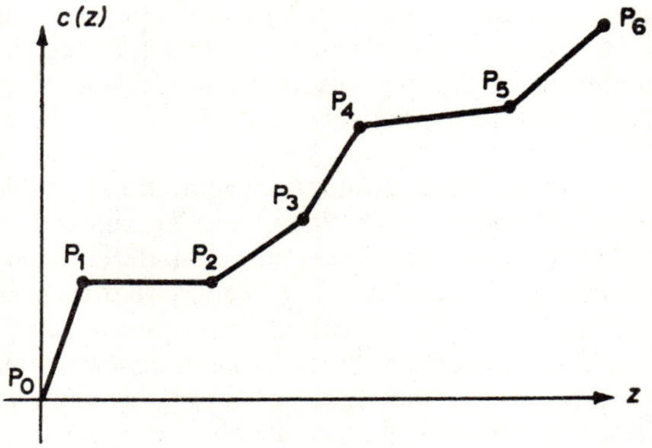

Figure 15.1

to say (15.1) (the convexity row) will appear explicitly, (15.2) (the reference row) will appear with z replaced if necessary by the linear function of the other variables of the problem that z represents, and the left hand side of (15.3) will be inserted in the objective function.

The difference between the integer programming and separable programming formulations lies in the way illegitimate combinations of λ-variables are excluded from the final solution. In integer programming the special rules for selecting the new basic variable are replaced by new constraints involving integer variables. The curve of $c(z)$ is a piecewise convex function, that is to say it is convex between P_0 and P_1, between P_1 and P_4, and between P_4 and P_6. If we can decide which of these pieces to use the problem reduces to an ordinary linear programming problem. We therefore introduce 3 zero-one variables δ_1, δ_2 and δ_3 representing the probabilities that the solution lies in each of the three possible ranges, and the constraints

$$\delta_1 + \delta_2 + \delta_3 = 1 \tag{15.4}$$

$$\left.\begin{aligned} \lambda_0 &\leqslant \delta_1 \\ \lambda_1 + \lambda_2 + \lambda_3 &\leqslant \delta_1 + \delta_2 \\ \lambda_2 + \lambda_3 + \lambda_4 + \lambda_5 &\leqslant \delta_2 + \delta_3 \\ \lambda_5 + \lambda_6 &\leqslant \delta_3 \end{aligned}\right\} \tag{15.5}$$

These constraints ensure that, whichever δ_i is chosen to be equal to 1, the λ_i corresponding to P_i outside the corresponding range must

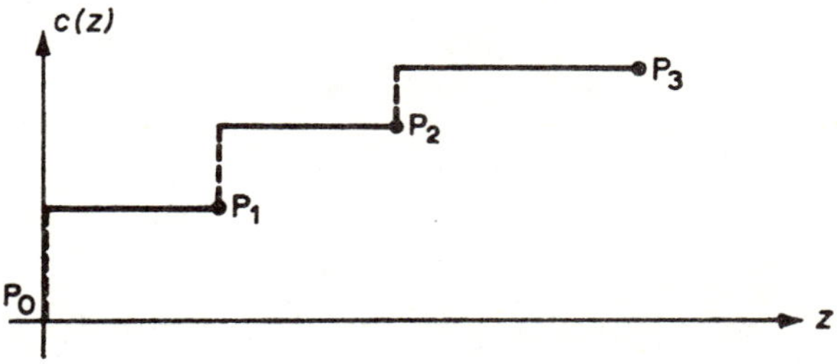

Figure 15.2

vanish. The fact that non-convex optimization problems can be formulated as mixed integer programming problems was pointed out by Markowitz and Manne (1957). This particular formulation is based on one given by Dantzig (1963).

A useful feature of this formulation is that one can get a good first trial solution to the problem by treating the δ_i as ordinary continuous variables and using separable programming.

The second method of representing a non-linear function is appropriate if the function $c(z)$ can conveniently be approximated by piecewise constant function, i.e. if the graph is as indicated in Fig. 15.2.

Again the co-ordinates of P_i are (a_i, b_i).

We can now treat the variables λ_i as zero-one variables, rewriting (15.2) as

$$\sum a_i \lambda_i \geqslant z \tag{15.6}$$

and can dispense with the constraints (15.4) and (15.5).

We can of course add a cost component proportional to z to this step-function.

It is usually expedient to retain the constraint (15.1), since the partially solved problem (with some integer variables allowed to take fractional values) will then be a closer approximation to reality, and less work will be involved in reaching the final solution, but this constraint is often not strictly necessary.

The third method of representing a non-linear function is appropriate if the function $c(z)$ can conveniently be approximated by a set of possibly disconnected line segments, with perhaps one or more isolated points, as in Fig. 15.3.

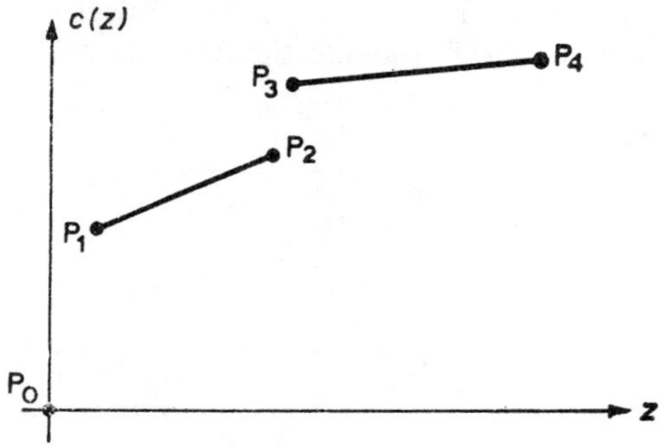

Figure 15.3

In practice the origin will often be an isolated point P_0, although P_1 may also have $z = 0$. The points P_2 and P_3 may coincide, but in the following analysis we denote the ends of the ith segment by P_{2i-1} and P_{2i}. Any isolated points other than the origin can be considered to have $P_{2i-1} = P_{2i}$.

We now introduce a zero-one variable δ_i for each line segment, and a continuous variable y_i for each line segment that is not an isolated point, and we write

$$\sum_i \delta_i = 1 \tag{15.7}$$

$$\sum_i a_{2i-1}\delta_i + \sum_i y_i = z \tag{15.8}$$

$$\sum_i b_{2i-1}\delta_i + \sum_i c_i y_i = c(z) \tag{15.9}$$

$$y_i \leqslant (a_{2i} - a_{2i-1})\delta_i \tag{15.10}$$

for all i such that $a_{2i-1} \neq a_{2i}$
where

$$c_i = (b_{2i} - b_{2i-1})/(a_{2i} - a_{2i-1})$$

What are the relative merits of these 3 formulations? The second minimizes the number of equations. This is important, but it is generally much more important to minimize the number of integer variables in the problem, so this formulation should not normally be used if one of the others gives an adequate approximation to $c(z)$ with fewer integer variables. The third formulation is usually rather more compact than the first, unless the function being approximated is piecewise convex (as indicated in the diagram for the first formulation).

15.4 Branch and Bound Methods for Mixed Integer Programming

The first integer programming method to be discussed is a *branch and bound* method for mixed integer programming that has been implemented in the LP/90/94 system. The code can also be used for pure integer programming, and it may prove to be the most generally effective of all presently known methods for all types of integer programming problem.

The method is based on the original work of Land and Doig (1960), but it incorporates ideas from Little, Murty, Sweeney and Karel (1963), Dakin (1965) and Driebeek (1966). It was described by Beale and Small (1965) One solves a sequence of ordinary linear programming problems in which upper and lower bounds are imposed on the values of all integer variables. Originally one has one problem in which these bounds are placed far enough apart to be sure to include the true solution. In general one has a list of alternative problems of this type that have been generated by previous steps of the algorithm. One also needs to keep a current best known feasible solution with its value of the objective function x_0 being maximized, say x_{0c}. If one has no ideas about this, one may start with $x_{0c} = -\infty$, but it may be better to select some plausible values for the integer variables and to solve for the continuous variables to get a finite value of $\bar{x}_{0c}$.

A general step of the algorithm is as follows—

(1) See if the list is empty. If so, the whole problem is solved, i.e. the current best known solution is the final solution. Otherwise take a problem out of the list and solve it.
(2) Consider the current value of the objective function. If this is less than or equal to x_{0c}, then the problem is of no further interest, and the step is complete.
(3) Otherwise test whether all variables that have to be integral are in fact within a suitable tolerance of being integral. If so, one has a new best known feasible solution and a new value of x_{0c}. The step is then complete.

(4) Both the above types of step remove a problem from the list without creating any new entries on the list, but there remains the situation when the current value of the objective function exceeds x_{0c} but the solution contains inadmissible fractions. Then we take some variable $X_i = \bar{a}_{i0}$, where $\bar{a}_{i0}$ is such an inadmissible fraction, and we add 2 new problems to the list, differing from the current one only in one of the bounds placed on X_i. In one problem the upper bound is replaced by $[\bar{a}_{i0}]$ and in the other problem the lower bound is replaced by $[\bar{a}_{i0}] + 1$. This completes the step.

An algorithm on these lines was proposed by Land and Doig (1960). It clearly must terminate at the optimum solution in a finite number of steps—since if the worst came to the worst one could continue until the permitted ranges of all integer variables in all problems had decreased to zero, in which case they must take integer values. At first sight it may seem rather ridiculous to try to solve real problems by such a pedestrian method, but there is an increasing amount of evidence that such methods can be very effective, if well organized on powerful computers, in situations where more high-brow methods run into difficulties.

The first encouraging thing about the algorithm is that its implementation on a computer is straightforward in principle if one has a spare magnetic tape, or other suitable backing-store, on which to record the relevant facts about those problems on which one is not currently working. (This may be called the stored list.) These problems have a number of rows equal to the number of rows in the original problem plus the number of integer variables, assuming that one uses new integer variables representing the amounts by which the original variables exceed their lower bounds. (The additional rows then define the permitted ranges of the integer variables.) The problems differ only in their right hand sides, so there is no question of storing a complete matrix with each problem on the list.

To minimize the time spent searching the tape, whenever 2 new problems are generated, one is selected for immediate attention and the other is put at the end of the stored list, overwriting the last problem selected from this list. Whenever a new problem is not generated one takes the last problem from the stored list to be processed next. Fortunately this strategy, chosen to simplify the computer storage problem, is desirable on mathematical grounds when combined with the rule described below for selecting the variable for branching.

In spite of the fact that the approach can conveniently be implemented, it could be very laborious if the variable X_i selected for branching is not chosen intelligently. Driebeek (1966) suggested that one should consider the effect on x_0 of small changes in each integer variable in turn. Sometimes this allows one to tighten the bounds on some integer variables, and we explore this very important point first. Using the same notation for the tableau elements as before, we see that the effect of increasing a non-basic integer variable x_j is measured by its reduced cost $\bar{a}_{0j}$ so x_j cannot be made greater than

$$U_j = [(\bar{a}_{00} - x_{0c})/\bar{a}_{0j}]$$

without making x_0 less than x_{0c}. So the upper bound on x_j can be reduced to U_j if the present bound exceeds it. This will of course be particularly useful if $U_j = 0$.

Similar calculations can be made for the basic integer variables X_i, using the cost ranging procedure of linear programming. The marginal cost δ_{Ui} of increasing X_i is given by

$$\delta_{Ui} = \min_{j,\bar{a}_{ij}<0} (\bar{a}_{0j}/|\bar{a}_{ij}|)$$

and the marginal cost δ_{Di} of decreasing x_i is given by

$$\delta_{Di} = \min_{j,\bar{a}_{ij}>0} (\bar{a}_{0j}/|\bar{a}_{ij}|)$$

Hence, if x_0 is to exceed x_{0c} we must have

$$n_{i0} - \left[\frac{\bar{a}_{00} - \delta_{Di}f_{i0} - x_{0c}}{\delta_{Di}}\right] \leqslant X_i \leqslant n_{i0} + \left[\frac{\bar{a}_{00} + \delta_{Ui}f_{i0} - x_{0c}}{\delta_{Ui}}\right]$$

where n_{i0} and f_{i0} are the integer and fractional parts of $\bar{a}_{i0}$, i.e. $n_{i0} = [\bar{a}_{i0}]$ and $f_{i0} = \bar{a}_{i0} - n_{i0}$.

This may make it possible to tighten either, or both, bounds on X_i for this problem.

At this point one (or more) of the new bounds on the basic integer variables may exclude the current trial solution. If so, the problem is resolved without any branching, but more often some branching will be necessary. A strategy that was successfully applied by Little, Murty, Sweeney and Karel (1963) to the travelling salesman's problem was to branch on that variable that made the worse of the two alternatives as bad as possible. This alternative can then be put in the stored list while the other alternative is explored. This strategy involves computing

$$L_{Ui} = \delta_{Ui}(1 - f_{i0})$$

and

$$L_{Di} = \delta_{Di}f_{i0}$$

for each basic integer variable with $f_{i0} \neq 0$, and branching on that variable that makes the larger of these quantities as large as possible.

The process can conveniently be illustrated by Example 1 given by Thompson (1964). This problem is to minimize z_2 subject to the constraints

$$66z_1 + 14z_2 \geqslant 1430$$

$$-82z_1 + 28z_2 \geqslant 1306$$

$$z_1 \geqslant 0, \qquad z_2 \geqslant 0 \text{ and both integral}$$

The problem is illustrated in Fig. 15.4.

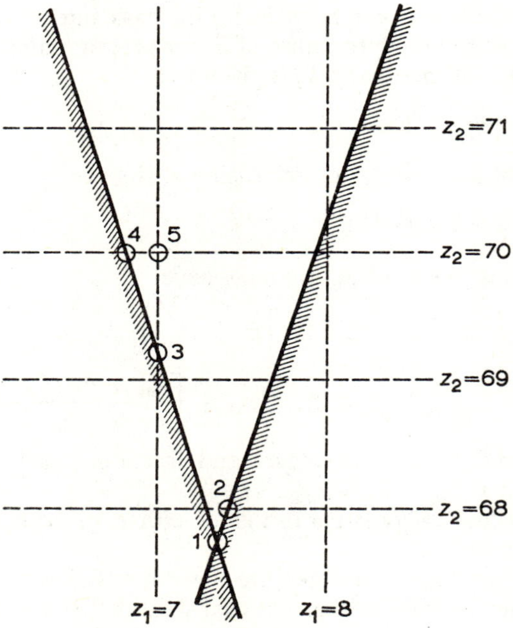

Figure 15.4

The continuous optimum is at the point marked 1, with $z_1 = 7{\cdot}26$, $z_2 = 67{\cdot}91$. The program realizes that z_2 cannot be less than 68 (i.e. the corresponding δ_{Di} is infinite because there is no j for which $\bar{a}_{ij} > 0$), so the lower bound on z_2 is increased to 68 and the next trial solution has $z_1 = 7{\cdot}29$, $z_2 = 68{\cdot}00$ (point 2). A branch is now necessary. It seems much cheaper to decrease z_1 than to increase it, so the stored list is set up to consider the possibility that $z_1 \geqslant 8$, which is seen to imply that the objective function $\geqslant 70{\cdot}07$. Meanwhile we explore the possibility that $z_1 \leqslant 7$. This leads to the point marked 3, with $z_1 = 7{\cdot}00$, $z_2 = 69{\cdot}14$. We can then impose the constraint $z_2 \geqslant 70{\cdot}0$, which takes us to the point marked 4, with $z_1 = 6{\cdot}82$, $z_2 = 70{\cdot}0$. A second branch is now necessary. It seems much cheaper to increase z_1 than to decrease it; so the possibility $z_1 \leqslant 6$, which is seen to imply an objective function of at least 73·86, is added to the stored list, while we immediately work on the possibility that $z_1 \geqslant 7$. This leads to the point marked 5, with $z_1 = 7{\cdot}00$, $z_2 = 70{\cdot}00$. We therefore have a feasible solution. Both of the alternatives on the stored list can now be rejected as involving a worse value of the objective function, and the procedure terminates.

15.5 Extensions to the Branch and Bound Code

Three additional features are available in the LP/90/94 branch and bound code. One avoids the necessity for extra rows defining the permitted ranges of zero-one variables—since branchings on such variables can more easily be recorded using flags. The other is to mark some such variables (with names ending in the characters / =) as more suitable for forcing to one than for forcing to zero. One will never branch on such a variable in such a way as to consider the branch in which the variable equals zero first. This facility may be used for covering variables, i.e. integer variables that must sum to unity. One then makes much more progress towards an integer solution by forcing such a variable to 1 than by forcing it to zero. The facility may also be used if one has an *a priori* reason for thinking that a variable will in fact be unity in the final solution.

The third special feature restricts the amount of searching if one is prepared to accept a final solution that may not be the very best possible but must be within a specified percentage of the best possible. This involves defining a factor f just greater than unity if x_0 is expected to be positive (or just less than unity otherwise), and modifying the criteria of Section 15.4 to exclude all possibilities that cannot produce a value of the objective function better than fx_0.

15.6 Martin's Version of the Method of Integer Forms

Another approach, that has successfully solved some quite large pure integer programming problems, is Martin's version of Gomory's method of integer forms—see Gomory (1958), Gomory (1963*a*) and Martin (1963). This algorithm will solve problems where all the variables have to be integers, and all the coefficients in the constraints are integers. In practice it is important that they should be small integers, since the method becomes inefficient when the determinant of the basis becomes large.

The method is a cutting-plane method. That is to say one first solves the problem ignoring the requirement that the variables must be integers, and if the final solution is not integral one constructs an additional constraint that is not satisfied at the current trial solution but that must be satisfied at any genuinely feasible solution, and resolves the problem. To understand in more detail how this works, suppose that the problem is to maximize x_0, and that the final tableau reads

$$x_0 = \bar{a}_{00} + \sum \bar{a}_{0j}(-z_j)$$

$$X_i = \bar{a}_{i0} + \sum \bar{a}_{ij}(-z_j)$$

(We use the same notation as the Chapter 13, since we again have the possibility of introducing additional non-basic variables during the calculations.)

Suppose further that

$$\bar{a}_{ij} = n_{ij} + f_{ij}$$

where n_{ij} is an integer (not necessarily non-negative) and $0 \leqslant f_{ij} < 1$.

Now suppose that X_i takes a non-integral value in the current trial solution, i.e. that $f_{i0} \neq 0$, and consider the expression

$$s = -f_{i0} + \sum f_{ij} z_j$$

This must be an integer, since it differs from $-X_i$ by an integer. On the other hand it cannot be less than $-f_{i0}$ since the expression $\sum f_{ij} z_j$ must be non-negative, and the smallest integer not less than $-f_{i0}$ is zero. So s must be a non-negative integer, and it can be introduced as a new non-basic variable of the problem.

This cut was derived from the expression for a single basic variable in the tableau. But Gomory (1963) showed that a similar cut can be derived from an (positive or negative) integer combination of basic variables; on the other hand he also showed that the total number of distinct cuts of this type is $D - 1$, where D is the absolute value of the determinant of the basis. He showed that one can often (though not always) derive all these cuts by considering simple multiples of a single basic variable.

In Martin's version of the algorithm the cut is chosen as follows. Choose some basic variable X_i such that $\bar{a}_{i0}$ is non-integral. Now choose a pivotal column z_j such that $\bar{a}_{0j}$ is minimized over all columns for which $f_{ij} \neq 0$. Next derive the cut from the expression for that multiple of X_i for which the fractional part of the coefficient of z_j takes the smallest possible positive value. Then use this coefficient as a pivot, even though it may destroy dual feasibility.

Note that the new value of D equals the old D multiplied by the absolute value of the pivot. The pivot has been chosen to be a small fraction, so D will be greatly reduced. If $D = 1$ the trial solution must be integral, and it is quite likely that the trial solution will be integral at this point, whether or not $D = 1$. If the trial solution is not integral, further cuts are imposed in the same way until it becomes integral, and no attempt is made to restore non-negativity until an all-integer trial solution has been achieved.

Many people have been puzzled about why this particular strategy has been so successful. A major problem in mathematics is to find some theoretical insight into the efficiency of iterative numerical methods, and it is hard to see how this problem will ever be solved at all completely. At one time I thought Martin's success was due entirely to his boldness in writing a code that was capable of attempting a problem with more than about 100 variables. Now I think that this is only part of the story. The point is that the method takes advantage of the primal and dual degeneracy that is present in most practical integer programming problems. In particular, the decision to pivot in the selected column, and thereby bringing D right down, pays off because

(*a*) it will not destroy dual feasibility, except in an irrelevant lexicographical sense, if the current reduced cost of z_j is zero;
(*b*) even if it does destroy dual feasibility, the primal degeneracy may well be such that dual feasibility is restored by a set of pivot operations in rows with a constant term of zero, and this does not make the solution non-integral.

Although this algorithm, as implemented in the LP/90/94 system, has solved a number of problems containing thousands of variables, it cannot be guaranteed to solve all integer programming problems. The presence of an appreciable number of large coefficients in the original equations is apt to make the determinant of the basis large, and to cause difficulties.

Sometimes one can reduce the determinant of the basis, and thereby improve the performance of the code, by adding additional constraints derived from original constraints by λ-transformations, see Gomory (1963*b*). If one has a constraint of the form

$$a_{i0} + \sum a_{ij}(-z_j) \geqslant 0$$

where all n_{ij} are integral, and if $a_{ij} = \lambda n_{ij} + f_{ij}$, where λ is any positive number (not necessarily integral) and $0 \leqslant f_{ij} < \lambda$, then

$$s = n_{i0} + \sum n_{ij}(-z_j) \geqslant 0$$

If the a_{ij} are rather large, then it may be possible to choose a λ that makes all the n_{ij} much smaller, and if the slack on the original constraint is basic the determinant of the basis will be smaller.

15.7 Partial Enumeration Methods

Partial enumeration represents another approach to integer programming problems consisting entirely of zero-one variables. It is easy to program, and is therefore convenient for use in a subroutine to solve small problems of this kind. The approach has been extended to apply to more general types of integer programming problem, but these extensions deprive the approach of some of its simplicity and therefore its attractiveness. The original work on this approach is due to Le Garff and Malgrange (1963), Balas (1964), Glover (1965) and Freeman (1966). The approach is closely related to the branch and bound method discussed earlier, but here we require all trial solutions to be integral—although they are only feasible if the inequality constraints are all satisfied; this is the opposite tactic to the one described in Section 15.4.

We assume that all constraints are of the form

$$y_i = b_i + \sum_j a_{ij}x_j \geqslant 0$$

and that the objective function to be maximized is

$$y_0 = b_0 + \sum_j a_{0j}x_j$$

We assume that all the variables x_j must be either 0 or 1. (If we had a variable x_k that could lie between 0 and $2^{N_k} - 1$ we could replace x_k by N_k zero-one variables representing the binary digits of x_k, i.e.

$$\left. x_k = \sum_{i=0}^{N_k-1} 2^i x_{ki} \right)$$

We may also assume without loss of generality that $a_{0j} \leqslant 0$, since otherwise we could replace x_j by $1 - x_j$.

As in the original branch and bound process we have a current best known solution with its corresponding value of y_0, say y_{0c}. We also have a set of sub-problems, in each of which the variables are divided into 3 sets—

S_0: the set of variables assigned the value zero
S_1: the set of variables assigned the value one
S_2: the set of unassigned variables provisionally set equal to zero

We also consider the current values $v_0, v_1, v_2, \ldots$ of $y_0, y_1, y_2, \ldots$, and quantities $U_1, U_2, \ldots$ representing the maximum possible values of $y_1, y_2, \ldots$ obtainable by changing the values of the variables in S_2. So in fact

$$U_i = v_i + \sum_j \max(0, a_{ij})$$

where throughout this exposition j will be considered as ranging over all values such that x_j is in S_2.

Initially we put $y_{0c} = -\infty$ and have one sub-problem with all variables in S_2.

A general step of the algorithm can be described as follows—

(1) Take a sub-problem from the list. If $v_0 \leqslant y_{0c}$, abandon it. Otherwise if all $v_i \geqslant 0$ for $i \geqslant 1$ we have a new best known solution. There is nothing more to be done with this sub-problem. All $a_{0j} \leqslant 0$, so it is unprofitable and unnecessary to give any variable in S_2 a non-zero value.

(2) Otherwise if $a_{0j} \leqslant y_{0c} - v_0$ for any j, put x_j in S_0 and revise the values of the U_i. This is legitimate because any solution found from this sub-problem with $x_j = 1$ can be no better than one we have found already.

(3) If any $U_i < 0$, the sub-problem cannot have a feasible solution and should be dropped. Furthermore if $U_i + a_{ij} < 0$ for some i, we may put x_j in S_0 and revise the U_i accordingly since the sub-problem would be infeasible with $x_j = 1$. If any variable is assigned to S_0 in this way, continue to look at each constraint in turn until all have been considered after the last assignment to S_0 was made (or until some $U_i < 0$).

(4) Now put x_j in S_1 for all j such that $U_i - a_{ij} < 0$ for some i, since the sub-problem would be infeasible with $x_j = 0$. If there is any such x_j, the step is completed when the v_i and U_i have been updated.

(5) If no x_j can be assigned to S_1 in stage 4, then a branch must be made. We take some variable in S_2 and assign it to S_1, at the same time setting up a new sub-problem that is the same as the current one except that this variable is assigned to S_0.

The choice of variable for branching is theoretically immaterial. Balas suggests taking that variable which when increased to 1 (keeping everything else constant) increases at least one negative v_i and makes the greatest net decrease in the sum of infeasibilities, i.e. in

$$\sum_{i>0} \max(0, -v_i)$$

Note that this greatest net decrease may conceivably be negative. Ir. H. Schipper has implemented this suggestion, and found that for the problems he had to solve it was important to give preference in the case of ties to the variable with the least negative value of a_{0j}.

Whichever branching strategy is adopted, it is relatively easy to keep track in the computer of the set of sub-problems that remain to be explored if after branching one always works on the new problem with the extra variable in S_1, and if one always takes the last new sub-problem to have been created when the current sub-problem does not lead to a branch. This is the same tactic that was recommended in Section 15.4.

15.8 The Choice between Integer Programming Methods

Three out of many approaches to integer programming have been described in this chapter. Each of the three has been applied successfully to the solution of real problems, but none can be relied on to give the optimum solution to an arbitrary integer programming problem in a reasonable length of time—even if we restrict the number of integer variables to say 50. Some people will conclude from this that integer programming is an unreliable technique, but it seems fairer to conclude merely that it has to be used intelligently. The branch and bound approach has an important property, that is shared to some extent by the partial enumeration approach, that it will usually produce a good solution—which may even turn out to be the optimal solution—even if one does not feel justified in spending the time to explore all alternatives thoroughly enough to reach a guaranteed optimal solution. With this approach one should try to assess the number of branches that will be required to drive the solution to the continuous problem to an integral solution, since this is likely to have a major influence on the number of branches that must ultimately be explored. If the number seems likely to be excessive one may be able to do better by reformulating the problem.

16 Decomposition

16.1 What Is Decomposition?

The decomposition principle is an approach to the solution of certain types of large linear programming problems. It was devised by George Dantzig and Philip Wolfe, see Dantzig and Wolfe (1960), (1961) and Dantzig (1963). Specifically, it is a method of solving

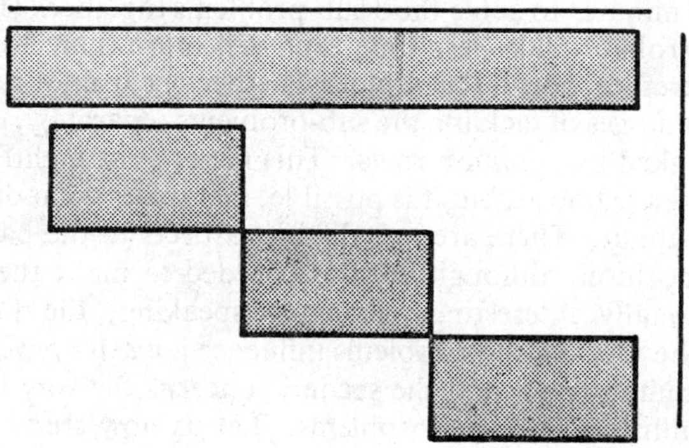

Figure 16.1

problems with a structure that can be represented schematically as in Fig. 16.1. This is intended to indicate that the problem breaks up into separate sub-problems, of which there are 3 in the diagram, except for a relatively small number of *common rows*, or equations involving variables from more than one sub-problem.

Almost all large linear programming problems can be written in this way. This is because linear programming problems only become large when one has to make a combined study of several similar operations spread out in either space or time (or both). The sub-problems may then represent different production centres that compete for the use of scarce raw materials, or to satisfy a market whose size is assumed to be fixed. The common rows may impose limits of the use of each raw material used at more than one centre or on the total amounts to be made of each product at all centres.

If one is working in an industry in which seasonal factors affect sales, or supplies of raw materials, it may be necessary to set up different sub-problems representing the same production centre in different seasons. One may then have common rows expressing the fact that the stock of each commodity left over at the end of one season is equal to the stock available at the start of the next season.

So much for the source of decomposable problems, but how should one solve them? If there were no common rows other than the objective function, the sub-problems would be separate linear programming problems. One could solve them as one large linear programming problem, but this would be inefficient. Suppose it takes 10 minutes on some computer to solve each sub-problem separately then it would take 30 minutes to solve 3 sub-problems separately. But the time taken to solve a linear programming problem varies roughly as the cube of the number of constraints, so one might expect it to take about 270 minutes to solve the 3 sub-problems together. (In practice it would probably take less time, but still more than 30 minutes.)

It is, therefore, natural to wonder whether one cannot retain some of the advantages of tackling the sub-problems separately, even when they are linked by common rows. This is not as straightforward as one might have hoped, but it is possible, and this is what decomposition is all about. There are two distinct aspects to the basic theory of decomposition, although both are needed to make the principle computationally interesting. Roughly speaking, the first aspect concerns the way the sub-problems influence a *master problem* based on the common rows, and the second concerns the way the master problem influences the sub-problems. Let us now study these two aspects in more detail.

16.2 The Master Problem

The first aspect of the theory of decomposition is based on the fundamental fact that a convex polyhedron can be represented either as the intersection of a set of half-spaces or as the set of all possible non-negative linear combinations of its vertices.

Please do not be put off by the long words in the last paragraph, because the concept is really quite simple. A half-space is the set of points that satisfy a linear inequality. The intersection of several sets is defined as the set of points in all of them. When the feasible region of a linear programming problem is defined by a set of linear inequalities it is being defined as the intersection of half-spaces. Alternatively, this region can be defined in terms of its vertices, since it consists of all possible centres of gravity obtainable by putting non-negative weights at its vertices. We can dispense with the constraints of any sub-problem, and instead say that the variables of the sub-problem must take values that can be expressed as linear combinations of other variables representing weights associated with the vertices of the feasible region of the sub-problem.

Perhaps the easiest way to appreciate just what this involves is to take a miniature example in which it is a straightforward matter to

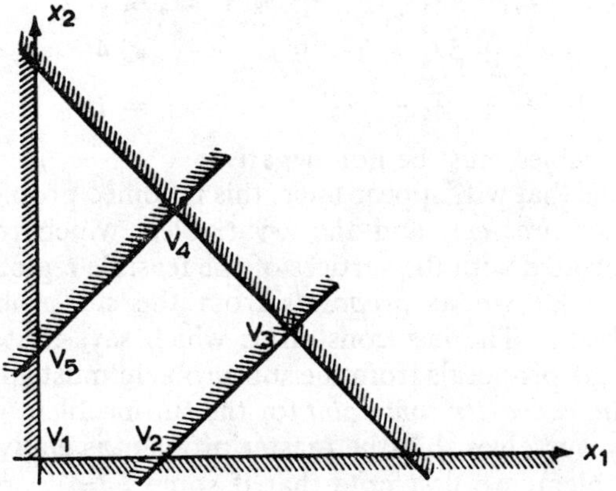

Figure 16.2

enumerate all these vertices. It is usual in practical decomposition work to have several sub-problems, but this is not theoretically necessary. Let us, therefore, consider the following problem.

Maximize x_0 subject to the following constraints—

$$\begin{aligned} x_0 - x_1 - x_2 + x_3 - x_4 &= 0 \\ 2x_1 + x_3 + 2x_4 &\leqslant 5 \\ x_1 + 2x_2 - x_3 &\leqslant 4 \\ x_1 + x_2 &\leqslant 3 \\ x_1 - x_2 &\leqslant 1 \\ x_1 - x_2 &\geqslant -1 \end{aligned}$$

where all the variables must be non-negative.

In this problem we may regard the last 3 inequalities as representing a sub-problem, together with the non-negativity requirements on the variables of the sub-problem, i.e. x_1 and x_2. The feasible region for this sub-problem is represented in the (x_1, x_2) plane as shown in Fig. 16.2.

The feasible region reduces to a pentagon, with 5 vertices marked V_1, V_2, V_3, V_4 and V_5. They correspond to the points (0, 0), (1, 0), (2, 1), (1, 2) and (0, 1) respectively.

We therefore assert that the original problem can be replaced by the following problem.

Maximize x_0, subject to the following constraints—

$$
\begin{aligned}
x_0 \quad - \lambda_2 - 3\lambda_3 - 3\lambda_4 - \lambda_5 + x_3 - x_4 &= 0 \\
2\lambda_2 + 4\lambda_3 + 2\lambda_4 \qquad + x_3 + 2x_4 &\leqslant 5 \\
\lambda_2 + 4\lambda_3 + 5\lambda_4 + 2\lambda_5 - x_3 \qquad &\leqslant 4 \\
\lambda_1 + \lambda_2 + \lambda_3 + \lambda_4 + \lambda_5 \qquad &= 1
\end{aligned}
$$

where all variables must be non-negative.

For reasons that will appear later, this modified problem is known as the *master problem*, and the λ-variables, which represent the weights associated with the vertices of the feasible region of the sub-problem, are known as *proposals* from the sub-problem to the master problem. The last constraint, which says that the weights attached to the proposals from the sub-problem must add up to 1, is known as the *convexity constraint* for the sub-problem.

To satisfy ourselves that the master problem is equivalent to the original problem, we first note that if some $\lambda_i = 1$ and the other $\lambda_i = 0$, then the contributions of the proposals to the common rows, i.e. the first 3 constraints, represent the contribution that the variables x_1 and x_2 would make if they took the values represented by the corresponding vertex of the feasible region of the sub-problem. Similarly any interior point of this region is represented (possibly in many ways) as a positive linear combination of proposals satisfying the convexity constraint. Conversely, any point that does not satisfy the constraints of the sub-problem is not representable in this way.

Let us now compare the master problem with the original problem.

We have been able to dispense with all the constraints and all the variables of the sub-problem. In this case we have saved 2 variables and 3 constraints. In exchange we have had to accept one new variable corresponding to each vertex of the feasible region of the sub-problem, and one new equation—the convexity constraint—for each sub-problem. In this case we have had to add 5 variables and 1 constraint.

The solution of practical problems by these means would now be straightforward, except for two difficulties—

(1) In a real problem, although the number of equations saved by going from the original problem to the master problem may be

considerable, the number of possible proposals is generally very large indeed. So the principle would be computationally hopeless if all these proposals had to be derived explicitly at the start of the program.

(2) When the master problem has been solved, one knows the weights associated with each proposal from a sub-problem, but one does not immediately know the values of the variables of the sub-problem.

These two difficulties are discussed in the next two sections.

16.3 Sub-problems

The second aspect of the basic theory of decomposition concerns the method of deriving relevant proposals from the sub-problems during the course of the computation.

The idea motivating this is the fact that an optimal solution to a linear programming problem remains optimal if some or all of the constraints are withdrawn, but the variable terms in such constraints are multiplied by suitable Lagrange multipliers, or π-values, and added to the objective function. In particular, if the common rows are treated in this way, the problem decomposes into separate sub-problems that can be solved separately. This is why the name decomposition was applied to the principle. The difficulties about applying this idea are

(1) It is not a straightforward matter to select the right π-values
(2) Even if one knew the right π-values, the optimal solutions to the decomposed sub-problems are not unique, and in general only one set of these optimal solutions actually satisfies the constraints defined by the common rows.

Nevertheless the idea of replacing the common rows by suitably weighted additions to the objective functions in the sub-problems can usefully be applied as follows. One solves a *restricted master problem*, which is the same as the complete master problem except that many of the proposal variables are omitted. One may even start without any proposals at all: the master problem will then be infeasible, if only because the convexity constraints cannot be satisfied, but one can start with the sum of infeasibilities as an auxiliary objective function in the usual way. Having solved the restricted master problem, one has a set of π-values on the common rows. One can then ask, for each sub-problem in turn, which of all the proposals that one could (conceptually) write down in a complete master problem has the most negative reduced cost at this stage. This question can be formulated as a linear programming problem, or sub-problem. The kth sub-problem has the same constraints on the variables of the sub-problem as the original problem, and its objective function can be defined in terms of quantities r_{ik} representing minus the contribution of these variables to the common rows of the original problem. (The minus sign is not essential, but it simplifies the organization of the computations.) So r_{ok} represents minus the contribution of the variables of the kth sub-problem to the equation defining the original objective function, and r_{ik} (for $i \geqslant 1$) represents minus the contribution of these variables to the left hand side of the ith constraint. Corresponding to any vertex of the feasible region of the sub-problem, we have a proposal in the complete master problem with coefficient $-r_{ik}$ in the ith row, together with a unit coefficient in the kth convexity row. The reduced cost of this proposal is $-\sum \pi_i r_{ik} + \pi_{sk}$, where π_{sk} is the π-value on the kth convexity row. Hence the proposal with the most negative reduced cost from this sub-problem is the one corresponding to the solution that maximizes $\sum \pi_i r_{ik}$. A vertex of the feasible region of the sub-problem that achieves this can be found by the simplex method in the usual way, and the coefficients of the corresponding proposal in the master problem can be taken from the corresponding values of the r_{ik}.

The decomposition procedure is therefore as follows. First solve the (restricted) master problem and find the corresponding set of π-values. Then solve each sub-problem in turn, using the expression $\sum \pi_i r_{ik}$ as the objective function, and add the corresponding proposals to the master problem. Now solve the master problem again, and repeat the whole process until none of the new proposals can profitably be made basic in the master problem. In this case the π-values on the common rows do not change, so no new proposals would be generated if one were to continue.

The step from one optimal solution of the master problem to the next, based on an extended set of proposals, is called a *major iteration*, to distinguish it from a normal iteration of the simplex method which we call a *minor iteration*.

It is clear that the procedure must terminate after a finite number of major iterations, since it is simply a way of carrying out the normal simplex method on the master problem in which some variables are excluded from entering the basis (because they have not been generated). Further, this termination cannot take place before the true optimum is reached, because the proposal generated from each sub-problem has the most negative reduced cost of all possible proposals from that sub-problem. If even this is not worth introducing, then neither is any other proposal.

Let us now solve the problem introduced in Section 16.2 by decomposition. Because of the key role played by the π-values, we use the inverse matrix method, in the product form, for both the master problem and the sub-problem.

We start with a master problem containing only its natural variables x_3, x_4, s_1 and s_2, so it reads

$$\begin{aligned}
x_0 + x_3 - \;\; x_4 \qquad\qquad &= 0 \\
x_3 + 2x_4 + s_1 \qquad &= 5 \\
-x_3 \qquad\qquad + s_2 &= 4 \\
0 \qquad\qquad\qquad\qquad &= 1
\end{aligned}$$

The corresponding A-matrix is

$$\begin{bmatrix} 1 & 1 & -1 & & \\ & 1 & 2 & 1 & \\ & -1 & & & 1 \end{bmatrix}$$

and the right hand side vector $\mathbf{b}$ is

$$\begin{bmatrix} 0 \\ 5 \\ 4 \\ 1 \end{bmatrix}$$

The initial ordered list of basic variables is

$$x_0, s_1, s_2, A_3$$

The basis is a unit basis, so the current right hand side vector $\boldsymbol{\beta} = \mathbf{b}$.

We now form a row vector $\mathbf{c}$ to represent the fact that we would like to reduce the sum of infeasibilities by reducing A_3, so

$$\mathbf{c} = [0 \quad 0 \quad 0 \quad -1]$$

and this is also the π-vector. Multiplying $\boldsymbol{\pi}$ into each column of $\mathbf{A}$ in turn (other than the first column corresponding to the dummy variable x_0) we find that all variables have a zero reduced cost, and no progress can be made without additional variables.

We therefore turn to the sub-problem, which we write as

$$\begin{aligned}
r_{01} \qquad - \;\; x_1 - \;\; x_2 \qquad\qquad\qquad &= 0 \\
r_{11} \quad + 2x_1 \qquad\qquad\qquad\qquad &= 0 \\
r_{21} + \;\; x_1 + 2x_2 \qquad\qquad\qquad &= 0 \\
x_1 + \;\; x_2 + s_3 \qquad\qquad &= 3 \\
x_1 - \;\; x_2 \qquad + s_4 \qquad &= 1 \\
x_1 - \;\; x_2 \qquad\qquad - s_5 &= -1
\end{aligned}$$

The corresponding A-matrix, which we call $\mathbf{A}_S$ to distinguish it from the A-matrix in the master problem, is

$$\begin{bmatrix} 1 & & & -1 & -1 & & & \\ & 1 & & 2 & & & & \\ & & 1 & 1 & 2 & & & \\ & & & 1 & 1 & 1 & & \\ & & & 1 & -1 & & 1 & \\ & & & 1 & -1 & & & -1 \end{bmatrix}$$

and the right hand side vector $\mathbf{b}_S$ is

$$\begin{bmatrix} 0 \\ 0 \\ 0 \\ 3 \\ 1 \\ -1 \end{bmatrix}$$

We start by introducing the slack variable s_5 into the basis, so our first transformation matrix is

$$\mathbf{T}_{1S} = \begin{bmatrix} 1 & & & & & \\ & 1 & & & & \\ & & 1 & & & \\ & & & 1 & & \\ & & & & 1 & \\ & & & & & -1 \end{bmatrix}$$

The initial ordered list of basic variables is

$$r_{01},\ r_{11},\ r_{21},\ s_3,\ s_4,\ s_5$$

and the current right hand side

$$\boldsymbol{\beta}_S = \mathbf{T}_{1S}\mathbf{b}_S$$

$$= \begin{bmatrix} 0 \\ 0 \\ 0 \\ 3 \\ 1 \\ 1 \end{bmatrix}$$

We therefore have a feasible solution to our sub-problem, and can concentrate on maximizing $\sum \pi_i r_{ik}$ to provide the best proposal for the master problem. At this stage $\pi_i = 0$ for all common rows, the only non-zero π-value being in the convexity row. So our row-vector $\mathbf{c}_S = (0, 0, 0, 0, 0, 0)$. Hence $\boldsymbol{\pi}_S = \mathbf{c}_S\mathbf{T}_{1S} = (0, 0, 0, 0, 0, 0)$; and multiplying this into all columns of $\mathbf{A}_S$, other than the first 3 columns corresponding to the dummy variables r_{01}, r_{11} and r_{21}, we again find that all variables have a zero reduced cost and we have an optimal solution.

So far, we have covered a lot of paper, though we have not had to do much arithmetic, without making any obvious progress; but we can now add a proposal to the master problem. The values of r_{01}, r_{11} and r_{21} at the optimum solution to the sub-problem are all zero, so the new proposal has zero coefficients in these rows, but it has a unit element in the convexity row. It is the variable λ_1 of Section 16.2, and the A-matrix now reads

$$\begin{bmatrix} 1 & 1 & -1 & & & \\ & 1 & 2 & 1 & & \\ & -1 & & & 1 & \\ & & & & & 1 \end{bmatrix}$$

Multiplying the π-vector for the master problem into the new column, we obtain a reduced cost of -1, so we bring λ_1 into the basis. The vector

$$\boldsymbol{\alpha} = \mathbf{a} = \begin{bmatrix} 0 \\ 0 \\ 0 \\ 1 \end{bmatrix}$$

Now taking ratios of the elements of $\boldsymbol{\alpha}$ with the corresponding elements of $\boldsymbol{\beta}$ we find the $p = 3$, and our new elementary transformation matrix

$$\mathbf{T}_1 = \begin{bmatrix} 1 & & & \\ & 1 & & \\ & & 1 & \\ & & & 1 \end{bmatrix}$$

The new ordered list of basic variables is

$$x_0, s_1, s_2, \lambda_1$$

and the right hand side

$$\boldsymbol{\beta}' = \mathbf{T}_1\boldsymbol{\beta} = \begin{bmatrix} 0 \\ 5 \\ 4 \\ 1 \end{bmatrix}$$

We now have a feasible solution to the master problem and for the next iteration

$$\mathbf{c} = [1, 0, 0, 0]$$

so $\boldsymbol{\pi} = \mathbf{c}\mathbf{T}_1 = [1, 0, 0, 0]$

Multiplying $\boldsymbol{\pi}$ into the columns of $\mathbf{A}$, we obtain the reduced costs

$$1, -1, 0, 0, 0$$

We select the fourth of these numbers, and bring x_4 into the basis.

We must now form $\boldsymbol{\alpha} = \mathbf{T}_1\mathbf{a}$, where

$$\mathbf{a} = \begin{bmatrix} -1 \\ 2 \\ 0 \\ 0 \end{bmatrix} \quad \text{so} \quad \boldsymbol{\alpha} = \mathbf{T}_1\mathbf{a} = \begin{bmatrix} -1 \\ 2 \\ 0 \\ 0 \end{bmatrix}$$

Comparing this with the elements of $\boldsymbol{\beta}$, we find that $p = 1$, and our new elementary transformation matrix

$$\mathbf{T}_2 = \begin{bmatrix} 1 & \frac{1}{2} & & \\ & \frac{1}{2} & & \\ & 0 & 1 & \\ & 0 & & 1 \end{bmatrix}$$

The new ordered list of basic variables is

x_0, x_4, s_2, λ_1

and the new right hand side

$$\boldsymbol{\beta}' = \mathbf{T}_2\boldsymbol{\beta} = \begin{bmatrix} 5/2 \\ 5/2 \\ 4 \\ 1 \end{bmatrix}$$

For the next iteration

$$\mathbf{c} = [1, 0, 0, 0]$$

and $\boldsymbol{\pi} = \mathbf{c}\mathbf{T}_2\mathbf{T}_1 = [1, \frac{1}{2}, 0, 0]$

Multiplying $\boldsymbol{\pi}$ into the columns of $\mathbf{A}$, we obtain the reduced costs

$3/2, 0, 1/2, 0, 0$

None of these is negative, so we can make no further progress without obtaining another proposal from the sub-problem.

In the sub-problem we take the π-values on the common rows as the corresponding components of $\mathbf{c}_S$, so $\mathbf{c}_S = (1, \frac{1}{2}, 0, 0, 0, 0)$ and $\boldsymbol{\pi}_S = \mathbf{c}_S\mathbf{T}_{1S} = (1, \frac{1}{2}, 0, 0, 0, 0)$. Multiplying $\boldsymbol{\pi}_S$ into the columns of $\mathbf{A}_S$, we obtain the reduced costs $0, -1, 0, 0, 0$.

We select the second of these numbers, and bring x_2 into the basis.

We must now form the vector $\boldsymbol{\alpha}_S = \mathbf{T}_{1S}\mathbf{a}$, where

$$\mathbf{a} = \begin{bmatrix} -1 \\ 0 \\ 2 \\ 1 \\ -1 \\ -1 \end{bmatrix} \quad \text{so} \quad \boldsymbol{\alpha}_S = \begin{bmatrix} -1 \\ 0 \\ 2 \\ 1 \\ -1 \\ 1 \end{bmatrix}$$

Comparing this with the vector $\boldsymbol{\beta}_S$ and remembering that we cannot pivot out any of the dummy variables r_{01}, r_{11} or r_{21} (since these are allowed to be negative), we put $p = 5$, i.e. we pivot in the bottom row. So our new elementary transformation matrix

$$\mathbf{T}_{2S} = \begin{bmatrix} 1 & & & & & 1 \\ & 1 & & & & 0 \\ & & 1 & & & -2 \\ & & & 1 & & -1 \\ & & & & 1 & 1 \\ & & & & & 1 \end{bmatrix}$$

The new ordered list of basic variables is

$$r_{01}, r_{11}, r_{21}, s_3, s_4, x_2$$

and the new right hand side

$$\boldsymbol{\beta}'_S = \mathbf{T}_{2S}\boldsymbol{\beta}_S = \begin{bmatrix} 1 \\ 0 \\ -2 \\ 2 \\ 2 \\ 1 \end{bmatrix}$$

For the next iteration we again put

$$\mathbf{c}_S = (1, \tfrac{1}{2}, 0, 0, 0, 0)$$

and $\boldsymbol{\pi}_S = \mathbf{c}_S\mathbf{T}_{2S}\mathbf{T}_{1S} = (1, \tfrac{1}{2}, 0, 0, 0, -1)$

Multiplying $\boldsymbol{\pi}_S$ into the columns of $\mathbf{A}_S$ we obtain the reduced costs

$$-1, 0, 0, 0, 1$$

We select the first of these numbers, and bring x_1 into the basis.

We must now form the vector $\boldsymbol{\alpha}_S = \mathbf{T}_{2S}\mathbf{T}_{1S}\mathbf{a}$ where

$$\mathbf{a} = \begin{bmatrix} -1 \\ 2 \\ 1 \\ 1 \\ 1 \\ 1 \end{bmatrix} \quad \text{so} \quad \mathbf{T}_{1S}\mathbf{a} = \begin{bmatrix} -1 \\ 2 \\ 1 \\ 1 \\ 1 \\ -1 \end{bmatrix} \quad \text{and} \quad \boldsymbol{\alpha}_S = \begin{bmatrix} -2 \\ 2 \\ 3 \\ 2 \\ 0 \\ -1 \end{bmatrix}$$

Comparing this with the elements of $\boldsymbol{\beta}_S$, we find that we must put

$p = 3$. So our new elementary transformation matrix

$$\mathbf{T}_{3S} = \begin{bmatrix} 1 & & & 1 & & \\ & 1 & & -1 & & \\ & & 1 & -3/2 & & \\ & & & 1/2 & & \\ & & & 0 & 1 & \\ & & & 1/2 & & 1 \end{bmatrix}$$

The new ordered list of basic variables is

$$r_{01}, r_{11}, r_{21}, x_1, s_4, x_2$$

and the new right hand side

$$\boldsymbol{\beta}'_S = \mathbf{T}_{3S}\boldsymbol{\beta}_S = \begin{bmatrix} 3 \\ -2 \\ -5 \\ 1 \\ 2 \\ 2 \end{bmatrix}$$

For the next iteration we again put

$$\mathbf{c}_S = (1, \tfrac{1}{2}, 0, 0, 0, 0)$$

and

$$\boldsymbol{\pi}_S = \mathbf{c}_S\mathbf{T}_{3S}\mathbf{T}_{2S}\mathbf{T}_{1S} = (1, \tfrac{1}{2}, 0, \tfrac{1}{2}, 0, -\tfrac{1}{2})$$

Multiplying $\boldsymbol{\pi}_S$ into the columns of $\mathbf{A}_S$, we obtain the reduced costs

$$0, 0, \tfrac{1}{2}, 0, \tfrac{1}{2}$$

None of these is negative, so we have an optimal solution. We can now add another column to the A-matrix in the master problem. Its entries in the common rows are the negatives of the corresponding coefficients in $\boldsymbol{\beta}_S$. We would normally call this Proposal No 2, but here we note that it is the variable λ_4 of Section 16.2. The A-matrix now reads

$$\begin{bmatrix} 1 & 1 & -1 & & & & -3 \\ & 1 & 2 & 1 & & & 2 \\ & -1 & & & 1 & & 5 \\ & & & & & 1 & 1 \end{bmatrix}$$

Multiplying the π-vector for the master problem into the new column, we obtain a reduced cost of -2, so we bring λ_4 into the basis. The vector

$$\mathbf{a} = \begin{bmatrix} -3 \\ 2 \\ 5 \\ 1 \end{bmatrix} \quad \text{so} \quad \boldsymbol{\alpha} = \mathbf{T}_2\mathbf{T}_1\mathbf{a} = \begin{bmatrix} -2 \\ 1 \\ 5 \\ 1 \end{bmatrix}$$

Comparing this with the elements of $\boldsymbol{\beta}$, we find that $p = 2$, and our new elementary transformation matrix

$$\mathbf{T}_3 = \begin{bmatrix} 1 & & 2/5 & \\ & 1 & -1/5 & \\ & & 1/5 & \\ & & -1/5 & 1 \end{bmatrix}$$

The new ordered list of basic variables is

$$x_0, x_4, \lambda_4, \lambda_1$$

and the new right hand side

$$\boldsymbol{\beta}' = \mathbf{T}_3\boldsymbol{\beta} = \begin{bmatrix} 41/10 \\ 17/10 \\ 8/10 \\ 2/10 \end{bmatrix}$$

For the next iteration

$$\mathbf{c} = [1, 0, 0, 0]$$

and

$$\boldsymbol{\pi} = \mathbf{c}\mathbf{T}_3\mathbf{T}_2\mathbf{T}_1 = [1, 1/2, 2/5, 0]$$

Multiplying $\boldsymbol{\pi}$ into the columns of $\mathbf{A}$, we obtain the reduced costs

$$11/10, 0, 1/2, 2/5, 0, 0$$

None of these is negative, so we can make no further progress without obtaining another proposal from the sub-problem.

Back in the sub-problem, we again take the π-values on the common rows as the corresponding components of $\mathbf{c}_S$, so

$$\mathbf{c}_S = (1, 1/2, 2/5, 0, 0, 0)$$

and

$$\boldsymbol{\pi}_S = \mathbf{c}_S\mathbf{T}_{3S}\mathbf{T}_{2S}\mathbf{T}_{1S} = (1, 1/2, 2/5, -1/10, 0, -3/10).$$

Multiplying $\boldsymbol{\pi}_S$ into the columns of $\mathbf{A}_S$ we obtain the reduced costs

$$0, 0, -1/10, 0, 3/10$$

So we select the third of these numbers, and bring s_3 into the basis.

We must now form the vector $\boldsymbol{\alpha}_S = \mathbf{T}_{3S}\mathbf{T}_{2S}\mathbf{T}_{1S}\mathbf{a}$, where

$$\mathbf{a} = \begin{bmatrix} 0 \\ 0 \\ 0 \\ 1 \\ 0 \\ 0 \end{bmatrix} \quad \text{so} \quad \mathbf{T}_{2S}\mathbf{T}_{1S}\mathbf{a} = \begin{bmatrix} 0 \\ 0 \\ 0 \\ 1 \\ 0 \\ 0 \end{bmatrix} \quad \text{and} \quad \boldsymbol{\alpha}_S = \begin{bmatrix} 1 \\ -1 \\ -3/2 \\ 1/2 \\ 0 \\ 1/2 \end{bmatrix}$$

Hence $p = 3$ and our new elementary transformation matrix

$$\mathbf{T}_{4S} = \begin{bmatrix} 1 & & -2 & & & \\ & 1 & 2 & & & \\ & & 1 \quad 3 & & & \\ & & 2 & & & \\ & & 0 & 1 & & \\ & & -1 & & & 1 \end{bmatrix}$$

The new ordered list of basic variables is

$$r_{01}, r_{11}, r_{21}, s_3, s_4, x_2$$

and the new right hand side

$$\boldsymbol{\beta}'_S = \mathbf{T}_{4S}\boldsymbol{\beta}_S = \begin{bmatrix} 1 \\ 0 \\ -2 \\ 2 \\ 2 \\ 1 \end{bmatrix}$$

(We note in passing that this simply reverses the previous pivot step in the sub-problem: $\mathbf{T}_{4S}\mathbf{T}_{3S} = \mathbf{I}$.)

For the next iteration we again put

$$\mathbf{c}_S = (1, 1/2, 2/5, 0, 0, 0)$$

and

$$\boldsymbol{\pi}_S = \mathbf{c}_S\mathbf{T}_{4S}\mathbf{T}_{3S}\mathbf{T}_{2S}\mathbf{T}_{1S} = (1, 1/2, 2/5, 0, 0, -1/5)$$

Multiplying $\boldsymbol{\pi}_S$ into the columns of $\mathbf{A}_S$, we obtain the reduced costs

$$1/5, 0, 0, 0, 1/5$$

None of these is negative, so we have an optimal solution. We can now add another column to the A-matrix in the master problem. It is the variable λ_5 of Section 16.2, and the A-matrix now reads

$$\begin{bmatrix} 1 & 1 & -1 & & & & -3 & -3 \\ & 1 & 2 & 1 & & & 2 & \\ & -1 & & & 1 & & 5 & 2 \\ & & & & & 1 & 1 & 1 \end{bmatrix}$$

Multiplying the π-vector for the master problem into the new column, we obtain a reduced cost of $-1/5$, so we bring λ_5 into the basis. The vector

$$\mathbf{a} = \begin{bmatrix} -1 \\ 0 \\ 2 \\ 1 \end{bmatrix} \quad \text{so} \quad \boldsymbol{\alpha} = \mathbf{T}_3\mathbf{T}_2\mathbf{T}_1\mathbf{a} = \begin{bmatrix} -1/5 \\ -2/5 \\ 2/5 \\ 3/5 \end{bmatrix}$$

Hence $p = 3$, and our new elementary transformation matrix

$$\mathbf{T}_4 = \begin{bmatrix} 1 & & & 1/3 \\ & 1 & & 2/3 \\ & & 1 & -2/3 \\ & & & 5/3 \end{bmatrix}$$

The new ordered list of basic variables is

$$x_0, x_4, \lambda_4, \lambda_5$$

and the new right hand side

$$\boldsymbol{\beta}' = \mathbf{T}_4\boldsymbol{\beta} = \begin{bmatrix} 25/6 \\ 11/6 \\ 4/6 \\ 2/6 \end{bmatrix}$$

For the next iteration

$$\mathbf{c} = [1, 0, 0, 0]$$

nd

$$\boldsymbol{\pi} = \mathbf{c}\mathbf{T}_4\mathbf{T}_3\mathbf{T}_2\mathbf{T}_1 = [1, 1/2, 1/3, 1/3]$$

Multiplying $\boldsymbol{\pi}$ into the columns of $\mathbf{A}$, we obtain the reduced costs

$$7/6, 0, 1/2, 1/3, 1/3, 0, 0$$

None of these is negative, so we can make no further progress without obtaining another proposal from the sub-problem.

Back in the subproblem, we again take the π-values on the common rows as the corresponding components of $\mathbf{c}_S$, so

$$\mathbf{c}_S = (1, 1/2, 1/3, 0, 0, 1/3)$$

Multiplying $\boldsymbol{\pi}_S$ into the columns of $\mathbf{A}_S$, we obtain the reduced costs

$$0, 0, 0, 0, \tfrac{1}{3}$$

None of these is negative, so we already have an optimum solution to the sub-problem. This means that we have no new proposal to offer, and there is nothing more to be done in the master problem. The optimum value of $x_0 = 25/6$, is obtained by putting $x_4 = 11/6$, $\lambda_4 = 4/6$ and $\lambda_5 = 2/6$.

Returning now from the example to a general discussion, we note two mathematically trivial but practically important points. Firstly, although the optimum proposal is obtained by solving the sub-problems completely, a valid proposal is obtained from any feasible solution to a sub-problem, and in particular from intermediate basic feasible solutions obtained in the course of iterating from the final basis reached on the previous major iteration towards the optimum basis for the current π-values. In many problems the π-values oscillate significantly from one major iteration to the next, and the intermediate proposals are often more valuable in the long run than the final proposals obtained on early major iterations. In the worked example we could have saved one major iteration by making the proposal λ_5 when we first encountered it on the way to λ_4. Secondly, one may cut off each sub-problem after a certain number of minor iterations in each major iteration. Convergence is still assured if, whenever a major iteration produces no minor iterations in the master problem, one does not terminate if any sub-problem was cut off before reaching optimum. Instead one just carries on doing more iterations in all such sub-problems, starting where one left off last time.

16.4 Interpreting the Final Solution

There remains the problem of finding the values of the sub-problem variables from a solution to the master problem, where one is only given the weight attached to each proposal. This problem could obviously be solved by recording the values of the sub-problem variables associated with each proposal. This would be a rather tedious operation from a data processing point of view, since in the course of solving a large problem one generates an immense number of proposals, nearly all of which are rejected in the final solution.

An alternative approach is based on a possibly important alternative method of decomposing a problem having the structure with which we are operating. This is to divide each common row into separate constraints—one relating to the natural variables of the master problem if there are any, and another for each sub-problem relating to the variables of the sub-problem. The problem is of course to know how to divide the right hand sides of the original common rows between these new constraints, but we can easily compute what values are required to produce the current solution to the master problem. In each row we simply have to multiply the weight attached to each proposal by its coefficient in the row; then sum these products. We then solve the sub-problems using these right hand sides, treating all rows other than the original objective function as constraints. When we have an optimum solution to the whole problem, this process does not take long, since we start from a trial solution to the sub-problem that is optimum under the current shadow prices on the common rows, and we simply have to find another that satisfies the common row constraints. One may wish to do the same thing at an intermediate stage. There is no difficulty about this, but the process is apt to take a little longer.

16.5 Theoretical Interest in Decomposition

Some economists are interested in decomposition as a mathematical representation of decentralized planning. The central authority—the master problem—posts prices for the scarce resources available to more than one sub-problem, and the sub-problems submit optimal plans based on these prices. But note that the sub-problems are not allowed to implement these plans. The master problem makes a compromise plan based on all proposals submitted so far, and posts new prices to get more information from the sub-problems.

Some mathematicians are interested in decomposition as an example of the solution of a linear programming problem in which some variables (or some constraints) are generated automatically during the calculation as opposed to being written down explicitly to begin with. The first proposal on these lines was due to Ford and Fulkerson (1958). Other examples are discussed by Gomory (1963*c*), and Gilmore and Gomory (1961), and Dzielinski and Gomory (1965). It seems likely that this approach will find many further applications.

There is also some theoretical interest in the use of decomposition to solve non-convex non-linear problems. This has been studied by Fromovitz (1965). He points out that a *randomized strategy*, in which one chooses a mixture of different solutions with specified probabilities, may be better on average than any pure strategy if some constraints need not be satisfied for each individual component of the strategy provided that they are satisfied on average. Decomposition will treat the common row constraints as ones that need only be satisfied on average. The constraints within the sub-problems must be satisfied for each component of the strategy. Note that it is not normally feasible to have integer variables in a decomposition problem, since it would not normally be acceptable to have a solution that combined proposals with different values of integer variables.

16.6 Computational Experience

Some people are interested in decomposition primarily as a computational technique for solving large linear programming problems. Successful results have been achieved with codes using no special tricks on problems with very few common rows.

As the number of common rows increases, the problem becomes more difficult. Beale, Hughes and Small (1965) report the successful solution of problems decomposed with between 50 and 100 common rows. To achieve these results they used the procedures for making several proposals from each sub-problem in each minor iteration, and cutting off the sub-problems, mentioned in Section 16.3. They also found it possible to put several trial proposals from each sub-problem into the master problem initially, so that the master problem was able to find fairly realistic π-values on the common rows before any proposals had been generated automatically. Another device they found useful was to incorporate one of the sub-problems into the master problem: the idea being that it could adjust to accommodate any minor variations in the contributions of the other sub-problems to the common rows.

In many problems of this size it is necessary in practice to stop the calculations before reaching a complete optimum. This is less unsatisfactory than in normal linear programming because one has a definite upper bound to the additional improvement possible in the objective function. This is given by the sum of the reduced costs on the optimal proposals from each sub-problem. (It is derived theoretically by taking the composite objective function defined by the π-values on the common rows, and then imagining that the common row constraints—other than the convexity rows—do not have to be satisfied. The solution to this problem is trivial, and is obviously not less favourable than the solution to the real problem.)

Early experiences with problems containing more than 100 common rows have not been so satisfactory. Some such problems have been solved but only after many hours on the IBM 7090 or 7094 computers. It seems reasonable to hope that better results will be obtained with more experience of how to use all the additional features now available in decomposition codes.

A. C. Williams (1962) has shown that distribution sub-problems can be handled very compactly in the decomposition algorithm, and can be solved by inspection for any given set of π-values. This facility is available in the decomposition package for the LP/90/94 system, and in other codes.

The question of when to delete proposals from the master problem is not entirely clear. Theoretically it is only necessary to retain the proposals in the current basis, but it seems to help the master problem to have a number of other proposals on hand, to make the best use of the new material offered. The LP/90/94 system has a wide variety of *delete* options, i.e. ways of removing unwanted proposals from the master problem, for use both during the solution of a problem and when changing from one problem to another.

If a large number of initial trial proposals cannot conveniently be constructed, it is probably useless to put in just one proposal from each sub-problem. This will not provide realistic π-values on the common rows, and introduces awkward degeneracies into the master problem. One can use an externally given set of π-values for the first major iteration, but this will be lost afterwards. If one can estimate upper and lower limits for each π-value, one can prevent the master problem from producing "frivolous" π-values (through lack of a properly balanced set of proposals) by introducing suitably priced synthetic variables representing buying and selling the resources represented by the common rows.

16.7 Problem Formulation for Decomposition

It is hard to give a general description of good practice in the formulation of decomposition problems, but the following points should be noted.

(1) Do make a great effort to keep the number of common rows down, even if it means adding to the total number of rows in the problem.
(2) Remember that it is possible to have rows in the master problem that are not common rows (or convexity rows, of which there is one for each sub-problem). This means in effect that one can put one sub-problem into the master problem. This seems to be a good thing to do. Ideally the sub-problem so selected should have few extra rows, but it should represent a group of activities that can easily cope with moderate excesses or deficiencies in the contributions to (or from) the common rows that may be implied by the proposals thrown up from the other sub-problems. These two requirements tend to be contradictory, so one must make the best compromise possible. In practice the distribution activities are often selected for this treatment; this has the incidental advantage that all the information required from the final solution may be obtainable from the master problem without the need to use the procedure described in Section 16.4 for solving the sub-problems.
(3) Remember that bad scaling (having non-zero matrix elements very different from (1) in absolute value) is bad in ordinary linear programming, and is apt to be very bad in decomposition because of the way sub-problems are cut off before reaching optimum in each major iteration.
(4) Do take the sub-problems into your confidence, but do not ask them to make decisions that are better taken in the master problem.

As an example of the first of these points, one may know lower or upper bounds on the possible contribution of some sub-problem to some common row. If these are not represented in the sub-problem it may produce a large number of "frivolous" proposals that violate these bounds. One may get better proposals and a quicker solution by formulating these bounds as explicit constraints in the sub-problem, even if they are technically redundant.

The other point, about not asking the sub-problems to make unnecessary decisions, arises in particular if the sub-problems represent different plants and there are alternative sources of some raw materials used by more than one plant, or alternative markets for some products made by more than one plant. The sub-problem should not be asked to choose between these sources or markets. There should be a material balance row for the raw material or product for the plant, and the proposals should represent the best way for the plant to operate if it is to be a net user or producer of each material at some specified level (given whatever other conditions are represented by the π-values on the other common rows). The master problem can then decide how to provide or distribute this material in the light of proposals made from other plants.

16.8 Conclusions

The solution of very large linear programming problems, by decomposition or any other means, cannot yet be treated as a routine exercise in the same way as solving smaller problems. Careful attention to the formulation of the problem, in particular with respect to the number of common rows, is needed to avoid excessive computer running times. In some ways the state of decomposition as a practical process resembles the state of ordinary linear programming ten years ago, but there are grounds for hoping that decomposition will now progress in the same way as ordinary linear programming.

17 Stochastic Programming

17.1 Introduction

It has proved hard to develop methods for handling both inequality constraints and random errors in a single analytical model. Given an optimization problem, we usually have to start by deciding whether the constraints or the random elements are the more important. If the constraints are more important, we replace all random elements by their mean values for a mathematical programming model: if the random elements are more important, we either ignore the constraints or else abandon analytical optimization methods and simulate alternative possibilities.

This is a reasonable approach, but one may do better with a mathematical programming formulation that introduces at least a first approximation to the effects of random variables. Such a formulation will often involve more computing than the deterministic one, but this can often be handled efficiently by some standard non-linear programming technique. About the only convenient theoretical property of stochastic programming models is that in most formulations the resulting non-linear programming problem is convex—provided the problem is convex in the absence of uncertainties. So methods of finding a local optimum to a non-linear programming problem will find a global optimum to such problems.

On the other hand the data on the random elements are unlikely to be precise enough to justify a very elaborate calculation, and the models suggested below are derived with this fact in mind.

Some problems involving both constraints and random variables can be formulated in dynamic programming terms. But it is rare for a practical problem to have the special properties needed to make dynamic programming computationally effective.

So much for generalities, the next point to note is that, although it may be obvious in a general way that a particular real problem involves both constraints and random variables, it may not be obvious how to formulate this problem in a precise mathematical way. Here three types of formulation are discussed. They may be classified as

non-sequential stochastic programming
sequential stochastic programming
chance-constrained programming

Let us first summarize the assumptions common to all these formulations.

For convenience of exposition, we assume that, except for some random coefficients, we have a linear programming problem. There is no real difficulty in extending the ideas to some non-linear problems: indeed this may be computationally attractive, since if the problem is non-linear anyway the non-linearities introduced by the random variables may not make the problem any harder. But since stochastic programming is not yet widely used in practice, it seems prudent to concentrate on the logically simpler problems first.

Our next basic assumption concerns the nature of the uncertainties to be analysed. We assume that, although we do not know all the coefficients in the problem, we do know their probability distributions and (where relevant) their correlations or more generally their joint distributions. Again it seems sensible to treat the statistical problems of estimating the distributions as a separate exercise. Theoretically the optimum policy may depend on the precision to which the parameters of the distributions are determined, as well as on our best estimates of the parameters—so that for example we should work with a *t* distribution with some fixed number of degrees of freedom rather than a normal distribution (since a *t* distribution can be regarded as a mixture of normal distributions with a common mean but different variances, thereby allowing for the fact that the true variance may not be known exactly), but in practice these distinctions will be insignificant compared with the effects of other assumptions that must be made about the data.

Another basic assumption is that some variables, known as *first-stage variables* must be chosen before the true values of any random coefficients are revealed, while other variables may be chosen later. The term *non-sequential stochastic programming* has been used by Hadley (1964) to cover formulations in which no variables have to be chosen after the values of some random coefficients have been revealed but before the values of others are revealed, so all variables that are not first-stage variables can be considered as *second-stage variables*. This assumption greatly simplifies the problem, so let us first see what can be done with it.

17.2 Non-sequential Stochastic Programming

If all the random coefficients are in the objective function the problem is relatively easy. If all the variables are first-stage variables, then the mean value of the objective function is maximized by simply replacing the random coefficients by their mean values. Alternatively one may minimize the variance of the objective function for a given mean. This approach, pioneered by Markowitz, see Markowitz (1959), with particular reference to the selection of a portfolio of investments leads to a quadratic programming problem. One may doubt whether the uncertainties in predicting stock exchange prices are not too great to justify such an elaborate mathematical analysis. But if one has estimated the mean return and degree of risk associated with each individual possible investment, it is by no means easy to select a portfolio that takes proper note of the correlations between these risks. A quadratic programming study using a correlation matrix estimated from past data may therefore be useful.

If there are some second-stage variables, then one may want to know the probability that any particular solution will be optimal. This involves calculating the probability that all the reduced costs are non-negative, i.e. the probability that the values of the random coefficients regarded as a vector lie within some polyhedron. Such calculations are apt to be very laborious, so one should be sure that this is an appropriate formulation of the problem before embarking on them.

If the constraints include some random variables, we may wish to choose the first-stage variables so as to maximize the expected value of the objective function. See Dantzig (1955) and Beale (1955). It is easy to show that this involves maximizing a concave function of the first-stage variables, so there is no danger of reaching a local but not global optimum solution. If the joint distribution of the random elements is discrete, then the problem of choosing the first-stage variables and sets of second-stage variables for all possible circumstances becomes one vast linear programming problem. This consists of separate sub-problems except that the first-stage variables are linking variables. But the number of sub-problems, representing the number of possible combinations of values of the random variables, is likely to be discouragingly large. The problem is eased if the second-stage variables are such that the constraints can be divided into groups where no second-stage variable occurs in more than one group. The correlations between the values of random coefficients in different groups of constraints are then irrelevant, and for each group one can work with the probabilities of different combinations of coefficients in these constraints, without considering the values of coefficients in other constraints.

An extreme example arises when each group consists of a single constraint. Prospects of some effective computation in these circumstances are obviously much brighter. Particular attention has been paid to problems of this type with two further special features: firstly, the only random elements are in the right hand sides; and secondly, for each constraint separately, there is a cost for each unit by which the left hand side (considering only the first-stage variables) falls short of the random right hand side, and there is another cost for each unit by which the left hand side exceeds the right hand side. The random right hand side may represent a sales forecast, and the two costs then represent the per-unit costs of being out of stock when a demand is made and of having unsold stock at the end of the operation. Note that the solution does not depend on the correlations between the random coefficients—which is very important, since these correlations are rarely known at all exactly. If the second-stage variables are denoted by y_i and y_{-i}, the problem can be formulated as follows—

maximize the mean value of x_0, where

$$x_0 + \sum a_{0j}x_j + \sum f_i y_i + \sum (g_i - f_i)y_{-i} = 0$$

$$\sum a_{ij}x_j + \quad y_i - \qquad\qquad y_{-i} = \beta_i \quad (i = 1, \ldots, m)$$

and β_i is a random variable with mean μ_i and cumulative distribution function $F_i(\beta_i)$.

Note that g_i, which represents the sum of the unit costs of exceeding and falling short of the right hand side on the ith constraint, must be non-negative.

We can now eliminate the second-stage variables from the problem, by writing

$$E(x_0) = -\sum a_{0j}x_j - \sum H_i(z_i)$$

where

$$\sum a_{ij}x_j = z_i$$

$$H_i(z_i) = (\mu_i - z_i)f_i + g_i z_i F_i(z_i) - g_i \int_{-\infty}^{z_i} \beta_i \, dF_i(\beta_i)$$

Note incidentally that $dH_i/dz_i = -f_i + g_i F_i(z_i)$, a relationship that can easily be proved from first principles.

The functions $H_i(z_i)$ can conveniently be handled using the interpolation procedure developed for use in separable programming, but the special pivot-selection rules of separable programming are not needed, since the problem is convex.

17.3 Sequential Stochastic Programming

The present state of sequential stochastic programming can be illustrated by considering the following problem.

We wish to schedule the production of N products over T time periods. This problem may well be representable in linear programming terms, in which case it will have $2NT$ supply constraints of the form

$$s_{i,t} = s_{i,t-1} + p_{i,t} - x_{i,t} \tag{17.1}$$

$$x_{i,t} \leqslant d_{i,t} \tag{17.2}$$

where

$s_{i,t}$ denotes the stock of product i at the end of period t

$p_{i,t}$ denotes the production of product i in period t

$x_{i,t}$ denotes the sales of product i in period t

$d_{i,t}$ denotes the demand for product i in period t

which is assumed known.

There will of course be other production constraints that we do not need to consider explicitly here.

What happens if the $d_{i,t}$ are not known, but we can estimate probability distributions for them? The principal effects of the uncertainty are that

(1) We may need more stocks on hand in any time period, to guard against unforeseen extra demand.
(2) We shall on the average have more stocks carried forward into the next time period, as a result of unforeseen shortfalls in demand.

If the production constraints on different products did not interact, then the problem would be amenable to dynamic programming. This is unlikely to be so, but we can still obtain an approximate solution to the appropriate modification of the production policy to allow for the uncertainty as follows. We define $q_{i,t}$ as the average amount of product i available for sale in period t, averaged over all possible values of the random demands. We also re-define $p_{i,t}$ as the average production of product i in period t, and we have the equation

$$q_{i,t} = E(s_{i,t-1}) + p_{i,t} \tag{17.3}$$

We now make an assumption that is true when there are no random errors in the demand forecasts, though it is generally not strictly true if there are random errors. This may seem an unpromising step, but we shall see later how to allow at least approximately for the error in the assumption. The assumption is that the amount of product i available for sale in period t will always be precisely $q_{i,t}$. Given the probability distribution function for $d_{i,t}$, we can then compute $E(s_{i,t})$ as a concave function and $E(x_{i,t})$ as a convex function, both of $q_{i,t}$. If $a_{j,i,t}$ for $j = 1, 2, \ldots$ denote selected values of $q_{i,t}$, and $b_{j,i,t}$ and $c_{j,i,t}$ denote corresponding values of $E(s_{i,t})$ and $E(x_{i,t})$ respectively, then we can introduce a new set of non-negative variables $\lambda_{j,i,t}$, and we may write

$$\sum_j \lambda_{j,i,t} \qquad = 1 \tag{17.4}$$

$$\sum_j a_{j,i,t}\lambda_{j,i,t} = q_{i,t} \tag{17.5}$$

$$\sum_j b_{j,i,t}\lambda_{j,i,t} = E(s_{i,t}) \tag{17.6}$$

$$\sum_j c_{j,i,t}\lambda_{j,i,t} = E(x_{i,t}) \tag{17.7}$$

Using equations (17.5) and (17.6) we see that (17.3) can be rewritten as

$$\sum_j a_{j,i,t}\lambda_{j,i,t} = \sum_j b_{j,i,t-1}\lambda_{j,i,t-1} + p_{i,t} \tag{17.8}$$

Of all these equations, the only ones that need appear explicitly in the matrix used for calculation are (17.4) and (17.8), which replace (17.1) and (17.2) in the deterministic model. The left hand side of (17.7) will of course replace the right hand side in the objective function, multiplied by an appropriate profit factor to represent receipts from sales. (Note that we have not yet specified whether sales not met immediately are lost or backlogged with some penalty. If they are backlogged then $s_{i,t}$ must be regarded as negative if unfulfilled orders are outstanding, and the values of $c_{j,i,t}$ must include an allowance for delayed sales.)

The stochastic model has no more equations than the deterministic model. It does have more variables, but the number of additional variables can be kept down if we start with a coarse grid and use the interpolation scheme to add more variables where they are needed. This can again be done without using the special pivot selection rules of separable programming.

We must now consider what to do about the fact that the actual amount of product available may differ from $q_{i,t}$ by a random variable with zero mean. Although this problem has no simple solution the vital thing about it is that *a random addition to the supply of a product has exactly the same effect on the amount of unsold stock as a random subtraction of the same amount from the demand.* The loss of revenue due to lost or delayed sales is the same under both conditions, so this replacement of a random supply by a random demand does not affect the average receipts from sales as long as the mean of the distribution is zero.

This fact puts the problem into proper perspective. We are unlikely to know the demand distribution precisely, so there is no need to worry about getting a precise estimate of the variability in supply. How do we get a rough estimate of this variability? We have in effect to assess how the actual production levels, and the associated marginal costs of extra production, will depend on variations in stock levels at the beginning of each period. Two extreme cases can easily be analysed.

(*a*) Production may be essentially unconstrained, the marginal cost being independent of production level over all levels of activity. In this case an amount $q_{i,t}$ will be made available regardless of initial stocks, and the original analysis needs no modification. (This assumes we may regard the set of demands in one time period as being statistically independent of demands in previous time periods. Such an assumption may not be true, but it will rarely be justifiable to try to take advantage of any correlations in an analysis of this kind.)

(*b*) Production may be completely fixed by other considerations, so that it is uneconomic or even impossible to adjust it in the light of current stock levels. For example one may be producing the product at maximum capacity in this time period. Or one may not be producing it at all—perhaps because the necessary raw materials are not available, or because the production capacity is needed for other purposes. In this case the demand distribution for the product should be adjusted to represent the total variability in demand in this and all previous consecutive time periods during which production has been fixed in this way. Such a situation arises for example with a seasonal product for which one has to build up stocks in the off season. Let us suppose that no flexibility in production level is likely to be available during the peak season; and we want to estimate the appropriate level of stocks with which to enter the peak season. The probability of running out of stock during the last period of the peak season must then be computed using the assumed variability in demand for the peak season as a whole, and not simply the variability in demand for the last period.

In some cases a compromise between these assumptions of unconstrained and fixed production may be appropriate, but a detailed analysis of the problem is unlikely to be needed to produce a sensible plan of action for the first time period. Decisions for later time periods will in any case have to wait until more information is available.

17.4 Chance-constrained Programming

Charnes and Cooper (1959) have generalized stochastic programming by allowing each inequality constraint to be violated with some prescribed probability (say α_i for the *i*th constraint.) This may seem illogical, since when a constraint is unsatisfied one presumably has to pay some penalty (represented by second-stage or other variables in the previous formulations), which is likely to depend on the extent to which the constraint is violated. Theoretically this penalty should be weighed against the direct costs of activities that tend to reduce it, but sometimes the assessment of the appropriate penalty is so uncertain as to make this seem a meaningless exercise. All one really knows is that a strategy that violated the constraint very often would be unacceptable, and this knowledge is represented by the selection of an appropriate value of α_i. The argument is not unlike the argument for conventional statistical significance tests.

An example of a type of problem in which this approach seems justified has been published by Van de Panne and Popp (1963). This is a classical diet problem except that the amount of a nutrient in a given foodstuff is regarded as a normally distributed random variable with known means and variances. One then cannot be certain of meeting all the inequality constraints on the nutrients, but it seems not unreasonable to insist that each should be satisfied with some high probability, say 99%. We have done some computing on such problems, with uncertain analyses for several nutrients, using separable programming and interpolation.

17.5 Models for Uncertain Market Sizes

Many real problems to which one might hope to apply stochastic programming involve complications that are not discussed in any of the models considered so far. This is not a reason to despair of doing any useful quantitative work in such problems, since a very simplified model is often more useful than no model at all. However, it is a reason for being very careful about the precise nature of the assumptions made in the model—particularly about the relationships between the random elements and the decisions to be taken. It also means that we must be prepared to make many new types of model in this field.

For example, consider the problem of deciding what production policy to follow when a number of products can be sold in different markets at different prices, but the sizes of the different markets are unknown. If one could afford to wait and choose the policy only when the actual demands have been determined then of course there is no stochastic programming problem. Otherwise one needs to compute a curve of marginal expected revenue $f(x)$ from an extra unit of any product made as a function of the number of units x already being made. If there is only one market, this curve is obviously given by the formula

$$f(x) = p[1 - F(x)]$$

where p is the selling price and $F(x)$ is the probability that the demand is x or less (i.e. the distribution function for the demand). The problem is now essentially that considered in Section 17.2 above.

Now suppose that there are n markets for the product, but that we have to allocate the product to a specific market before one knows what the demand in this market will be. The problem is then fairly simple in principle, although one can no longer write down a simple formula for the solution: one allocates each extra unit of production to the market with the highest expected marginal revenue. If x_i denotes the amount of production allocated to the ith market with selling price p_i, then we have to choose the x_i such that

$$\sum_{i=1}^{n} x_i = x$$

and such that there exists some quantity λ, where

$$x_i = 0 \quad \text{if } p_i < \lambda$$

and otherwise

$$\lambda = p_i[1 - F_i(x_i)]$$

i.e.

$$F_i(x_i) = 1 - \lambda/p_i$$

The Lagrange multiplier λ is the required marginal expected revenue $f(x)$, so it is a straightforward matter in principle to determine the value of x corresponding to any given value of λ.

A mathematically more interesting situation arises if one has to choose the levels of production knowing only the probability distributions for the demands, but can choose one's markets in the light of actual demands; so that if for example one's hopes of selling a particular item in the best market were disappointed one can still offer it on the next market. To analyse this situation we must arrange the markets in decreasing order of profitability. We must also consider the cumulative distribution of the demands in the first m markets combined: let us denote this by $G_m(x)$. Then it is not difficult to see that the marginal expected revenue from an extra unit of production is given by the formula

$$f(x) = \sum_{i=1}^{n} p_i[G_{i-1}(x) - G_i(x)]$$

where

$$G_0(x) = 1.$$

To establish the truth of this formula we note that the probability of being able to sell another unit in the best market is obviously $1 - G_1(x)$, so the expected revenue from this market is

$$p_1(1 - G_1(x))$$

On the other hand the probability of being able to sell another unit in one or other of the best two markets is obviously $1 - G_2(x)$. Since we will choose the very best market whenever this is available, the probability that we will actually have occasion to sell in the second market is $G_1(x) - G_2(x)$. The rest of the formula follows by the same reasoning. The formula can of course be rewritten as

$$f(x) = p_i - \sum_{i=1}^{n} (p_i - p_{i+1})G_i(x)$$

where $p_{n+1} = 0$.

To estimate the cumulative distributions for combined markets in practice it is convenient to approximate them by normal distributions. It is easy, and therefore probably worth while, to allow the demands in different markets to be correlated. Let us therefore suppose that these demands have means μ_i and variances σ_i^2, and that a fraction r^2 is totally correlated between markets.

The mean of the total demand in the first m markets is then $\sum_{i=1}^{m} \mu_i$. The totally correlated part of the demand has a standard deviation equal to the sum of the standard deviations of the components, i.e.

$$r \sum_{i=1}^{m} \sigma_i$$

so the variance of this part of the demand is

$$r^2 \left(\sum_{i=1}^{m} \sigma_i \right)^2$$

The variance V_m of the total demand is then obtained by adding in the variances of the independent components, and is given by the formula

$$V_m = r^2\left(\sum_{i=1}^{m} \sigma_i\right)^2 + (1 - r^2)\sum_{i=1}^{m} \sigma_1^2$$

Appendix: Note on the LP/90/94 System

A.1 Introduction

C-E-I-R's LP/90/94 system is basically a system for solving linear programming problems with up to 1125 rows and an arbitrary number of columns (variables) on an IBM 7090 or 7094 computer. The system has been extended to provide facilities for separable programming and interpolation, quadratic programming, integer programming by either branch and bound or Martin's method, and decomposition. (Not all combinations of these features are possible: for example one cannot use more than one of quadratic, integer or decomposition at the same time.)

A brief description of the method of formulating problems for the LP/90/94 system is given to illustrate what is involved in using a production LP code. The data input format is based on the SHARE standard input for LP systems for the IBM 700 and 7000 series, and is used by many other systems.

There are two kinds of input to the LP operating system: data and operating instructions. Original data are entered on card images written in BCD (Binary-Coded Decimal) on a magnetic tape, known as the I-tape. The card images may have been loaded from real cards on peripheral card-to-tape equipment: but they are more often generated as card-images on tape by some other program. Instructions are normally entered via the on-line card reader on *agendum call cards*, though there is an agendum to read subsequent agenda as card images from a specified tape unit.

With this system a matrix generator program is primarily concerned with generating the I-tape. The agendum cards can be selected manually for each individual problem.

In this system the rows (or equations) and columns (or variables) are given names consisting of 6 Hollerith characters, of which the first must be blank or numeric (1–9). There is no objection to using some combination of characters both as a row name and as a column name in the same problem.

A.2 I-tape Data

There are three main types of data input cards: remarks, which have an asterisk in column 1, indicator cards which announce the kind of data following, and the intrinsic data. The following description lists some but does *not* give all the possible element format options.

1. TITLE CARDS
There should be at least one title card, and there may be any number. They must have an asterisk in Col. 1. The rest of the title, in columns 2–72, may be arbitrary.

2. ROW IDs
The next card announces the row identifications. It must be punched RØWbID in columns 1–6 (where b means blank). This is followed by one card for each row to be used on the problem. Rows may be of 4 kinds: objective functions, equalities, less-than-or-equal-to inequalities, or greater-than-or-equal-to inequalities. The row name is punched in columns 13–18, preceded by an indicator in column 12 to specify the type of row. The indicators are as follows:

0 or blank	for an objective function or equality
+	for a less-than-or-equal-to inequality (instructing the program to supply a positive slack)
–	for a greater-than-or-equal-to inequality (instructing the program to supply a negative slack).

The objective functions must precede all constraint rows.

3. BASIS HEADINGS (OPTIONAL)
Cards to modify the automatically created all-slack-and-artificial basis may be announced by an indicator card punched BASIS in columns 1–5. This is followed by cards that define a column name in 7–12 and a row name in columns 13–18. The slacks or artificials associated with the named rows will then be replaced in the initial basis by the named columns (as far as possible). Only changes from the slack basis are specified, so slack names should not be entered in columns 7–12. The pairing of row and column names is immaterial—it will not be preserved after inversion.

4. MATRIX ELEMENTS
The next card announces the matrix elements. It must be punched MATRIX in columns 1–6. The non-zero matrix elements are then punched, one per card, as follows

Cols. 1–6	Blank
Cols. 7–12	Column (or variable) name
Cols. 13–18	Row (or constraint) name
Col. 19	Sign of Element (b or + for positive, – for negative)
Cols. 20–23	Integer part of element
Col. 24	Decimal point
Cols. 25–30	Fractional part of element

Some variation in this format is permitted. In particular the sign of a negative element may come immediately before the first digit (where it will naturally occur if the number is produced by an F-format in a FORTRAN matrix generator). Also the decimal point may be shifted—though it is normally desirable to scale the problem so that this is not necessary.

Note that zero elements do not have to be specified.

All elements relating to a particular column must be together, but the row order within a column is immaterial.

5. RIGHT HAND SIDE ELEMENTS

The next card announces the right hand side elements (i.e. the nonzero constant terms). It is punched FIRSTbB in columns 1–7. The elements are then punched, one to a card, as the matrix elements, except that columns 7–12 are left blank. Multiple right hand sides can be supplied: each must be preceded by a header card punched NEXTbB,n, where n is the number of the right hand side. The values of n must lie between 2 and 9999 and must form an ascending but not necessarily consecutive sequence. There must be no blanks between the comma in column 7 and the first digit of n, but leading zeros are permitted.

6. END OF INPUT

The last non-zero element of the last right hand side must be followed by a card with EØF punched in columns 1–3.

NOTES

If the row name specified in column 13–18 of either a matrix or a right hand side element card is not in the list of names following the RØWbID card, then the element will be ignored, but there will be a message printed to say that the corresponding row is not used in the problem. This is not regarded as an error. If one or more elements of a column are separated from the rest, an error message stating that the vector is split will occur—unless the separated elements are all in the objective function rows, in which case they are suppressed and no message appears. If two or more elements in a column have the same row name, then a DUPLICATE ROW error message appears.

A.3 Agendum Cards

Control of the system is accomplished by means of agendum cards. The user's guide to the system must be consulted for details, but the following list of some of the more important agenda may give some feel for the system.

Agendum Name	*Brief Description*
ADDRHS	Adds one or more RHS to binary matrix from specified tape unit or card reader.
A. TØ. I	Translates binary matrix to BCD input tape formed.
CØMPILE	Compiles a report writing program for use by REPORT.

CØNTROLS	Sets values of controls parameters.
CØRRECT. BCD	Makes corrections to input or compile tape information.
CØST RANGING	Obtains the range over which the basic variables may be varied, one at a time, without requiring a change of basis.
DECØMP	Solves decomposed problem.
DIFFERENCE	Defines the difference between two RHS as a new RHS.
DØ.D/J	Computes and prints reduced costs.
DØ.PCR	Parametric programming on objective function.
DØ.PLP	Parametric programming on RHS.
EPSILØN	Zero RHS elements are replaced by specified (small) value.
FIX.VEC	The product of specified scalars and vectors is subtracted from a RHS to form a new RHS.
FLAGS	Delete or restore columns to problem.
GETØFF	Saves current solution on specified tape for use by RESTART.
HEADING	Starts new problem. Provides identification on output.
INPUT	Reads BCD input tape and converts to binary matrix tape (A-tape).
INTERPØLATE (or INTERP)	Interpolates among the special variables used by separable programming. Also corrects illegal combinations of special variables in the basis.
INVERT	Inversion routine. Accepts basis in core (Normally called automatically by NØRMAL)
MØDES	Sets modes for different ways of operating NØRMAL. In particular this indicates whether or not to use special rules for separable programming, or whether to use the quadratic, integer (branch and bound), or all-integer (Martin) algorithms.
NEW. BASIS	Replaces basis by basis specified on cards from card reader.
NØRMAL	Normal optimizing routine. (This automatically calls INVERT as required.)
ØUTPUT	Processes mediary tape into BCD on O-Tape for printing.
PICTURE	Pictorial representation of matrix.
RECØST	Forms linear combination of rows.
REPØRT	Produces report on solution, using procedure prepared by previous CØMPILE agendum.
RESTART	Restarts problem from tape created by GETØFF.
REVISE	Rows, columns and/or revised elements can be inserted or substituted in the binary matrix tape. (A-tape).
RHS RANGING	Obtains the range over which the RHS elements can

	be varied, one at a time, without requiring a change of basis.
SCALEM	Scales rows and columns so that magnitude of largest element in each row and column is unity.
SØLUTION	Provides full print-outs of current solution (on mediary tape).
TABLEAU	Provides full tableau (or parts of it).
TITLE	Changes output page headings.
UNRAVEL	Produces unscrambled solution on specified tape unit in a format suitable for reading into a FØRTRAN output analysis program.
UNSCALE	Restores scale factors used before SCALEM was called.
UNSCRAMBLE	Sorts the primal solution so that the basic vectors are in the same order as on the matrix tape.

References

A. J. Akeroyd (1966); "An application of separable programming," *Computer Journal* **8** pp 344–346.

E. Balas (1964); "Un algorithme additif pour la résolution des programmes linéaires en variables bivalentes," *C.R. Acad. Sc.* (*Paris*) **258** pp 3817–3820.

M. L. Balinski (1965); "Integer programming: methods, uses, computation," *Management Science* **12** pp 253–313.

E. M. L. Beale (1955); "On minimizing a convex function subject to linear inequalities," *J. Roy. Statist. Soc.* (B) **17** pp 173–184.

E. M. L. Beale (1959); "On quadratic programming," *Naval Research Logistics Quarterly* **6** pp 227–243.

E. M. L. Beale (1965); "Survey of integer programming," *Operational Research Quarterly* **16** pp 219–228.

E. M. L. Beale (1967); "Numerical methods," *Nonlinear Programming*, edited by Jean Abadie, pp 135–205, (North-Holland Publishing Company, Amsterdam).

E. M. L. Beale, P. J. Coen and A. D. J. Flowerdew (1965); "Separable programming applied to an ore purchasing problem," *Applied Statistics* **14** pp 89–101.

E. M. L. Beale, P. A. B. Hughes and R. E. Small (1965); "Experience in using a decomposition program," *The Computer Journal* **8** pp 13–18.

E. M. L. Beale and R. E. Small (1965); "Mixed integer programming by a branch and bound technique," *Proceedings of the IFIP Congress* 1965 **2** pp 450–451, edited by W. A. Kalenich (Spartan Press, Washington D.C., and Macmillan, London).

A. Charnes and W. W. Cooper (1959); "Chance-constrained programming," *Management Science* **6** pp 73–79.

R. J. Dakin (1965); "A tree-search algorithm for mixed integer programming problems," *The Computer Journal* **8** pp 250–255.

G. B. Dantzig (1951); "Maximization of a linear function of variables subject to linear inequalities," *Activity Analysis of Production and Allocation* Chapter XXI, edited by T. C. Koopmans (Wiley, New York).

G. B. Dantzig (1955); "Linear programming under uncertainty," *Management Science* **1** pp 197–206.

G. B. Dantzig (1963); *Linear Programming and Extensions* (Princeton University Press).

G. B. Dantzig and P. Wolfe (1960); "Decomposition principle for linear programming," *Operations Research* **8** pp 101–111.

G. B. Dantzig and P. Wolfe (1961); "The decomposition algorithm for linear programs," *Econometrica* **29** pp 767–778.

N. J. Driebeek (1966); "An algorithm for the solution of mixed integer programming problems," *Management Science* **12** pp 576–587.

B. P. Dzielinski and R. E. Gomory (1965); "Optimal programming of lot size, inventory and labor allocations," *Management Science* **11** pp 874–890.

L. R. Ford, Jr. and D. R. Fulkerson (1958); "A suggested computation for maximal multi-commodity network flows," *Management Science* **5** pp 97–101.

R. J. Freeman (1965); "Computational experience with a 'Balasian' integer programming algorithm," *Operations Research* **14** pp 935–941.

S. Fromovitz (1965); "Non-linear programming with randomization," *Management Science* **9** pp 831–846.

S. I. Gass (1964); *Linear Programming* (McGraw Hill, New York, 2nd Edition).

P. C. Gilmore and R. E. Gomory (1961); "A linear programming approach to the cutting stock problem," *Operations Research* **9** pp 849–859.

F. Glover (1965); "A multiphase-dual algorithm for the zero-one integer programming problem," *Operations Research* **13** pp 879–919.

R. E. Gomory (1958); "Outline of an algorithm for integer solutions to linear programs," *Bulletin of the American Mathematical Society* **64** pp 275–278.

R. E. Gomory (1963a); "An algorithm for integer solutions to linear programs," *Recent Advances in Mathematical Programming* pp 269–302, edited by R. L. Graves and P. Wolfe (McGraw Hill).

R. E. Gomory (1963b); "All-integer programming algorithm," *Industrial Scheduling* pp 193–206, edited by J. F. Muth and G. L. Thompson (Prentice Hall, Englewood Cliffs, N.J., and London).

R. E. Gomory (1963c); "Large and nonconvex problems in linear programming," *Proc. Sympos. Appl. Math.* Vol. XV, pp 125–139 (Amer. Math Soc., Providence, R. I.).

R. E. Griffith and R. A. Stewart (1961); "A non-linear programming technique for the optimization of continuous processing systems," *Management Science* **7** pp 379–392.

G. Hadley (1964); *Non-linear and Dynamic Programming* (Addison Wesley, Reading, Massachusetts).

H. Hancock (1917); *Theory of Maxima and Minima* (Ginn & Co, Boston, Massachusetts).

F. L. Hitchcock (1941); "The distribution of a product from several sources to numerous localities," *J. Math. Phys.* **20** pp 224–230.

L. V. Kantovorich (1939); "Mathematical methods in the organization and planning of production," Publication House of the Leningrad State University. Translated in *Management Science* **6** pp 363–422 (1960).

H. W. Kuhn and A. W. Tucker (1951); "Non-linear programming," *Proceedings of Second Berkeley Symposium on Mathematical Statistics and Probability* pp 481–492, edited by J. Neyman (University of California Press).

A. H. Land and A. G. Doig (1960); "An automatic method of solving discrete programming problems," *Econometrica* **28** pp 497–520.

A. Le Garff and Y. Malgrange (1963); "Résolution des programmes linéaires a valeurs entières par une méthode Booleienne «compacte»", *Proceedings of the 3rd International Conference on Operational Research* pp 695–701 (Dunod, Paris & English Universities Press).

C. E. Lemke (1954); "The dual method of solving the linear programming problem," *Naval Research Logistics Quarterly* **1** pp 36–47.

J. D. C. Little, K. C. Murty, D. W. Sweeney & C. Karel (1963); "An algorithm for the traveling salesman problem," *Operations Research* **11** pp 972–989.

H. M. Markowitz (1959); "Portfolio Selection" (*Cowles Commission Monograph No.* 16), (Wiley).

H. M. Markowitz and A. S. Manne (1957); "On the solution of discrete programming problems," *Econometrica* **25** pp 84–110.

G. T. Martin (1963); "An accelerated euclidean algorithm for integer linear programming," *Recent Advances in Mathematical Programming* pp 311–317, edited by R. L. Graves and P. Wolfe (McGraw Hill).

C. E. Miller (1963); "The simplex method for local separable programming," *Recent Advances in Mathematical Programming* pp 89–100, edited by R. L. Graves and P. Wolfe (McGraw Hill).

W. C. Mylander (1966); "Non-linear programming test problems," letter to the editor *Computer Journal* **8** p 391.

A. Orden (1956); "The transshipment problem," *Management Science* **2** pp 276–285.

D. M. Smith and W. Orchard-Hays (1963); "Computational efficiency in product form LP codes," *Recent Advances in Mathematical Programming* pp 211–218, edited by R. L. Graves and P. Wolfe (McGraw Hill).

G. L. Thompson (1964); "The stopped simplex method: I. Basic theory for mixed integer programming; integer programming," *Revue Française de Recherche Opérationelle* pp 159–182.

C. Van de Panne and W. Popp, (1963); "Minimum-cost cattle feed under probabilistic protein constraints," *Management Science* **9** pp 405–430.

A. C. Williams (1962); "A treatment of transportation problems by decomposition," *J. Soc. Indust. Appl. Math.* **10** pp 35–48.

R. B. Wilson (1963); "A simplicial algorithm for concave programming," Doctoral Dissertation, Graduate School of Business Administration, Harvard.

P. Wolfe (1959); "The simplex method for quadratic programming," *Econometrica* **27** pp 382–398.

P. Wolfe (1965); "The composite simplex algorithm," *SIAM Review* **7** pp 42–54.

P. Wolfe and L. Cutler (1963); "Experiments in linear programming," *Recent Advances in Mathematical Programming* pp 177–200, edited by R. L. Graves and P. Wolfe (McGraw Hill).

G. Zoutendijk (1960); *Methods of Feasible Directions* (Elsevier, Amsterdam).

Author Index

Subject Index